MULTIMODAL TRANSPORT RULES

MULTIMODAL TRANSPORT RULES

by

HUGH M. KINDRED

Professor of Law and Director,
Marine and Environmental Law Programme,
Faculty of Law,
Dalhousie University

and

MARY R. BROOKS

William A. Black Chair of Commerce and Director,
Centre for International Business Studies,
Faculty of Management,
Dalhousie University

KLUWER LAW INTERNATIONAL
THE HAGUE / LONDON / BOSTON

A C.I.P. Catalogue record for this book is available from the Library of Congress.

ISBN 90-411-0360-0

Published by Kluwer Law International,
P.O. Box 85889, 2508 CN The Hague, The Netherlands.

Sold and distributed in the U.S.A. and Canada
by Kluwer Law International,
675 Massachusetts Avenue, Cambridge, MA 02139, U.S.A.

In all other countries, sold and distributed
by Kluwer Law International, Distribution Centre,
P.O. Box 322, 3300 AH Dordrecht, The Netherlands.

Printed on acid-free paper

Cover: ANP Foto

to Sheila
and
to Mitch

Preface

The risks and responsibilities of multimodal operations are not well understood in the business and legal communities even though this form of transport has become a major means of delivering international trade in the last 25 years. This book offers an insight into the complex legal regimes governing multimodal transport and the equally subtle commercial influences operating in the market for multimodal services. Three sets of model rules have been fashioned by the international community between 1973 and 1992 to regulate multimodal business but the evidence of awareness, let alone use of them is slight. Our purpose in writing this book is to inform traffic managers, logistics service providers, unimodal operators, carriers and other executives involved with the transportation industry as well as their legal advisors about the Multimodal Rules. The book examines the differences between the Rules as well as the various needs and expectations of the parties to multimodal transport. It details the impacts of the alternative rules on current multimodal operations and provides the facts to make informed decisions about the liabilities flowing from a cargo casualty and about the preferable regime to apply prospectively in multimodal contracts.

Since there has been little documented experience with multimodal cargo casualties and even less litigation, we have been forced to analyze the application and operation of the Multimodal Rules from first principles. To provide a sense of practical reality we have discussed them in the context of four imagined yet typical case studies. In addition, in as much as the Multimodal Rules build on the experience of principles already applied in unimodal carriage, we have relied on sources and commentaries in those modes as authority, by analogy, for our analysis and conclusions. In this way we have sought to make a complex system plain and to provide a clear picture of the commercial risks and legal responsibilities involved in modern multimodal transport operations.

October 9, 1996

Hugh M. Kindred
Mary R. Brooks

Acknowledgements

The authors gratefully acknowledge the assistance of our students at Dalhousie University in the preparation of this book. In particular, we thank Danielle Foley, Robert Hollis, Michael Siltala and Lisa Van Buren for their tenacity and perseverance in the face of our obscure research requests.

We are also very thankful for the painstaking and cheerful secretarial and editorial help we have been given. Without the expertise of Kathleen Basque, Maggie Lapp, Janet Lord and Molly Ross, we could not have produced a camera-ready manuscript.

In addition, we wish to record our appreciation for those who supported our work financially—the Social Sciences and Humanities Council of Canada and the Centre for International Business Studies of Dalhousie University.

Table of Contents

Stand

List of Exhibits

CHAPTER 1

Responsibilities and Rules in Multimodal Transport

Introduction

Since the 1970s door-to-door services have dominated the market for the delivery of manufactured goods. Shippers and consignees appreciated the convenience, simplicity, security and efficiency of multimodal transport services and were prepared to pay for their benefits. Shipping lines quickly recognized the market potential for integrated transportation systems and moved decisively into providing multimodal services. In more recent years, this recognition has driven shipping lines either to acquire inland transport and terminal companies or to form strategic alliances with such companies; the goal is to achieve a seamless service for customers. As a result, freight forwarders and other intermediaries found their traditional business challenged by these new vessel-owning multimodal service operators and responded with the development of non-vessel and non-vehicle owning operations and integrated logistical support services. In today's transport environment, complex interrelationships bind together carriers, terminal operators, and multimodal service companies who may or may not provide carrying capacity of their own. Transport is no longer seen as a discrete business unit but as one element in a total logistics pipeline.

It was soon realized that this new network of relationships has greatly complicated the assignment of risks and liabilities. The number of intermediaries between the shipper and the actual carrier on any particular segment of a multimodal movement obscures the scope of commercial responsibilities for the cargo. In addition, the use of containers has led to a prevalence of concealed damage which, in spite of the insurance industry's best efforts, may not be attributed to any particular operator. Moreover, the prevailing regulation of carriers by unimodal regimes of international rules and of terminal operators by national systems of law has been unable to resolve the tangled web of multimodal relations. Each regime serves a piece of the multimodal movement; none governs the whole. Indeed, the segmentation of legal regimes has added to the commercial uncertainties. The different regimes apply different principles of responsibility and determine their own limits of liability for the carriers on each mode.

CHAPTER 1

Legal Responsibilities and Rules

Widespread appreciation of the uncertainties surrounding the distribution of risks in multimodal operations led to attempts to establish uniform principles of allocating responsibilities between cargo owners and those with whom they contract for complete door-to-door transportation service, namely multimodal operators. The term 'multimodal transport operator,' or 'operator' for short, is used throughout this book to refer to a company that contracts to carry goods by at least two different modes of transport and to assume responsibility for the complete performance of the agreed move. This description confirms that the operator acts as a principal to the transport contract, and not as an agent of either the cargo owner (shipper or consignee) or the carrier and cargo handlers who participate in the movement.[1]

The international attempts to establish rules governing the liability of multimodal operators involved decisions on several common matters that are essential elements in the regulation of all business relationships. The two most fundamental decisions and their impacts on multimodal transport constitute the core of this book. First, it was necessary to agree about the basis of liability of a multimodal operator. Second, the extent of liability of the defaulting operator had to be settled. A brief explanation of the implications of these legal concepts will serve as a foundation for the subsequent introduction of the alternative regimes for governing multimodal operations.

Basis of Operator's Liability

As to the basis of liability, the chief decision was a choice between holding the multimodal operator strictly responsible for all loss and damage to goods while in its custody (however caused) or liable only for preventable loss and damage resulting from its lack of care and attention. The former standard of strict liability provides greater protection for cargo owners since the multimodal operator is made to bear all the risks. In practice this is never the case as all regimes of strict liability excuse the carrier or operator for a few uncontrollable causes of loss such as *force majeure* (Act of God), shipper's own faults, and inherent vice or defects of the goods themselves. The alternative standard of fault liability allocates to the operator only those risks

---

[1] Compare the definitions surrounding multimodal transport in the UN Convention on International Multimodal Transport of Goods 1980 art.1, which appears in Appendix 3. Local pickup and delivery service by road provided by a unimodal carrier such as an airline company, the carriage of containerized goods by truck that happens to travel by roll-on/roll-off ferry, and similar movements by rail are not treated as multimodal transport operations for the purposes of this book.

2

associated with its own actions, leaving losses that arise from other sources to fall on the cargo owner. In practice, fault liability usually means the operator is only responsible for the consequences of the negligent acts and omissions that are committed by itself or its employees and agents.

In association with the standard of responsibility there is always a complementary issue about proof of the cause of loss. Once a cargo claimant has substantiated a loss, who should bear the responsibility of proving the injury is attributable to the operator? The issue has a significant impact on the allocation of risks in multimodal operations because the side which is made to bear the burden of proof must make an affirmative showing in order to avoid the consequences. In other words, if the operator is called upon to bear this onus, it must disprove its liability for the loss. If the cargo owner is made to do so, it must prove the operator's liability or it will have to absorb the loss itself. When the source of the loss or damage is uncertain or the evidence is weak, the party that bears the burden of proof is unlikely to satisfy it and so will also bear the risk of the loss.

Normally in legal actions claimants have to prove their claims, but historically carriers have been allotted the reverse onus of disproving their assumed irresponsibility. This assumption may have arisen because carriers are entrusted with exclusive control of the cargo owners' goods while they are providing the transport services. It means in practice that the carrier is typically presumed to be liable for all loss and damage until it proves it took reasonable precautionary care of the goods. If it was negligent in some respect, it must go further in its proof and show that its negligence was not the cause of the loss or damage in order to be exonerated of liability.[2] In multimodal movements the cargo is usually stuffed in sealed containers that are passed amongst many service providers, and so the task of discovering the source of concealed damage may become very difficult. As a result, the risk of failing to satisfy the burden of proof is that much greater.

Extent of Operator's Liability

Once the multimodal operator has admitted or been allocated liability, the measure of compensation payable to the cargo owner has to be determined. The fundamental decision to be taken on this matter is whether the extent of the operator's liability shall be the full loss or in some manner limited. Typically, national law leaves this issue to the contracting parties. That is to say, the law will grant full compensation unless the parties, in exercise of their freedom to contract, agree otherwise. They frequently do this by including clauses in their agreement that either disclaim responsibility or limit liability, or both. This practice was exceedingly common amongst

---

2   See Ld. Atkin's opinion in *The Ruapeha* (1925), 21 Ll. L.R. 310, at 315 (C.A.).

carriers in all modes until the adoption of international unimodal conventions. Now, where these apply, limited liability has been adopted as the operating principle. This choice affects the allocation of the risks of carriage in the sense that, although the carrier is held responsible for the loss in principle, the cargo owner may still have to bear that portion of the loss by which it happens to exceed the established limit or ceiling of liability.[3] But since these limits of liability are mandatory law, the corollary also holds true that the cargo owner is entitled to the limit of liability as the minimum compensation recoverable[4] and the carrier is prevented from enforcing any agreement or otherwise attempting to pay less than the stipulated rate of recovery.

Policy choices also have to be made about the quantification of compensation. It is self-evident that a multimodal operator that is held liable should pay for the loss or damage to the cargo itself, but for what other possible financial losses of the shipper should it be expected to provide compensation? If goods are delayed in delivery, usually no physical loss or damage is incurred but the loss of their use may seriously inconvenience their owner. Whether cargo is lost, damaged or delayed, the owner may have been put to considerable expense in reliance on delivery that turns out to be wasted money. Again, the cargo owner may have required the goods to fulfil its supply orders from third parties, or as inputs to production. In either case, the cargo owner may find itself in breach of contract or facing lost business and profits. When any of these kinds of losses can be causally related to the default of the operator, the cargo owner will want and expect to be paid compensation.

Yet at some point the chain of causation between the transport casualty and the economic injury will have to be cut because the consequent losses are judged to be too distantly connected to the operator. Typically carriers are liable for delayed delivery but have rarely had to compensate cargo owners for the loss of further business profits expected to be made from the goods. Once again, even though the operator is held liable, the cargo owner is made to bear a part of the risk of loss.

Segmental Carriers' Liabilities

In trying to deal with these issues on the international plane in a uniform manner, efforts were concentrated on the responsibilities of the multimodal operators, but not to the exclusion of the fact that many terminal and unimodal operators are inevitably involved in the performance of the

---

[3] The unimodal regimes usually permit the carrier and the shipper to agree upon higher limits of liability, typically for a higher freight rate.

[4] Always assuming the actual loss is equal to or greater than the limit of compensation.

contracted movement. When a multimodal operator accepts the shipper's business, it agrees to be responsible for the complete movement even though it is unlikely to carry the goods on its own vehicles or vessels for more than one stage. Many multimodal services are offered by sea carriers who subcontract the other connecting activities of carriage and transhipment. In response to this invasion of the traditional business of freight forwarders, some of them have reorganized their working methods to offer competing multimodal services. Since forwarders own neither vessels nor vehicles, they take responsibility for the whole movement but procure its performance entirely through others (acquiring the moniker of non-vessel owning common carriers, or NVOCs[5]).

When default in a multimodal movement occurs and a loss ensues, the cargo owner (or its insurer) only has to look to the operator for responsibility and recovery. Though the underlying actual carriers have a duty of care for the cargo, they have no contractual relations with the shipper, only with the operator. However, the operator will be very concerned about the conduct of the carriers to whom it subcontracted parts of the movement since it is responsible to the cargo owner for the consequences of their actions. Obviously it would like to pass back that liability to the defaulting carrier or terminal. Hence a very important distinction affecting the risks allocated to the multimodal operator impacts at this point. The ability to attribute the loss or damage to a particular carrier on a particular stage of the multimodal movement will significantly affect the liability the operator has to bear.

If the loss or damage cannot be attributed (or it occurred while the cargo was in the operator's own charge), the operator will probably have to absorb full liability. The risk of this degree of responsibility is enhanced by the likelihood that if it is not possible to pinpoint the cause or occasion of the loss to a particular stage of the movement, the operator will not be able to discharge the burden of proof towards the shipper, discussed previously, that the loss was not its fault. The risk that the operator will be held solely responsible is the greatest in the event of concealed damage to the cargo. When goods stuffed in a sealed container are delivered damaged, there may be less chance of determining when and where the injury was caused, compared to the physical loss of the goods for which an account can usually be made of the missing container or tampering with its seal.

When the loss or damage is attributable to a particular subcontracted carrier or terminal, the multimodal operator is entitled to claim an indemnity against the defaulter. Towards that subcontracted carrier the operator acts as though it was the shipper. Just as the true cargo owner can claim against the operator, so the operator can pursue the actual carrier for

---

5   Non-Vessel Owning Common Carrier (NVOC) is a US legal term which has now passed into common commercial usage.

breach of its subcontract. In this way the multimodal operator can shift the responsibility for attributed loss and damage onto the actual defaulting carrier. However, the multimodal operator's contract with the cargo owner and its subcontract with the actual carrier are different agreements which may contain different terms. For instance, the operator may have to accept general responsibility for the goods towards their owner while recognizing that the actual carrier has more limited liability. In the event of an attributed loss in this situation, the operator is not prevented from passing it back to the actual carrier but the operator will have to share the responsibility to the extent it exceeds the carrier's limit of liability. Operators bear this risk unhappily for the understandable reason that they are held liable in circumstances in which they can prove they were personally not at fault.

Existing Unimodal Regimes

The risk of bearing liability for the default of subcontractors, for which they do not have to answer fully or at all, is made more probable for multimodal operators due to the existence of internationally agreed liability regimes in all four modes of carriage. Air transport is almost universally regulated by the Warsaw Convention and its amending protocols. Sea carriage is widely governed by the Hague, Hague/Visby or Hamburg Rules. Road and rail transport in Europe are controlled by the CMR and COTIF conventions. There is also an international convention directed to the operators of transport terminals regarding their responsibilities at shipment and transhipment points between modes, but it has not yet come into force.[6] Each of these conventions sets out a distinct regime of carrier's responsibilities and liabilities for the mode of transport they govern. In addition, they differ in significant ways, especially in the limits of carrier liability.

Since these international conventions are imposed as compulsory law in those countries that adhere to them, multimodal operators have to respect them in their dealings with their subcontracted unimodal carriers. In other words, the terms of the multimodal operators' agreements with the actual carriers is largely established and controlled by the relevant unimodal regime. Hence, whenever loss or damage can be localized and attributed to one of the actual carriers, the multimodal operator may only be able to shift responsibility from itself to the limited extent of liability imposed by the governing unimodal convention. As a result, all attempts to create uniform principles of responsibility and liability between shippers and multimodal operators have to take into account the existing conventions governing the

---

[6] The full citation and status of each of these conventions is set out in Appendix 1: Table of International Unimodal Transportation Conventions.

unimodal carriers who, in combination, actually execute the desired movement of the cargo.

Multimodal Rules

The international solutions proposed for the liability issues of multimodal transport just outlined adopt different approaches and therefore can result in significantly different distributions of risk and responsibility for the same incident. In fact, three sets of model rules for the regulation of multimodal transport have been established by the international community since 1973.[7] The International Chamber of Commerce (ICC) devised the first significant set of rules, the *Uniform Rules for a Combined Transport Document* which were issued in revised form in 1975 (hereinafter ICC Rules 1975).[8] Like all ICC publications, they are not mandatory law but model contract terms. Hence they cannot override existing law, such as the unimodal conventions in countries where they have been implemented. The ICC Rules 1975 operate by voluntary incorporation by the multimodal operator into its standard trading terms. In practice the ICC Rules were accepted as the appropriate standard for the model combined transport bills of lading designed by such industry associations as BIMCO[9] and FIATA.[10]

Other interested parties, notably cargo owners and governments of developing countries, were not enthused by the industry's terms and conditions of operation. They successfully persuaded the United Nations Conference on Trade and Development (UNCTAD) to prepare a different set of mandatory rules. The resulting *UN Convention on International Multimodal Transport of Goods* (hereinafter MTC 1980)[11] was adopted in 1980. However, it has been ratified by too few states to bring it into force and currently languishes with very little governmental support. Yet the MTC 1980 remains significant because it contains a set of model rules which may

---

[7]   Prior to 1973 the chief attempts to establish uniform regimes internationally were the Tokyo Rules developed by the Comité Maritime International and the draft T.C.M. Convention worked out between the U.N. Economic Commission for Europe and the Intergovernmental Maritime Consultative Organization. These documents provided the basis for the ICC Rules 1975. See A. Diamond, 'Liability of the Carrier in Multimodal Transport' in C. M. Schmitthoff & R. M. Goode, eds., *International carriage of goods: some legal problems and possible solutions* (London: Centre for Commercial Law Studies, 1988) at 38; and R. De Wit, *Multimodal Transport, Carrier Liability and Documentation* (London: Lloyd's of London Press, 1995) at 147-60.

[8]   See Appendix 4.

[9]   The Baltic and International Maritime Council is the leading commercial shipping organization comprising shipowners, agents, brokers and others in the maritime industry.

[10]   The International Federation of Freight Forwarders' Associations. The acronym is formed from the French title of the organization.

[11]   See Appendix 3.

be incorporated voluntarily, like the ICC Rules, as part of the operator's standard trading conditions.

More recently a fresh attempt was made to resolve the unsettled questions about the allocation of risks and liabilities in multimodal transport. The new initiative was the combined effort of the secretariats of both UNCTAD and ICC, which developed a new set of *Rules for Multimodal Transport Documents* (hereinafter UNCTAD/ICC Rules 1992).[12] The new Rules were adopted in June 1991 and published with effect from January 1, 1992.[13] Like the other sets of rules on which they are based, these Rules are also voluntary and not mandatory. They also have the advantages of being able to reflect a longer experience with multimodal operations and to draw on the precedents provided by the previous separate models of ICC and UNCTAD.

Choice of Multimodal Regimes and Structure of the Book

In light of the introduction of the UNCTAD/ICC Rules 1992, it is appropriate to review their provisions and to assess their utility to the users and providers of marine transport services for whom they have been prepared. They present alternatives. In essence, a choice among three different standards of responsibility is presented. Hence, this book takes a comparative approach by analyzing the latest set of Multimodal Rules against the earlier individual efforts of the ICC and UNCTAD. It concentrates on two questions:

(1) How do the UNCTAD/ICC Rules 1992 differ from their predecessors?

(2) What influences significantly affect the choice of Multimodal Rules?

The answers to these questions depend upon the combined effect of the legal regimes established by the Multimodal Rules and their commercial appropriateness to current transport industry conditions. Since there is little knowledge of, and less experience with, the UNCTAD/ICC Rules 1992 to date, the assessment of their effects is bound to contain more projection than practice. So, as a way to give the discussion increased resonance with reality, the operation of the three sets of rules will be contrasted in the detailed context of four practical case studies.

To this end, Chapter 2 provides an overview of the current business practices and attitudes of the different parties to a multimodal movement. It

---

[12] See Appendix 2.

[13] At which time the ICC Rules 1975 were formally withdrawn by the ICC but they are still available in older transport documents and may continue to be incorporated by contracting shippers and operators.

provides the commercial context of modern multimodal operations to which the Multimodal Rules are to be applied. Chapter 3 explains the principal considerations of these rules; in particular it outlines the approaches in each set of rules to the central questions about the basis and the extent of liability of the multimodal operator. It ends with a description of the four case studies and their use to elucidate the operational impacts of the Rules. These chapters supply the background for understanding the detailed consideration of each case separately in the successive Chapters 4, 5, 6 and 7. Next Chapter 8 gathers up the other elements involved in substantiating, or dissolving, the multimodal operator's legal liability under the Rules. It is intended to round out the discussion of the application of the Multimodal Rules.

Following these legal analyses, the final chapter assesses the commercial reasons for choosing between the different sets of Multimodal Rules. It provides some background on claims handling and claims experience as a basis for understanding how the Multimodal Rules may be used to control the risks involved in multimodal operations. It concludes with projections about the choice of Multimodal Rules facing each of the interested parties as a means of managing the commercial risks and legal liabilities in multimodal transport.

CHAPTER 2

Business Practices in Multimodal Transport

Introduction

> In 1979, less than 1 per cent of all containerized cargo in world transport moved intermodally under a through bill of lading; today, most containerized cargo does.[1]

The penetration of containerization as a method of transporting traded goods is a well recognized fact throughout the transport world. The amount of general cargo not moving via more than one mode has dropped precipitously since the 1970s. International multimodal transport is now an established business practice and domestic intermodal traffic is following in its path.

The move to containerization and to multimodal transport are not the only changes evident in international trade today. Trade liberalization has transformed global opportunities for business through the implementation of the Canada–US Trade Agreement, the North American Free Trade Agreement, the European Single Market and many other regional trade agreements as well as through the completion of the Uruguay Round of the General Agreement on Tariffs and Trade. International business on all fronts has become increasingly fluid and dynamic as it adjusts to the accelerating pace with which new opportunities are presented and the intensification of global competition. The results are not yet known as firms continue to grapple with their choice and implementation of a wide variety of potential business solutions, such as downsizing, re-engineering and so on.

The business structures designed to service the needs of trade are increasingly varied and the roles and responsibilities of both traders and facilitators of trade have become more and more fragmented. This chapter will be devoted to exploring the commercial context of the relationship between traders and facilitators of trade in the course of employing multimodal transport to meet their business needs. Its purpose is to establish an understanding of the current business environment and the commercial practices of each of the interested parties—shippers and consignees, carriers and multimodal transport operators, as well as those

---

1   G. Muller, *Intermodal Freight Transportation*, 3d ed. (Lansdowne, VA: Eno Transportation Foundation and Intermodal Association of North America, 1995) at 123.

who service each of them—in order to comprehend their likely approach to and perspectives on the risks and responsibilities assumed under the Multimodal Rules.

The decision as to the choice of appropriate Multimodal Rules will have distinct impacts. Each interested party will have a differing perspective depending on whether it is a cargo owner, a carrier (who may be a multimodal operator or a subcontracted actual carrier) or a third party logistics service provider (filling a role either as an agent for the cargo owner or as a multimodal operator). It is not just the role of each party which influences the choice of Multimodal Rules; it is also relevant whether a party seeks actively to choose the set of Multimodal Rules to be applied or passively to accept those chosen by the other party or parties to the transaction. The purpose of the book is to assist each of the parties in making a more informed choice about the set of Multimodal Rules applicable to the transport contract. Therefore, this chapter is organized to explore the business decisions taken about multimodal transport from the viewpoints of first cargo interests, then third party logistical service providers (TPLs) acting as agents for cargo owners, carriers and, finally, TPLs acting as multimodal operators. It begins, however, with a review of the growth of third party logistical services because the development of this type of business has made these perspectives more complex and difficult to comprehend.

Rise of Third Party Logistics

Third party services have long been available for the limited purposes of freight contracting (called freight forwarding) and customs clearance, but companies offering a broader range of logistical services have appeared only in the past two decades. Not only has third party logistics become more widely available in terms of the range of services on offer but the usage of such services has also grown dramatically. To understand why such services have developed will assist in appreciating the points of view of the third party logistics service providers and their clients.

Although third party logistics is a relatively new phenomenon in North America, the concept developed in Europe much earlier.[2] The European origin of logistics outsourcing (or contract logistics as it is sometimes called) has been traced to the late 1960s and early 1970s when food merchandisers began to seek more efficient and timely means of

---

2   E.J. Bardi & M. Tracey, 'Transportation Outsourcing: A Survey of US Practices' (1991) 21: 3, International Journal of Physical Distribution and Logistics Management, 15; and H. L. Randall, 'Outsourcing Logistics in Europe' [November/December 1991] Journal of European Business 21.

moving perishables from suppliers to retail markets.[3] It has also been argued that the more fragmented nature of the retail industry in Europe may have encouraged the rise of this industry, while in the United States transport regulation and anti-trust guidelines prevented many transport firms from developing such services to broaden their business activities.[4] Transport deregulation in the early 1980s effectively opened the way to the formation of broad-based TPLs in North America. In the past decade or so, the 'new-age' TPL has been driven by a competitive marketplace and the opportunities afforded by restructured manufacturers to provide a wider range of services.

The economic reality of the 1990s is that TPLs bring specific expertise and economies of scale to bear on the logistical problems faced by cargo owners. The result is higher quality logistics services at a cost lower than would be incurred with in-house service provision.[5] Recently, third party logistics has been described as

> the use of external companies to perform logistics functions which have traditionally been performed within an organization. The functions performed by the third party firm can encompass the entire logistics process or selected activities within that process.[6]

Exhibit 2.1 contains a list of typical functions which may be supplied by a TPL. There is no common set of services offered by TPLs. At one end of the continuum a TPL may offer as little as would a traditional freight forwarder acting as an agent of the cargo owner and contracting for carriage. At the other end, the TPL may provide as much as would a shelf-to-shelf logistical management firm which undertakes whatever services are required of it. A TPL may offer a full range of services but be contracted by

---

3   E. Canna, 'Contract Logistics for a Mass Retailer' (1988) 30 American Shipper. This source has been cited in a sufficient number of journals to have acquired a life of its own. R. C. Lieb, R. A. Millen & L. N. Van Wassenhove, 'Third Party Logistics Services: A Comparison of Experienced American and European Manufacturers' (1993) 23: 6 International Journal of Physical Distribution and Logistics Management 35 at 43 question Canna's conclusion by noting that a similar response did not occur to American food firms facing a similar situation.

4   R. C. Lieb et al., ibid. at 43-44. D. J. Bowersox 'The Strategic Benefits of Logistics Alliances' (1990) 90:4 Harvard Business Review 36 at 38-40 identified four dominant forces creating an environment where logistic alliances could flourish: (1) deregulation of transportation, (2) the explosion of information technology, (3) the emphasis on leaner organizations and the propensity to seek external expertise, and (4) the escalating competitive environment.

5   The rationale for the development of third party logistical service firms is well-explored in the academic literature. Refer to Bardi & Tracey, supra note 2 at 16 and Ellram & Cooper, infra note 25 for examples. O'Laughlin et al., infra note 7 at 10 reports that total logistics costs have been reduced by as much as 40 to 50 per cent by integration.

6   R. C. Lieb et al., supra note 3 at 35.

different cargo owners for differing services on this continuum. This fragmentation of service offerings greatlycomplicates the discussion of risks and responsibilities in multimodal transport. In particular, it is essential to take into account that a TPL may act as an agent for the cargo owner, as a multimodal transport operator that subcontracts all of the transport, as an operator with transportation assets to undertake carrier responsibilities, or some combination of these roles.

Exhibit 2.1:
Typical Logistics Functions

- Transportation—Inbound and Outbound
- Work-in-Process Inventory Management
- Finished Goods Inventory Management
- Finished Goods Warehousing
- Logistics Systems Planning
- Logistics Information Systems
- Shipment Consolidation
- Carrier Selection
- Warehouse Management
- Order Processing
- Customer Service and Product Returns
- Sourcing and Purchasing
- Product Assembly or Installation
- Logistics Administration including Freight Payment or Freight Bill Auditing, Claims Processing, ...

There is no agreement on what services belong on this list; perhaps it might be said that it includes whatever the cargo owner wishes to purchase.

In the eyes of shippers, the traditional freight forwarder who contracts with a carrier or carriers for transport services on behalf of a cargo owner is perceived to operate much like a travel agent. Although the forwarder receives a discounted or wholesale price for the space contracted from a carrier, the cargo owner will perceive this to be a 'commission' for securing the sale of space. More importantly, such an arrangement is thought by most shippers not to cost any more than would have been incurred had it arranged its own transport. In addition, for a small fee some forwarders will take care of the documentation and/or customs clearance, both onerous tasks in the eyes of many shippers. The use of traditional freight forwarding services is therefore seen by many cargo interests as a bargain, and the cargo owner expects the provider of these services to represent its best interests.

A TPL may identify and purchase transport services both on its own account (e.g., as an NVOC) or on behalf of a client company (i.e., a shipper or consignee). If the situation is one of 'own account,' the cargo space may be sold piecemeal to several clients to service the consolidation market or on-sold to another TPL, although this is not a common practice.

The degree of reliance on TPLs has varied between North America and Europe. 'While many US-based companies have long been accustomed to performing many of their logistics operations in-house, European firms have relied more on third parties for such services.'[7] In Europe, the commonest tasks sought from TPLs are warehouse management, shipment consolidation, fleet management and order fulfillment.[8] Among American companies there is less commitment to third party services[9] but similar task requirements.[10] The use of TPLs is still growing in Europe as firms increasingly relinquish in-house logistical functions to TPLs.[11] But users are becoming more demanding and more imaginative responses are being required of TPLs.[12] This situation is being replicated in North America, albeit lagging in adoption.

The pattern of third party usage (and hence the issues surrounding TPL choice of Multimodal Rules) is expected to continue in the future. The demand for out-sourced services is growing dramatically. A study by Peat Marwick Stevenson and Kellogg[13] in Canada identified two types of third party firms emerging in the marketplace: (1) firms which provide a range of transportation services including traffic management; and (2) those which focus on providing the full complement of logistics services, including customer service, warehousing and information technology. The study found, for example, that more than 65 per cent of companies are using thirdparty transportation and more than 60 per cent are using third party import/export freight forwarders and customs brokers. The consumer

---

7   K. A. O'Laughlin, J. Cooper & E. Cabocel, *Reconfiguring European Logistics Systems* (Oak Brook, IL: Council of Logistics Management, 1993).

8   R. C. Lieb *et al.*, *supra* note 3 at 38. Freight payments and customs clearance have been outsourced traditionally and were not included in the study.

9   *Ibid.* at 36.

10 *Ibid.* at 38. The only statistically significant differences were in the greater use by Europeans of logistics service firms for the tasks of order fulfillment and product returns.

11 O'Laughlin *et al.*, *supra* note 7 at 65 attribute this to European deregulation and changing user requirements. It is noted at 76 that the development of logistics services is not uniform within Europe and at 83 that the extent of subcontracting of carriage differs between North America and Europe as well.

12 *Ibid.* at 68.

13 Reported in R. B. Lennox, 'Third Party Logistics: The Next Wave' [January 1993] Materials Management and Distribution 16.

packaged goods and chemical sectors tend to use third parties more heavily than primary industries. Although the study predicted significant growth in the use and types of third party services by cargo interests, it also identified that some companies rue the loss of control of the customer interface accompanying outsourcing. This reason was found to be the largest single factor inhibiting wholesale adoption of outsourcing.[14]

Greater future use of TPL services by cargo owners in both Europe and the United States is expected.[15] Greater interest in outsourcing logistics has been documented in food/consumer goods, chemical, health care, and automotive sectors of industry.[16] It can be concluded that the final shape of cargo owner/operator/TPL relationships has not finished evolving and that the relative power balance held by each in the relationship has yet to be determined. A more open but more fragmented marketplace for logistical operations can be expected to develop.

Over this complex business environment, the choice of rules to govern multimodal responsibilities is superimposed. Each of the parties involved in the transport of goods has a differing perspective depending upon their role in the relationship. Those roles will now be examined in order to understand the firm-specific view likely to be held about the choice of, and the anticipated readiness to adopt the responsibilities defined in, the Multimodal Rules.

Cargo Owner Perspectives on Multimodal Transport

The business practices of many cargo owners have evolved dramatically since the 1970s. For a very few, time has stood still. Prior to the early 1980s, it could be said that many cargo owners had very little interest in the risks and responsibilities of delivering their product. The primary thrust of their business was production and, unless there was a customer complaint, few firms were concerned about what happened to the product once it passed through the factory door. Although this statement is no longer as widely applicable, cargo owners today can still be classified as those who are inattentive or disinterested in the logistics aspects of product delivery and

---

14 F. Aertsen, 'Contracting Out the Physical Distribution Function: A Trade-Off between Asset Specificity and Performance Measurement' (1993) 23: 1 International Journal of Physical Distribution and Logistics Management 23 at 25 identifies the following list of managerial reasons why firms do not contract out distribution: less direct contact with the customer, dependency, loss of control, and differences between the transaction channel of the client and distribution channel of the service provider.

15 R. C. Lieb *et al.*, *supra* note 3 at 43.

16 B. J. LaLonde and A. B. Maltz, 'Some Propositions About Outsourcing the Logistics Function' (1992) 3: 1 The International Journal of Logistics Management 1, Table 4 at 5.

those vigilant in all aspects of the delivery of their goods to the final customers (a growing group discussed second).

Disinterested Cargo Owners

Those manufacturers disinterested in the distribution aspect of the business often choose to sell their product FOB or use other 'F' or 'E' terms.[17] These terms infer that the buyer agrees to take responsibility for most, if not all, of the transport arrangements. Such firms often believe that the company and its customers are best served by allowing those with greater expertise in transportation to handle that aspect of completing the execution of a contract of sale. The management of distribution and logistics, therefore, may be delegated to either the buyer or the seller, depending on the particular strength of the parties in the negotiation of a contract of sale and the preferences of each for control of logistics activities. It may occur that neither party has much interest in arranging these activities and, by default, the management of logistics falls to the weaker party.

Over the past two decades, some manufacturing companies in North America, particularly small ones, opted to convey the responsibility for managing transport, and the accompanying insurance, to the buyer or, if required to provide product on a delivered basis, to a freight forwarder. Alternatively, larger companies, or those with in-house expertise, tried to gain competitive advantage by controlling the distribution in-house and garnering distributive efficiencies. Some buyers, in contrast, preferred to control distribution so that they would gain potential distributive efficiencies.[18] Other buyers merely wanted to control the insurance arrangements, in order to minimize the challenges faced in cases of cargo damage, and so required CFR terms in the sale contract.[19]

---

[17] The allocation of risks and responsibilities is determined by the terms of the contract of sale, and executed by the terms and conditions of the contract of carriage. Following an agreement between buyer and seller as to which party would be responsible for arranging and paying for transport and insurance, the contract of sale would note these terms of trade. For a complete explanation of the lettered terms of trade in standard usage, and the responsibilities and obligations of each, refer, for example, to *Incoterms 1990* (Paris: International Chamber of Commerce, 1990).

[18] If a firm has significant in-house expertise in negotiating transport contracts and prices, the total delivered price will be less, thereby affording greater profits for the firm. Anecdotal evidence suggests the Japanese have often followed this approach. The big Japanese trading houses have often been able to make more cost-effective distribution arrangements with shipping lines associated with the trading house than might be available to non-Japanese firms with no relationship. North Americans who trade with Japanese firms therefore are often inclined to 'trade away' distribution control in the course of negotiating a contract of sale.

[19] CFR indicates that the shipper's price includes the cost of transport but not insurance. Those consignees having solid relationships with insurers or insurance brokers find CFR terms

During the 1980s, North American manufacturers, in particular, sought to follow the advice of management gurus Tom Peters and Robert Waterman, Jr. and 'manage what you do best.'[20] As a result, there was an ever-increasing use of TPLs. As firms divined their 'core competencies'[21] and spun off existing in-house expertise or otherwise outsourced the balance of their business needs, the emergent trend in the 1990s became one in which key logistics decisions are now frequently made by TPLs.[22] It should be noted, however, that willingness to use TPLs varies by industry sector.[23]

Anecdotal evidence indicates that many cargo owners have never examined the back of their transport document but assume that someone else (a freight forwarder, a contracted TPL or an insurer, for example) is looking after their interests. In any case, the complete standard trading terms of the multimodal operator are often simply made available for viewing at the company's offices. Then a short-form document can be issued incorporating the terms by reference. Shippers seldom visit the offices of the operator to examine the terms. As booking and documentation activities tend to be conducted by phone and fax, and increasingly by electronic data interchange, the first time a cargo owner examines the full details of the contract with the multimodal operator may be when there is a claim for loss or damage.

There is a tendency among cargo owners to rely on the word of, and personal relationship with, the multimodal operator's sales personnel that the terms of carriage are standard in the industry. Small shippers and consignees also perceive, correctly, that they have little clout in altering the standard business practices of large multinational companies like shipping lines and insurance providers. This belief results in the potential for cargo owners to be poorly positioned in cases of dispute.

With the exception of those companies controlling their own logistical systems with an eye to detail, or those with explicit monitoring programmes for TPL purchases, the situation can best be summed up as 'ignorance is bliss.' Given the rapid growth of small businesses in many developed country economies, the education of cargo owners cannot be considered complete. The primary challenge for this group of cargo owners will be to

---

meet their needs for a delivered product but leave them free to control the insurance arrangements.

[20] Peters and Waterman noted that excellent firms 'stick to the knitting' and focus their energies on doing what they do best. T. J. Peters & R. H. Waterman Jr., *In Search of Excellence: Lessons from America's Best-Run Companies* (New York: Harper & Row, 1982).

[21] C. K. Pralahad & G. Hamel, 'The Core Competence of the Corporation' (1990) 3 Harvard Business Review 79.

[22] Discussed in greater detail in the next section.

[23] O'Laughlin *et al., supra* note 7 provide an excellent review of the needs of and situation faced in several industry sectors in Europe.

identify the means by which they will be able to minimize the risks inherent in the delegation of responsibility to TPLs with respect to that group's choice of Multimodal Rules.

Attentive Cargo Owners

Not to be misleading, only some cargo owners are disinterested in the logistics aspect of the business of competing internationally. Many firms are now recognizing that they must pay closer and closer attention to the details of distribution and logistics as their particular sector of industry faces significant competitive change. The packaged goods industry[24] is a notable example. It has been commercially squeezed into paying attention to logistics details by the sheer force of competition in the global marketplace. Technology has improved product shelf-life so that convenience foods, for example, can compete in more than just the domestic market, and production technologies demand ever larger volumes to improve economies of scale. This industry has globalized and, at the same time, the balance of power in the distribution channel has shifted so that many manufacturers no longer have the clout they once did. The dominant force in many sub-sectors of packaged goods distribution in the developed world is the large retailer, offering a product mix finely tuned by the information extracted from UPC scanner data. Store loyalty is maintained by store brands and promotion schemes. Smaller retailers must innovate just to compete. In this environment, the manufacturer (or the retailer) must squeeze every efficiency from the distribution channel; there is no room for delay or service failures on the part of the transport companies used. Close attention to detail makes shippers and consignees in this industry sector a challenge for multimodal operators, TPLs and insurers alike. The fine print on all contracts is scrutinized and transport companies are chosen based on monitored performance. How service failures are handled by the TPL or the operator becomes a key factor in attracting and retaining business.

In order to gain greater control of all competitive elements and to streamline operations, some cargo owners have implemented supply chain management systems or strategic alliances with TPLs or carriers.[25] Recent

---

[24] This industry consists of a variety of consumer goods from household products through food and beverages to toiletries and over-the-counter pharmaceuticals. The industry is typically dominated by large international, if not global, companies selling well-known branded products. Examples of firms in this industry include Procter & Gamble, Pepsico, Unilever, Nestlé and SmithKline Beecham.

[25] Supply chain management focuses on the control and management of inventory throughout the entire supply chain from raw inputs to ultimate customer. It therefore involves the examination of relationships with all parties involved in the supply chain. Refer to L. M. Ellram and M.C. Cooper, 'Supply Chain Management, Partnerships, and the Shipper–Third Party Relationship' (1990) 1:2 The International Journal of Logistics Management 1. J. D.

trends in the transport industry indicate that strategic alliances between carriers and cargo owners are increasing in number.[26] Cargo owners still cannot assume that such alliances will ensure that the choice of Multimodal Rules in the documentation will serve their best interests. Although many countries have legislation affecting the freedom of carriers and, by extension, multimodal operators to contract out of their obligations, it is still the cargo owner's responsibility to identify acceptable transport terms and conditions. Many do so by confirming that the transport document of a proposed carrier or TPL meets their insurer's requirements.

To summarize this discussion on the business practices of cargo owners, it should be clear that their views on the choice of Multimodal Rules will depend on (1) the degree to which the cargo owner has delegated (and in some cases even abdicated) responsibility for arranging and managing multimodal transport to TPLs, (2) the extent of attention paid by the cargo owner to the transportation documentation under which the product is carried, and (3) the particular demands of the industry sector in which the cargo owner must conduct business. A few closing remarks may be made about each of these factors.

In cases where responsibility for the arrangement of multimodal transport has been delegated, the cargo owner relies on the TPL to provide advice and to protect its interests in the event of a service failure. Therefore, its interests are intertwined with those of the TPL. It should not be assumed, however, that these two sets of interests are compatible, even in situations where formal logistics alliances are in place or the cargo owner is the captain in a supply chain management system.

At the extreme, the risk the cargo owner runs in delegating too much control of the logistics to a TPL is not that dissimilar to the risk an investor incurs when too busy to thoroughly examine the investments proposed by a financial planner. The investor may discover too late that the planner advised the purchase of those investments which provided the planner with the highest commission income. The trust the cargo owner must have in the TPL is the glue for the relationship, but it must be subjected to scrutiny on a regular basis or it will run the risk of becoming grounded by complacency.

On the other hand, cargo owners with control of the logistics decisions (or monitoring programmes in place for TPL services) have the means available to minimize their risk through conscious examination of their own particular circumstances. This ability is a prerequisite to making an informed choice of a particular set of Multimodal Rules. Such risk

---

Lewis, *The Connected Corporation: How Leading Companies Win through Customer-Supplier Alliances* (New York: The Free Press, 1995) provides guidance on all types of supplier alliances.

26 J. J. Gentry, 'Strategic Alliances in Purchasing: Transportation is the Vital Link' [Summer 1993] International Journal of Purchasing and Materials Management 11.

minimization strategies for cargo owners will be more fully explored in Chapter 9.

As has already been noted, there remain those cargo owners who are distracted in their logistics handling and thus lay themselves open to business losses through inattention to documentary details, both in the agreement of sale and in the transport contract. Few manufacturers examine the fine print of transport contracts arranged on their behalf, but accept the documents provided as standard for the service. It is quite ironic that many manufacturers will negotiate extremely tough terms with buyers in the development of a contract of sale, bitterly arguing in favour of their own standard conditions, but do not consider that the clauses on a contract of carriage might be worth reviewing prior to use. Shippers tend to accept the third party's or operator's transport document as issued without considering that they may negotiate the use of an alternate document or clause(s). This tendency works in favour of the multimodal operator whose choice of Multimodal Rules is implemented by default.

There is significant potential for the size of this group of inattentive cargo owners to grow, as the outsourcing trend expands beyond logistics and component supply to include many areas of operations viewed previously as part of the core business. The net result is an increase in the number of smaller, newer businesses selling goods and services globally who likely lack the requisite knowledge of transport contracts. Additionally, the scrutiny that was once given to transport contracts in-house in large global companies may now be outsourced to a TPL, whose activities may or may not be subjected to audit. This trend raises questions concerning which party takes responsibility for examining the choice of Multimodal Rules on behalf of the cargo owner and, once made, whether or not that choice has been implemented to the satisfaction of the cargo owner. The choice itself depends on the circumstances of the particular industry faced by the company; this is the third consideration.

The circumstances may influence it to favour one set of Multimodal Rules over another chosen by companies in other industries. In branded goods sales, for example, the success of all participants in the supply chain depends upon the ability of the chain to deliver product timed to match marketing and promotion events. This means that provisions concerning delay and liability for delay will play an important role in this industry's choice of Multimodal Rules. The automotive sector, as another example, has witnessed continuing pressure in favour of just-in-time production and delivery systems implemented on a global scale. Hence, provisions with respect to consequential economic loss and the ability to break the limits of liability on aggregate loss are likely to be of more interest to this sector. The chemicals industry,[27] as it commonly ships hazardous cargo multimodally, will have concerns that differ from both the previous examples.

Because of these different industry concerns, four case studies have been developed to explore not only the variations in the Multimodal Rules with respect to losses, both physical and economic, but also with respect to differing industry circumstances faced by cargo owners. These cases explore the variations of simple cargo loss or damage, seasonal retail supply failures, and just-in-time operations that suffer from disrupted production and resultant diminished earnings. They provide a range of situations covering the full continuum of likely business losses. The structure of these case studies will be reviewed further in Chapter 3.

TPLs as Agents of Cargo Owners

The perspective on the choice of Multimodal Rules for a TPL will depend on whether it is acting as an agent for the cargo owner or as a multimodal operator for its own account. Furthermore, the point of view of the TPL will be coloured by the type of relationship it has with cargo owners and carriers. A TPL may conduct its business either on a transaction-by-transaction basis or within a strategic logistical alliance. The perspective of the TPL as operator (and possibly partner in a strategic alliance) is discussed later in the Operator Perspectives section of this chapter, while the TPL as agent of the cargo owner (within a transaction-by-transaction relationship) is briefly discussed below. Also, it should be noted that a single TPL may deal with a single cargo owner in both roles for different shipments.

When the TPL is serving as an agent of the cargo owner, it ought to serve the best interests of the cargo owner. However, the reality may be different.[28] For example, the price of third party services has an influence on the commercial relationship between the TPL and the cargo owner and, hence, on the potential for the interests of each to diverge in the choice of Multimodal Rules. TPLs have the ability to charge the cargo owner what the market will bear, with little relation to cost but, in doing so, they run the risk that some 'comparison shopping' by cargo owners will take place. Similarly, cargo owners might seek to spread market risk by using more than one TPL. Ultimately, these competitive pressures result in some TPLs concluding that customer loyalty is temporary. Such a conclusion can encourage the TPL to maximize its total volume of transactions on the assumption that some

---

27 O'Laughlin *et al.*, *supra* note 7 Chapter 15 focus on the needs and requirement by the chemicals industry of TPLs.

28 Data in support of the discussion in this and the next paragraph were collected during the interviews conducted for the study reported in M. R. Brooks, 'Understanding the Ocean Container Carrier Market—A Seven Country Study' (1995) 22 Maritime Policy and Management 39.

customers will migrate eventually to an alternate TPL. As a result, the TPL's allegiance in this type of situation will tend to be to the carrier, since its transport prices (tariffs) and services will ultimately determine the TPL's profitability across its total transactional customer base, rather than to the cargo owner whose fickleness, rightly or wrongly, is assumed.

In addition, traditional TPLs (operating as agents) do not choose carriers solely based on the terms on the back of their transport documents. Performance on service elements plays a not insignificant role. For example, how late the carrier will accept consolidated shipments or whether the carrier will allow transport to begin without complete and finalized documentation (thereby granting the forwarder time to complete the documentation package after departure of the goods) may be determining factors in the TPL's decision. Thus the TPL's choice of carrier may have more to do with its own service needs than with the best interests of its client cargo owner despite the codes of conduct assumed by professional associations.

There is the further complication in the third party logistics market that many carriers have decided to enter as competitors to non-asset-owning TPLs.[29] TPLs can now be classified as those which own transportation assets and those which do not.[30] As noted by Sheffi, asset-owning logistics providers have an inherent potential conflict between their customers' interests and their own.[31] This conflict increases the onus on the cargo owner to pay even closer attention to the details of the decisions made by an asset-owning TPL working as its agent.

To conclude, although TPLs acting as agents rather than operators are usually assumed to represent their principal's interests in the choice of Multimodal Rules, no such assumption should be made.

Operator Perspectives on Multimodal Transport

Carriers

The carrier referred to in this section may be the multimodal operator or a subcontractor to the operator. As the company which sets the standard

---

[29] The use of the term 'third party' implies an external and arm's length relationship between the buyer and the seller of the goods. The carrier will be classified as a third party service provider even when it is not at arm's length in its relationship with the cargo owner with respect to the contract of carriage. A recent listing of the top 50 TPLs in the United States noted that 28 of the 50 were asset-based TPLs (Anonymous, 'Top 50 Third-Party Logistics Providers' [July 1996] Inbound Logistics 32.).

[30] Y. Sheffi, 'Third Party Logistics: Present and Future Prospects' (1990) 11: 2 Journal of Business Logistics 27 at 34.

[31] *Ibid*. at 35.

terms and conditions on the back of the transport document, a unimodal carrier has the ability to establish them in its favour. The same carrier may also choose to be a multimodal operator and so it will negotiate the terms and conditions of carriage with the others in the logistics chain. The impact of the terms and conditions applying to the multimodal movement depends on the negotiating skill and clout of each individual carrier and cargo handler in the logistics chain. Without specific requests by the TPL or the cargo owner, it is the carrier's choice of Multimodal Rules and standard contract terms which will govern the cargo owner's commercial outcome in cases of claims for loss, damage, delay or other economic losses.

Thus, the choice of Multimodal Rules actually adopted by the multimodal operator will depend predominantly on the bargaining power each unimodal carrier can muster in its negotiations. That power varies widely and is dependent, in part, on the perceptions of the different parties. For example, ocean carriers are viewed as a potential weak player by land-based carriers, because the marine mode is a preferred target in dispute resolution; arresting a ship can force a quick settlement compared to the hazards in bringing claims against land-based carriers. On the other hand, ocean carriers have complained that railroads, because many are self-insured, have extremely low limits of liability and often, in their agreements with shipping lines, are able to impose those limits because of their natural monopoly on low cost, long distance land transport.[32]

The essential issue in commercial practice is whether the Multimodal Rules desired by the operator, the shipper or the consignee are incorporated into the transport documents[33] used. This itself is very much dependent on the entity whose documentation is issued and how many different documents that entity may maintain and issue. The terms and conditions may or may not be the same from document to document. Because certain customers may have specific preferences spelled out in their contracts of sale or alliance agreements, an operator may keep documents meeting those needs on hand. Therefore, a carrier or TPL may offer a selection of documents. It is not usual for cargo interests to specify deletion of a clause or clauses in the documents in the course of making a booking.

In the final analysis, the Multimodal Rules applicable will depend on the type of document requested by the cargo owner, if any, and the carrier's or TPL's available documents. In practice, few cargo interests examine the fine print of contracts arranged on their behalf, but accept the documents provided as standard for the service. There is commercial pressure on the operator to issue a transport contract matching the terms of the letter of

---

32 From interviews undertaken in examining this issue.

33 The term 'transport document' as used in this book does not include container or equipment interchange receipts as discussed in Chapter 5 under Proof of Loss. It refers to bills of lading, waybills and combined transport documents as evidence of a contract of carriage.

credit; otherwise, shippers tend to accept the third party's or operator's transport document as issued without considering that they may negotiate the use of an alternate document or clause(s). This tendency works in favour of multimodal operators minimizing the risks they face.

As well as the variety of transport documents on offer by the operator, the practice of issuing documents also varies. For example, some ocean carriers, in attempts to control their risks as multimodal operators, insist that trucking firms not issue a transport document so its liability cannot be limited. One US trucking company interviewed reported that, even when foreign carriers, freight forwarders and NVOCs issue through bills of lading, the company always issues its own document and presents the customer with both the through document and its own unimodal one. The through bill of lading is treated as the document of record for purposes of evidencing the business terms and conditions, but the unimodal document advises the customer that the trucking company is responsible only for its leg of the journey. The benefit of this practice to the trucking firm is that it requires the multimodal operator issuing the through document to prove that the damage could only have occurred on its leg of the movement.

The trucking company justifies its practice by arguing that most customers insure their goods and expect the insurance coverage to be in place whether two documents are issued or one. The fact that the trucking company has issued a unimodal document limits the ability of the insurance company to collect from the trucking company without proof of attribution to that leg of the movement. The trucking company argues that it is not necessarily important to the shipper that the insurance company is unable to collect on subrogation.[34] (This opinion assumes that insurance premiums will not be raised eventually as a result.)

The above example is not the only instance where more than one transport document may exist for a single movement. Anecdotal evidence has also been gathered that some US NVOCs will issue more than one bill of lading for the same movement, e.g., a US port-named bill plus an ocean bill,[35] so that each party involved in the carriage contract has the documentation it specified and the contract of sale requirements are met. According to one US NVOC interviewed, if the claimed amount is small, the

---

[34] Subrogation is defined by Lloyd's Training Centre, *An Introduction to Lloyd's Market Procedures and Practices* (London, 1987) at p. xxxiii as 'the right of the underwriter to take over the insured's rights following payment of a claim to recover the payment from a third party responsible for the loss.' The amount able to be recovered through subrogation may be limited.

[35] For example, the shipper is required to provide a bill of lading with a US port named in it in order to gain a preferential advantage of some type. The product is actually moved via a Canadian port because the tariff is cheaper. One bill is issued naming the port as Chicago as evidence for the preferential subsidy and the ocean bill names Montreal. The product may actually be moved by rail from Chicago to Montreal before being loaded on a vessel. Clearly not all multimodal business is entirely ethical.

existence of two bills is not problematic and the dispute is often resolved out of court. The size of the claim, and possibly even the size of the subcontracted carrier, may be critical elements in this point of view.[36]

Furthermore, the US trucking company mentioned above supported its practice of issuing two bills by noting that US railroads argue that liability resides with the last carrier in the logistics chain, most often a trucking company. Clearly, the allocation of risk between carriers is subject to the paper trail each puts in place to limit its liability, and the willingness or reluctance of one carrier to act on behalf of all as a true multimodal transport operator, as intended in the MCT 1980.

TPLs as Multimodal Operators

To discuss the perspective of the TPL as operator, it is first important to determine whether the TPL and the cargo owner have an alliance[37] in which the conditions of doing business have been determined by negotiation. Unlike the transactional tensions noted above in the TPLs as Agents of Cargo Owners section, there is greater interest in a cooperative and win-win association between TPLs and their client companies in negotiated supply chain management relationships.[38] The TPL is part of the cargo owner's team and therefore its interests should align with those of its partner. Hence the carrier(s) is more likely to be contracted on the basis of conditions which best serve the interests of the cargo owner. In these cases, the choice of Multimodal Rules reasonably can be expected to meet the needs of the cargo interests.

However, TPLs may also have negotiated alliance agreements with carriers, or indeed be carriers themselves. In these instances, their interests can be expected to align with those of the carrier, discussed previously. The same can be said of those TPLs in the role of operator in a transactional relationship.

In conclusion, no assumptions can be made about the perspective of the TPL except that it will depend on the particulars of the situation and its pre-existing contractual arrangements. It can confidently be said that further evolution of the relationships between cargo interests and TPLs and between TPLs and carriers will occur.

---

36 In the US, many cargo owners insure on an open form basis; the cargo interest then runs into difficulty when it is argued that this arrangement insures them for only one leg of a multiple-leg shipment because each leg is governed by its own bill of lading. Small carriers may believe that it is unlikely they will be censured by large insurers for such a practice; the losses may not be sufficient to warrant insurers 'blacklisting' such carriers.

37 The alliance relationship between suppliers and customers has been the subject of much academic investigation in the last decade. Refer to Bowersox, *supra* note 4 for example.

38 See Ellram & Cooper, *supra* note 25.

Insurance Dimensions

In addition to the perspectives outlined above for each of the parties with a direct role in contracting transport, there is the confounding element of their individual relationships with insurers.

Anecdotal evidence seems to suggest that cargo owners often purchase insurance cover against potential losses without examining the fine print of the insurance policy (not unlike their reaction when faced with a transport document). Most shippers and consignees, but not all, know of the limitations of liability imposed in contracts of carriage and the resulting requirement for adequate cargo insurance. In practice, cargo owners do not often declare the value of the goods shipped because, if it appears on the face of the bill of lading or waybill, the freight rate may be significantly higher. Shippers often prefer to arrange for marine insurance separately so as to reduce the freight paid. In doing so, it is expected that the liability of the operator will be significantly limited. Thus, it has become customary for the shipper or the consignee to purchase insurance cover for the full value of the cargo, or a little more,[39] and for the complete transport move.

However, shippers or consignees get into difficulty when the contract of sale specifies trade terms involving less than full responsibility for the total multimodal move. It is not common but there is anecdotal evidence of cargo owners assuming that the other party has insured the full move. To illustrate the problem, consider a contract of sale between a seller in Chicago and a buyer in Ghent on the terms CIF (Cost, Insurance and Freight) Rotterdam. The consignee could mistakenly assume the insurance arranged by the seller covers the transport risks to the inland delivery point at Ghent, especially if the consignee arranges for inland transport from Rotterdam to be undertaken by the multimodal transport operator chosen by the seller. At the heart of this issue is the cargo owner's understanding of the responsibilities implied in the particular trade term specified in the contract of sale, and the point in the transaction at which the risk of loss or injury to the goods will be transferred from seller to buyer. In North American experience it seems that many cargo owners are not familiar with their responsibilities under Incoterms 1990 or whatever set of standardized terms is employed in the contract of sale. If accurate, this fact provides an additional explanation for the high usage of TPLs by shippers and consignees in this market.

The final point worth noting is that cargo owners are not always sophisticated buyers of insurance. They buy cargo insurance from a broker without necessarily further examining the company which is supplying the insurance or the fine print of the contract. In fact, they may not be fully

---

[39] It is customary practice for many shippers to purchase insurance cover for the invoice value of the cargo plus 10 per cent.

cognizant of the way the insurance cover is provided or activated. The purchase of insurance may be made from a trusted agent/broker, not necessarily the one whose policy provides the best cover for the particular client. When an incident occurs, the broker does not get involved but passes the claim on to the insurer.[40] It is not uncommon for a shipper, upon making a loss or damage claim, to find that the cover it purchased is not what it assumed.

For instance, a shipper may find its open policy does not cover it for particular carriers (who issue unapproved bills[41]), for losses incurred by subsequent carriers (because they may have purchased insurance for the first carrier without recognizing that more than one was being used) or for particular legs of the move (because they were not careful about the terms of their own contract of sale and used FAS when FCA would have been more appropriate[42]). Many shippers believe they avoid the problems by purchasing warehouse-to-warehouse insurance cover but, as a result, may pay for more insurance than is required.

Final Comments

The role and place of third party logistical service firms is currently dynamic. However, it would be unreasonable to expect that cargo owners and TPLs will share a common interest in the choice of Multimodal Rules, except in situations where there is an alliance or partnership between them. It is most unlikely that the interests of cargo owners and third parties will converge in those cases where third party services have been purchased from a transport-owning TPL.

This chapter has laid out the complexity of the business environment in which the choice of Multimodal Rules has to be taken by each party in the logistics chain. By default, the operator's choice of terms and conditions as set out on the back of the transport documentation will apply. Once issued, the operator will be bound by the terms and conditions of the transport document in its dealings with the cargo owner. The operator may find itself

---

[40] The only time the broker may get involved is if the broker acts as a settlement agent on behalf of the insurer.

[41] For instance, the Through Transit Club issues a list of unapproved bills.

[42] FAS indicates that the shipper's price quote includes the cost of delivering the goods Free Alongside Ship while FCA implies that the quote only covers those cost elements incurred in delivering the goods to the first carrier. If a buyer is arranging insurance for an FAS move, that insurance will only cover the goods from the ocean loading terminal; the move by the trucking company from the factory to the ocean terminal will remain uncovered unless insurance is purchased by the shipper. Clearly FCA terms are more suitable in cases of multimodal moves as there is alignment between the responsibility for carriage (by the multimodal operator) and the insurance contract.

in difficulty if the wording of the multimodal document does not match the wording of any unimodal documents issued by its subcontracted actual carriers.

For the cargo owner, different Multimodal Rules may have different commercial outcomes. Therefore, the next chapter will introduce four case studies developed to illustrate the differences between the Multimodal Rules under a variety of circumstances. All parties in the logistics chain can then determine for themselves what will be the best choice of Multimodal Rules given the typical business environment in which they work.

CHAPTER 3

The International Rules of Multimodal Transport

Introduction

A noticeable feature of the international Multimodal Rules is their complexity. Given the variety of multimodal services, the diversity of roles and interests among transportation users and providers, and the fragmentation of the industry described in the previous chapter, perhaps it should not be surprising that the governing legal regimes turn out to be complex. To ease the way to understanding them, this chapter explains the principal elements of the Multimodal Rules. It first surveys the Rules generally and then each set individually, emphasizing the key issues surrounding the core question of liability. It also sets out the structure of the four case studies that will be used to elucidate the operation of the Rules. Subsequent Chapters 4-7 will expose in detail the effects of each set of Rules on multimodal operations through their comparative application to the four illustrative cases.

Common Considerations in the Multimodal Rules

Since multimodal transport became widespread and commonplace in the 1970s, three sets of international rules for its regulation have been issued.[1] Their common objective is to distribute the risks incident to multimodal transport between the cargo owner and the contracting operator. Each does this by establishing the scope of responsibilities of the parties and the limit of liability of the operator in the event of default. They are constructed around a similar format, following the experienced pattern of the unimodal conventions on which they are modelled.

Each set of Multimodal Rules begins with a group of general articles that describe the scope of their application, define the terms used in the body of provisions, and deal with the documentary forms of the multimodal contract on which the rules operate.[2] Then they address the liability of the operator, including its employees and agents, as a matter of both contractual

---

1   Prior attempts to regulate multimodal transport are referred to in Chapter 1, note 6.
2   The principal provisions affecting the application and execution of the Rules are discussed in Chapter 8.

obligation and civil duty (tort). The elements of this liability are typically dealt with in three parts: the basis of liability, the extent of liability, and the period of responsibility.[3] The Rules also fix the shipper's responsibilities towards the operator, before closing with some miscellaneous provisions concerned with such matters as notices of loss, time bars on legal actions and implementation generally.

The key sections of the Rules, and the core of concern in this comparative review of them, are the provisions about the basis and extent of the multimodal operator's liability. Fixing the basis of liability involves a decision whether the operator shall be held responsible for every casualty that befalls the goods while they are in its charge, i.e., strict liability, or only for loss that is caused through the carelessness of the operator, its employees and agents, i.e., fault liability. As described in Chapter 1, carriers and now, by the Multimodal Rules, operators are generally held liable for a loss on the presumption that it was their fault until they prove otherwise.

Loss in this context is a generic word that has various shades of meaning which can be confusing. Loss can be used to refer to the whole range of economic injury that may befall a cargo owner when the cargo becomes a casualty. It may also be used to refer more narrowly to a particular kind of injury to the goods. In the context of the basis or scope of the multimodal operator's responsibility, loss is one of a trio of risks (loss, damage and delay) to which cargo is exposed. All three sets of multimodal rules therefore deal with the basis of the operator's liability for loss, damage or delay. They draw a distinction, however, between loss of and damage to the cargo, since these are physical casualties, and delay in delivery which is not. The physical destruction of the goods resulting from their loss or damage deprives the cargo owner of their use permanently, while delay in delivery only causes temporary deprivation. The Rules consequently set a common basis of liability for physical loss and damage, and a separate one for delay. Furthermore, the separate standard of responsibility for delay is not the same in all three sets of rules.

The Rules make a further distinction for localized injury, i.e., cargo injury that can be shown to be the result of an event which occurred on a particular segment of transportation. By localizing the cargo injury it becomes possible to attribute responsibility among the actual segmental carriers and cargo handlers. In principle, all physical loss and damage should be attributable to a specific incident during the movement of the goods, but it is not always possible to establish the moment and cause of a casualty. Goods found broken when unpacked from a container at destination are an obvious example of damage whose precise cause may

---

[3] The period of responsibility is ordinarily all the time the multimodal operator has the goods in its charge from the moment they are received from the shipper until the occasion when they are delivered at their ultimate destination. See Chapter 8 under Period of Responsibility.

never be determined. The multimodal operator remains responsible under the Rules whether the damage is localized or not, but the basis of liability varies in its detailed application when the loss can be attributed to a particular subcontracted carrier. Then the multimodal operator may be allowed to excuse itself from responsibility in those circumstances when the actual carrier is exempt from liability according to the unimodal convention governing that segment of carriage. However, the Multimodal Rules only adopt this approach partially and thus the three sets of rules differ in the way and the extent to which they govern the operator's responsibility for attributable loss and damage.

The extent of the multimodal operator's liability, following the example of the unimodal conventions, is limited. The main problem has been and is how to fix limits that seem reasonable to both cargo interests and operators. In addition, in order to operate this liability regime, it is also necessary to establish how the cargo is to be valued and whether or not the limits may be exceeded.

As to the basis of valuation of the goods, the general approach applied in sales transactions[4] has been either explicitly or implicitly adopted in the Multimodal Rules. That is to say, the goods are assessed according to the market, or commodity exchange, value they would have had at their destination had they arrived in a timely manner and a sound condition. In other words, the value equals the sum of money the cargo owner would require to replace the goods at the point of delivery, and so is often known as the principle of arrived sound market valuation. When the goods are lost the cargo owner requires full compensation for their value. But when they are only damaged, the cargo owner must also account for their residual value, if any.[5]

The Multimodal Rules also adopt a common approach to claims exceeding the limits of liability. They will be allowed exceptionally but only when the multimodal operator has abused the goods and its trust to care for them. The operator will forfeit the benefit of limiting its liability if the cargo loss results from a personal act or omission of the operator done with intent to cause the loss, or recklessly with the knowledge that the loss would probably result. Such wilfully wrongful conduct is hardly to be expected of a multimodal operator that hopes to prosper.

Establishing the actual limits of liability is the most contentious task since, regardless of the multimodal operator's legal responsibility, the cargo

---

[4] See, e.g., M.G. Bridge, *Sale of Goods* (Toronto: Butterworths, 1988) at 761-772; A.G. Guest, gen. ed., *Benjamin's Sale of Goods* 3d ed. (London: Sweet & Maxwell, 1987) at 783-794; H. McGregor, *McGregor on Damages* 15th ed. (London: Sweet & Maxwell, 1988) at 680-685; W. Tetley, *Marine Cargo Claims* 3d ed. (Montreal: Yvon Blais, 1988) at 323-328.

[5] The cargo owner must mitigate its losses. See Bridge, *ibid.* at 746-761; H. McGregor, *ibid.* at 168 fwd.; S.M. Waddams, *The Law of Damages* 2d ed. (Toronto: Canada Law Book, 1991 looseleaf) at 15-1 fwd.

owner may go more or less substantially uncompensated for its loss. Since the Rules make distinctions in the basis of the operator's responsibility between lost and damaged goods and delayed goods, and between attributable and unattributable damage, the limit of the operator's liability is also divided into matching elements with individual maxima that are separately assessed. But that is as far as the Multimodal Rules follow a common approach. The actual limits of liability vary in assessment and application that can make substantial differences in the compensation payable in individual cases. The differences of detail in the legal provisions in the three sets of rules may not attract the attention of the commercial parties, but the bottom line of the compensation calculations most certainly will.

In addition to compensation for lost, damaged or delayed goods, the owner may also make a claim for consequential losses. Deprivation of the goods may mean the business of the cargo owner cannot go forward and so it may reasonably assert that a portion of its expected profits have been lost. In limited circumstances, the general law about contracts allows such a claim for consequential loss, so it is to be expected that the Multimodal Rules would address this aspect of compensation as well. In fact, only the latest set, the UNCTAD/ICC Rules 1992, regulate the issue of consequential loss and then only to the extent of establishing a limit of liability referable to the freight paid.

Exhibit 3.1:
Common Considerations of Liability in the Multimodal Rules

1. What is the kind of cargo injury?—Loss, damage or delay

2. What is the basis of liability for loss, damage or delay?—Depends on whether the cause of cargo injury can be localized.

3. What is the extent of liability for loss, damage or delay?—Depends on

   - the value of the cargo injury
   - the applicable limit of liability
   - whether additional business losses were suffered and are compensable
   - whether an aggregate limit of liability applies
   - whether the limits of liability may be exceeded

The division of the operator's limited liability into itemized categories of compensation also raises a question as to whether there is an overall ceiling to the total compensation payable. In other words, is there a separate limit to the aggregated liability of the operator? In the absence of any provision in the ICC Rules 1975, it has to be assumed that the operator's total liability is the aggregate of the relevant individual assessments. In the other two sets of rules, a limit of aggregated liability is fixed by differing references to the value of the goods upon their total loss. Hence these Rules impose a general limit on the sum of the individual assessments of limited liability of the operator.

In conclusion, the key considerations in allocating risk and apportioning liability under the Multimodal Rules are summed up in Exhibit 3.1.

ICC Rules 1975

In light of these general distinctions in the incidence of liability, more may now usefully be said about each set of multimodal rules individually. Chronologically, the first of the three sets of model rules for the regulation of multimodal transport under consideration was the ICC's *Uniform Rules for a Combined Transport Document*.[6] They were published in their revised and final form in 1975.[7] They were subsequently withdrawn on entry into effect of the UNCTAD/ICC Rules 1992 on January 1, 1992, but they remain in commercial usage on old forms of transport documents. More importantly, they are part of the base of experience for comparative assessment of the greater utility of the more recent Rules. The ICC Rules 1975 were created expressly because no international convention then existed to regulate multimodal, as opposed to unimodal, transportation.[8] But, unlike the unimodal conventions, the ICC Rules 1995 were only established as model contract terms. This status has two important effects.

First, the transport industry is not required to abide by them. A multimodal operator may choose to incorporate them in its standard trading conditions and form contracts or it may ignore them in favour of terms of its own making.[9] This study proceeds on the assumption that the Multimodal Rules are incorporated in the operator's trading conditions because the discussion is about how well they operate. In the event of a dispute, the court will usually enforce such a choice of governing rules unless it is contrary to a mandatory law or the public policy of the forum.

Second, the ICC Rules 1975, as contract terms, cannot override existing law. This means that they must allow for existing unimodal rules established by international convention in those countries where they are applied. Even where they do not operate, there is likely to be mandatory national law that does impact on the performance of particular segments of the multimodal movement. For instance, while air carriage of goods to the

---

6 The ICC Rules 1975 appear in full in Appendix 4.
7 See ICC Publication No. 298.
8 See the introduction to ICC Publication No. 298.
9 See ICC 1975 rules 1(a) and 2(c).

United States is governed by the international standards of the Warsaw Convention, the intermodal transport of the cargo to its final place of delivery by interstate road or rail services is subject to federal American law about these modes of transport.

In the event of an unattributed loss, the basis of liability adopted by the ICC Rules 1975 is the standard of presumed fault of the multimodal operator. This standard was chosen because it was already a common principle in modern unimodal carriage laws. But the standard is subject to a lengthy litany of excuses which the operator may try and prove.[10] If, however, the loss can be localized, the ICC Rules 1975 apply no special rule of their own. Instead, they refer the question of responsibility to the unimodal convention governing the stage of the movement where the loss occurred, or failing the implementation of that convention in the country concerned, they defer the issue to the relevant local law.[11]

It follows from this decision about the basis of liability that the extent of the operator's liability for attributed physical losses has also to be determined by the compulsory or contractually incorporated unimodal rules, or failing them, the appropriate local law. But where the source of the loss or damage to the goods is unattributable, the ICC Rules 1975 had to set their own limit on the operator's liability. This was established at the rate of 30 Poincaré gold francs per kilogramme of the goods, unless a higher value was declared by the shipper.[12]

The ICC Rules 1975 contain no provisions about consequential losses or aggregate liability. They also exclude compensation for delay in delivering the goods, except to the extent that such loss can be localized to a particular segment of transport in which a unimodal convention or national law compulsorily imposes liability.[13] This was an unfortunate provision since the idea of attributing delay to a particular stage is obscure. True, an individual carrier may run into difficulties so that its journey may be slower than usual, but on another leg of the movement a different carrier may act with extra dispatch. Thus, whether there is delay in delivery is only determinable at the moment of delivery, yet it is referable to the continuous passage of time during all the individual stages of transport throughout the whole movement. Consequently, trying to attribute delay to a particular carrier is not a sensible way to deal with this type of loss.

---

[10] See rules 5(e) and 12.

[11] See rules 5(e) and 13.

[12] See rule 11.

[13] See rule 14.

UN Multimodal Transport Convention 1980

The second set of Multimodal Rules is contained in the 1980 UNCTAD sponsored *United Nations Convention on International Multimodal Transport of Goods* (MTC 1980).[14] UNCTAD's purpose was to correct the lack of mandatory uniform law by the creation of a new and separate multimodal transport convention. As an intergovernmental agreement, the Convention will have the force of law once it has come into effect; this requires ratification by at least 30 states and currently only a few have given their support. In spite of this, the MTC 1980 is not irrelevant. First, just as the ICC Rules 1975 established model contract terms, so the rules of the MTC 1980 may be used as standard trading conditions.[15] Second, because it is an intergovernmental agreement, it creates expectations of compulsory standards of conduct against which all the efforts of business associations and other non-governmental organizations to regulate multimodal transport may be judged. Thus, the MTC 1980 currently has the same voluntary status as the ICC Rules 1975 and may usefully be compared with them on the same plane of operation, namely industry acceptability.

Since the MTC 1980 was written as potential law, its authors were able to specify the standards of responsibility without the restraint of existing unimodal laws. However, the drafters chose to make the Convention operate on the same principle of liability as those unimodal conventions and the earlier ICC Rules 1975. That is to say, the multimodal operator is presumed at fault in the event of loss and will be held responsible unless it can be shown that all measures reasonably required to avoid the incident and its consequences had been taken. This basis of liability applies to the operator regardless of whether the loss can be localized or not.[16]

The MTC 1980 sets its own limits of liability using two alternative standards. For goods lost or damaged, the cargo owner may claim up to 920 SDR per package of goods or 2.75 SDR per kilogramme by weight, whichever is more favourable.[17] (A SDR or Special Drawing Right is the notional unit of account employed by the International Monetary Fund in the daily valuation of a basket of major currencies for exchange purposes.) These levels of liability are relatively low, being comparable to, but not much higher than, the limits established by the most recent unimodal standard for the carriage of goods by sea.[18] The application could produce inequality in

---

14 The Convention appears in full in Appendix 3.

15 UNCTAD itself prepared a draft model multimodal transport contract based on the Convention which it provisionally code-named UN-Multidoc.

16 See MTC 1980 art. 16.

17 See arts. 18 and 31.

18 I.e., the Hamburg Rules, cited in Appendix 1, which set limits of liability of 835 SDR per package or 2.50 SDR per kilogramme, whichever is higher. See art. 6.

compensation among shippers who have suffered a loss, depending on whether their contracts for transportation were multimodal or segmented ones. Since the levels of liability for physical loss and damage established by the unimodal conventions for air, road and rail transport are significantly higher than for sea carriage, the shipper of goods under a multimodal contract incorporating the rules of the Multimodal Convention would be greatly prejudiced. Consequently the MTC 1980, like the ICC Rules 1975, was also made to refer to the existing unimodal laws. However, the references are significantly different.

First, if there is no sea leg in the multimodal movement, the MTC 1980 substitutes the higher limit of liability of 8.33 SDR per kilogramme.[19] This is a rate of compensation commensurate with the international law for carriage by road under the CMR Convention.[20] Even this level of compensation would prejudice a multimodal shipper compared to a shipper by rail or air since the limits of liability in those modes can be considerably greater. Thus, as a second variant on the level of liability fixed by the MTC 1980, a cargo owner who can localize the loss to a particular stage of the multimodal movement may claim compensation according to the unimodal convention or national law governing that stage if it would provide a higher limit.[21]

In result, the MTC 1980 offers cargo interests a graduated scale of compensation. Unattributable damage in a movement involving a sea leg is treated comparably to loss at sea. In the absence of sea carriage, the damage will be compensated alike to a loss by road. But if the damage can be localized, it will be assessed in accordance with the rules of the mode to which it is attributed, provided they would be beneficial to the cargo owner. Thus the ICC Rules 1975 and the MTC 1980 both invoke the underlying unimodal laws but for different reasons and, more importantly, in comparably different ways.[22]

Loss resulting from delay in delivery is treated separately by the MTC 1980. The complications of the ICC Rules 1975 of trying to attribute the delay to a specific stage of transportation is avoided by imposing the liability on the multimodal operator. The limit of liability, however, is not applied by reference to the quantity or weight of the cargo but according to the freight (i.e., the price paid for the transport service). The multimodal operator is liable up to 2.5 times the freight for the goods delayed, but not so as to exceed the total freight paid under the contract.[23] For example, if there are 5 units and the freight per unit of goods is $1,000 but 3 were shut out of

---

[19] See MTC 1980 art. 18(3).

[20] Cited in Appendix 1. See art. 23.

[21] See MTC 1980 art. 19.

[22] The effects of the different approaches are drawn out in Exhibit 5.4 in Chapter 5.

[23] See MTC 1980 arts. 16 and 18(4).

a fully laden ship and so delayed until a later sailing, the maximum compensation for delay that the cargo owner might recover would be the lesser of 3 units x $1,000 freight per unit x 2.5, which equals $7,500, or the total freight, i.e., 5 units x $1,000 which equals $5,000. So the operator's liability in this situation would be limited to a ceiling of $5,000.

While the MTC 1980 contains no provision for consequential losses, it does fix a limit of aggregate liability.[24] Thus the sum of compensation for lost, damaged and delayed goods may not exceed the limit of liability for the total loss of the goods.

UNCTAD/ICC Rules 1992

Upon the failure of the Multimodal Convention to attract more rapid support among governments and so to come into effect, the UNCTAD Secretariat began to look for other ways to forward its objectives, including the promotion of uniform and equitable provisions concerning the liability of multimodal transport operators.[25] In the result the UNCTAD Secretariat established a joint working party with the ICC and other industry parties to draft a set of model rules based on the substantive articles of the Multimodal Convention. The end product was the UNCTAD/ICC Rules for Multimodal Transport Documents (UNCTAD/ICC Rules 1992),[26] which demonstrate a moving compromise between the two sponsors and between the two previous models. The UNCTAD/ICC Rules were adopted in June 1991 and published with effect from January 1, 1992.[27] Like the ICC Rules 1975 and the MTC 1980 to date, they are voluntary and not mandatory.[28] Their persuasiveness stands on the same footing as the previous two efforts to regulate multimodal transport, namely their acceptability to all sectors of the industry.

As to the basis of liability for loss, damage and delay, the UNCTAD/ICC Rules 1992 adopt the principle of presumed fault of the multimodal operator common to the other two sets of rules. Thus the operator will be held liable unless it proves the loss resulted through 'no fault or neglect' of its own, its employees, agents and subcontractors. No distinction is drawn between attributed and unattributed loss in regard to the basis of responsibility, except in two particular situations. When the multimodal movement includes a marine segment, the operator has two special defences for losses at sea. It will be excused from liability if the loss

---

24 See art. 18(5).
25 See the preamble to the MTC 1980, reproduced in Appendix 3.
26 The UNCTAD/ICC Rules 1992 appear in full in Appendix 2.
27 See ICC publication No. 481.
28 UNCTAD/ICC 1992 rule 1.1.

was caused by the 'act, neglect, or default of the master, mariner, pilot or the servants of the carrier in the navigation or in the management of the ship,' or through 'fire, unless caused by the actual fault or privity of the carrier.'[29] In essence, the former permits the multimodal operator to plead, as a sufficient excuse from responsibility, the negligence of its subcontracted sea carrier, while the latter exempts it from liability for loss by fire, absent the personal neglect of the sea carrier.

These two exceptional exclusions of responsibility for loss were not in the original draft of the UNCTAD/ICC Rules 1992 but were added later before their final adoption. They were drawn directly from the older law for carriage by sea,[30] which expresses these protections of the carrier uniquely among the unimodal conventions. Their inclusion in the UNCTAD/ICC Rules 1992 is an unfortunate step away from the objective of a multimodal regime that establishes one uniform standard of responsibility for the cargo throughout the movement. In this way, modal differences are allowed partially to project segmented carriage into multimodalism once more.

Some observers will be even more scornful about the contents of these exceptional provisions, pointing to their unique and much criticized application in marine transportation. The multimodal operator's exemption from liability for loss resulting from the sea carrier's negligence in navigation of the ship will be viewed as particularly offensive since it directly contradicts the general principle of responsibility, which is grounded in just such fault or neglect.

On the extent of liability, the UNCTAD/ICC Rules 1992 occupy the middle ground between the other sets of rules. Like the MTC 1980, the UNCTAD/ICC Rules 1992 set a low measure of liability for unattributable loss related to the limits established for sea carriage. Following the pattern of the MTC 1980, alternative limits by unit and weight are provided. These are set at 666.67 SDR per package as enumerated in the carriage document or 2 SDR per kilogramme by weight,[31] thus matching the ceilings of liability under the Hague/Visby Rules[32] for marine transportation. In the absence of a sea leg in the multimodal movement, the UNCTAD/ICC Rules, again like the MTC 1980, establish the considerably higher limit of 8.33 SDR per kilogramme,[33] by reference to the CMR Convention for road transport.[34]

---

[29] Rule 5.4. The operator remains responsible for ensuring that due diligence was used to make the carrying vessel seaworthy at the commencement of the voyage.

[30] Known as the Hague Rules. See Appendix 1 and the discussion of these provisions in Chapter 5 after note 27.

[31] UNCTAD/ICC 1992 rule 6.1.

[32] As amended by the SDR Protocol 1979. See Appendix 1 and Exhibit 5.4 in Chapter 5.

[33] UNCTAD/ICC 1992 rule 6.3.

[34] See Appendix 1 and Exhibit 5.4 in Chapter 5.

When the loss is attributable to a particular stage, the UNCTAD/ICC Rules 1992 adopt the approach of the ICC Rules 1975. That is to say, the limit of liability is ascertained by reference to the applicable unimodal convention or, failing one, the compulsory national law for that stage.[35] The UNCTAD/ICC Rules also set separate limits of liability for delayed delivery and consequential losses.[36] In both cases the limit is the total freight paid, which is a fractional amount of the value of the goods. Finally, the UNCTAD/ICC Rules 1992 establish an overall limit of liability for the aggregate loss of the cargo owner and this limit is fixed at the maximum compensation if the total loss of the goods had occurred.[37]

The UNCTAD/ICC Rules 1992 thus set limits of liability that fall below the MTC 1980 in several respects. The basic limit for unattributable damage is only approximately two-thirds of the rate of compensation under the MTC 1980, the permitted recovery for delay is 2.5 times less and, for the first time, a ceiling is placed on the amount payable for consequential losses. These significant reductions in recovery for losses is disturbing for cargo owners. It is also surprising to see lower limits of liability being set 12 years after the MTC 1980 was concluded when it is obvious that inflation has and continues to reduce substantially the value of the compensation permitted.[38] In addition, the severe limits set by the UNCTAD/ICC Rules 1992 on compensation for delay and other consequential losses run counter to the increasing importance of these risks with the growing adoption by international commerce of just-in-time and similar logistical systems to support more agile global production.

Comparative Liability under the Multimodal Rules

The combined effort of UNCTAD and ICC to find an acceptable middle standard of liability for multimodal operations invites comparison of the effects of the three sets of rules for shippers and operators. Why the first two sets of rules have not found general favour with all sectors of the industry, and whether the latest rules will fare better, depends in good part on the application of their complex liability regimes. To facilitate understanding, a summary of the key features of all three sets of rules as they affect both the

---

[35] UNCTAD/ICC 1992 rule 6.4.

[36] Rule 6.5.

[37] Rule 6.6.

[38] As to the extent that inflation has ravaged the value of the fixed SDR ceilings of compensation, see UNCTAD, *The Economic and Commercial Implications of the Entry into Force of the Hamburg Rules and the Multimodal Convention* (New York: United Nations, 1991) UN Doc. TD/B/C 4/315/Rev. 1, at 13-15.

Exhibit 3.2: Basis of Multimodal Operator Liability

ICC Rules 1975	Multimodal Convention 1980	UNCTAD/ICC Rules 1992
Lost or Damaged Goods Rule 5(b), (c) & (e)—MTO assumes liability also for employees, agents and sub-contractors, subject to particular rules for unattributed damage and delayed goods, below.	Art. 15—MTO assumes liability also for employees, agents and subcontractors.	Rule 4.2—MTO assumes liability also for employees, agents and subcontractors.
Unattributed Damage Rule 12—MTO presumed at fault unless it proves: (i) fault of shipper (ii) defective packing or marks (iii) inherent vice of goods (iv) unavoidable work stoppage (v) nuclear accident (vi) any other cause beyond its 'reasonable diligence' to prevent or avoid.	Art. 16—MTO presumed at fault unless it proves it and its employees, agents and subcontractors 'took all measures that could reasonably be required' to avoid loss.	Rule 5.1—MTO presumed at fault unless it proves 'no fault or neglect' by itself, its employees, agents or subcontractors.
Attributed Damage Rule 13—MTO liable according to compulsory or incorporated modal rules or national law about basis of liability.	No special rule about basis of liability. Above principle for unattributed damage also applies to attributed damage.	No special rule about basis of liability, except: Rule 5.4—MTO is additionally excused on sea or waterways leg if loss caused by: (i) error in navigation or management of the ship, or (ii) fire, unless due to fault and privity of carrier, provided MTO proves due diligence was exercised to make ship seaworthy.
Delayed Goods Rules 5(b), (c), (f) and 14—MTO liable only for localized delay, according to compulsory modal rules or national law.	Art. 16—Above principle for unattributed damage also applies to delay.	Rule 5.1—MTO liable for delay on above principle for unattributed damage but only when shipper demanded timely delivery.

basis of responsibility and the extent of liability of the multimodal operator has been drawn up in two comparative tables (Exhibits 3.2 and 3.3). The tables display how the Rules take account of the various kinds of business losses that may be incurred upon default in performance of the agreedmultimodal transportation. They permit comparison of the differing degrees of liability which attach for physical damage to the goods, for delay in delivery, and for consequential commercial loss arising from damage or delay, such as lost production, delay in project completion or lost sales. They also highlight the interplay between the multimodal rules and the unimodal laws according to whether the loss can or cannot be attributed to a particular segment of the movement. They provide a useful point of reference for the subsequent analysis of the multimodal case studies described in the next section.

Four Cases of Multimodal Operations

Multimodal transport is employed in very many different commercial situations. The possibilities are as diverse as the products being moved are various. As international trade liberalizes, so multimodal movements become even more widespread and complex. Hence in the application of any of the three multimodal liability regimes, a very wide range of contingencies have to be taken into account. These contingencies involve not only the intermodal arrangements for a particular multimodal movement, but also the different kinds of casualties that can occur and the full range of commercial consequences that may flow from those losses.

The combination of intermodal cargo handlers and segmental carriers is important because the character and location of their functions will determine what underlying unimodal rules or national law will have to be referred to. For instance, if the main part of the multimodal movement is by air rather than by sea, the Warsaw Convention rather than the Hague or Hague/Visby Rules will be called into operation and the level of compensation for, say, a total loss is apt to be much greater. Again, if rail is the carrying mode when the loss occurs, it will be necessary to consider where the casualty happened in order to determine if the rules in the convention concerning rail transport will apply. Since the convention is only in force in an area roughly congruent with continental Europe, recourse must be had to national law regarding a rail accident in, say, North America or Japan.

Exhibit 3.3: Limitation of Multimodal Operator Liability

ICC Rules 1975	Multimodal Convention 1980	UNCTAD/ICC Rules 1992
Basis of Valuation Rule 11(a) and (b)—Arrived sound commodity exchange/market value, unless damage localized when modal rules apply.	(No provision)	Rule 5.5—Arrived sound commodity exchange/market value.
Lost or Damaged Goods **Unattributed Damage** Rule 11(c)—Limit of 30 frs/kg (approximately 2 SDR/kg) – Unless higher value declared.	Art. 18—Limit of 920 SDR per enumerated package or 2.75 SDR/kg whichever higher –Plus container itself if not owned by MTO –But if no sea leg, 8.33 SDR/kg –Unless greater limit agreed.	Rule 6—Limit of 666.67 SDR per enumerated package or 2 SDR/kg whichever higher –But if no sea leg 8.33 SDR/kg –Unless higher value declared.
Attributed Damage Rule 13—Limit set by compulsory or incorporated modal rules or national law.	Art. 19—Apply compulsory or incorporated modal rules or national law if limit is higher than MTC rule, above.	Rule 6.4—Limit set by compulsory or incorporated modal rules or national law.
Delayed Goods Rule 14—Only for localized delay as set by compulsory modal rules or national law —subject to limit of freight for that stage, unless contrary to modal rule or national law.	Art. 18(4)—limit of 2.5 times freight for the goods delayed –But not exceeding total freight for the contract.	Rule 6.5—Limit of total freight.
Consequential Loss (No provision)	(No provision)	Rule 6.5—Limit of total freight.

continued on next page

Exhibit 3.3 (continued)

ICC Rules 1975	Multimodal Convention 1980	UNCTAD/ICC Rules 1992
Aggregate Liability (No provision)	Art. 18(5)—Limited to limit of liability for total loss of goods, not including consequential loss.	Rule 6.6—Limited to limit of liability for total loss of goods.
Breaking Limits of Liability Rule 17—Unlimited if MTO acted with intent or recklessly, knowing of probable damage.	Art. 21—Unlimited if MTO acted with intent or recklessly, knowing of probable damage.	Art. 7—Unlimited if MTO acted with intent or recklessly, knowing of probable damage.

The kinds of casualties and their commercial consequences are also significant because the Multimodal Rules draw distinctions in legal outcomes pursuant to the sort of injury that is suffered. Thus different limits of liability may be applied according to whether the cargo owner sustains physical loss or damage to the goods, delay in their delivery and thus use, or reduced expectations of commercial profit, or a combination of these kinds of injury.

As different cargo owners, because of the particular circumstances of their industry or company, have differing experiences with physical or economic loss, it is to be expected that their choice of Multimodal Rules would vary with the type of injury incurred and with the context of that loss. For example, for a small business, how the different Rules treat physical loss or damage to the cargo itself is likely to be the core issue of concern. Such a company would be less concerned about the complexities of the economic losses and more interested in the way in which the choice of Multimodal Rules would directly impact the claim for the injured cargo. Alternatively, the choice of Multimodal Rules may be assessed differently for a business for which timely delivery is a necessity, such as a seasonal business, or from one in which the co-ordinated relationship is put at risk by loss or delay, as is the case with just-in-time manufacturing operations. Therefore, to illustrate the full impact of the three sets of Multimodal Rules, four cases were developed, two to examine the choice of Rules in the context of simple loss or damage to the cargo (Cases 1 and 2), one to explore the differences in handling timeliness of delivery issues (Case 3) and one to examine the likely way in which each set of Multimodal Rules would manage consequential business loss (Case 4). As the Rules differ in the way in which they are applied when cargo damage cannot be localized in contrast to when it can, Case 2 was developed as a variant of Case 1 to explore this aspect. For convenience, the types of loss and their influence on the legal outcomes in these four Cases are structured diagrammatically in Exhibit 3.4.

Exhibit 3.4:
Types of Loss in the Four Cases

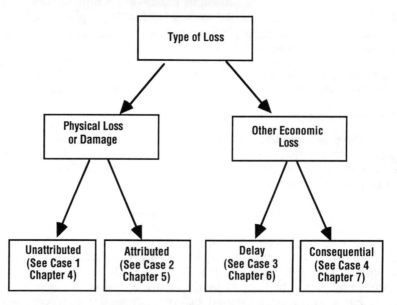

Case 1 involves an international movement of heavy metal machinery by a combination of road, rail and sea transport. At destination, concealed damage to some packages of machinery is discovered but the incident giving rise to this injury cannot be localized and attributed to any particular carrier. Hence liability and compensation will be governed exclusively by the Multimodal Rules in application between the cargo owner and the operator. Thus the Case affords the opportunity of comparing the effects of the Rules in the event of unattributed damage.

By contrast, Case 2 concerns the same illustrative movement but in this instance the two packages of machinery went missing. The cargo owner is able to demonstrate that they were stolen in transit so there is a partial loss of, rather than damage to, the cargo. By pinpointing where the theft occurred, the unimodal regimes of segmented carriage as well as the Multimodal Rules may be engaged. In addition, the operator may be able, in effect, to shift all or some of the liability onto the carrier or cargo handler in whose charge the machinery was when it was stolen. Thus, this Case allows for a more complex comparison, involving in addition the modal laws and rules in the jurisdiction of the attributed loss. By the end of these two Cases, the full ramifications of the Multimodal Rules should be apparent for instances of physical loss or damage.

Exhibit 3.5:
Comparative Characteristics of the Four Cases

Characteristics	Case 1	Case 2	Case 3	Case 4
General Circumstances	Unattributed Damage	Attributed Loss	Delay	Consequential Loss
Specific Circumstances	Broken Goods	Theft of Goods	Late Delivery When Date Specified	Damaged Goods Causing Further Business Losses
Modes: Truck Rail Sea Air	✓ ✓ ✓ X	✓ ✓ ✓ (✓)	(✓) ✓ ✓ (✓)	✓ X ✓ X
FCL/LCL[1]	FCL	FCL	LCL	FCL
Ratio of Freight/Value of Goods Relevant[2]	No	No	Yes	Yes

Notes
[1] FCL = Full container load; LCL = Less than container load.
[2] The significance of this ratio will become apparent in Chapters 6 and 7.

In Case 3 the problem is delay in delivery. A toy manufacturer filled an order to supply a foreign department store by a fixed date. The multimodal operator engaged to deliver the order understood the timetable for delivery. Since the shipment was late in arriving, the whole of the seasonal pre-Christmas market for the particular toys was lost. Unlike loss and damage *en route*, delayed delivery does not result in an injury to the cargo itself, but does deny any beneficial use of it at least temporarily. Thus the cargo owner may state a claim for financial loss, which will have to be settled by the separate provisions of the Multimodal Rules for delay. Hence, this Case permits a review of the differing liability for delay depending on which set of rules is applied.

Case 4 involves the accumulation of business losses as a consequence of physical loss, damage or delay to the cargo. A manufacturer, which closely times its schedule of deliveries of component parts so as to reduce the need to hold safety stock, has a long-standing arrangement with a multimodal operator for its shipments from overseas. When one of three containers of components was damaged in transit, the manufacturer was unable to use the contents of the other two, had to shut down its plant and lay off its workers temporarily, and lost a major contract to a competitor. The manufacturer may claim compensation for all of these injuries and the degree of its success will depend on the different provisions in the Multimodal Rules. Hence the Case allows a comparison between the three sets of rules regarding consequential business loss and aggregate liability.

The different features of the four Cases are summed up in Exhibit 3.5. Each Case will be described separately in detail and then assessed against the three different multimodal regimes in the successive Chapters 4, 5, 6 and 7.

CHAPTER 4

Liability for Unattributed Damage to Goods

Case 1: Unattributed Damage to Goods

A 40' dry van container said to contain 28 packages of metal machinery weighing 19,460 kg. and measuring 28.53 cubic m. was shipped on a Combined Transport Bill of Lading by Overseas Shipping Co. Limited (OverCo), a multimodal operator. The shipment, originating in Lansing, Michigan, was transported from the exporter's factory by Landfast Ltd., a trucking firm working on behalf of OverCo, to the rail yards at Detroit. From the rail terminal, the container was transported by Railfast Inc. to the Port of Montreal; it arrived at Speed Terminal 14 hours before OverCo's next sailing closed and was allocated a slot on the apron. The container was loaded and the ship sailed on an uneventful voyage to Rotterdam, where it was unloaded. After 6 hours in Rotterdam's European Container Terminal, the local road transport firm of van Lines b.v., under a contract to haul all of OverCo's cargoes through that port, picked up the container and carried it over the Belgian border to Turnhout. There it delivered the container to the warehouse of Trucs Belges de Turnhout S.A. (TrucSA), the consignee. When the container was opened, 2 packages of the 28 were found damaged and the machinery within them was broken. TrucSA, which had bought the goods on an Ex Works (EXW) basis, claims the damage occurred in transit. It has contacted OverCo and given notice of its claim.

Introduction

In this illustrative Case the consignee, TrucSA, has suffered a relatively simple loss. It claims that two of the 28 packages of metal machinery delivered are damaged. Thus TrucSA's injury is a partial physical loss of the cargo. It does not expect any other business losses. Ordinarily, TrucSA would receive compensation to the full value of the two missing packages of machinery out of insurance, which would normally have been arranged before shipment of the goods. However, satisfaction of TrucSA's claim in this way does not affect the question of liability for the loss because the insurance company that compensates TrucSA is subrogated to its claim against the responsible parties. This simply means the insurance company may stand in the place of TrucSA to recover as much as it can to offset the insurance monies it has had to pay out. But the insurer's recovery is limited to the claim that TrucSA could bring and is subject to all the defences to which TrucSA would be exposed.[1] Hence the discussion here will proceed as if the cargo claimant is directly pursuing the multimodal operator (as indeed it would in the rare circumstance that no insurance had been effected).

The legal analysis also assumes that the Combined Transport Bill of Lading issued by the multimodal operator, OverCo, incorporated one of the three sets of Multimodal Rules. The discussion will proceed as if each set of rules were to be applied in turn. The object of this discussion is to compare the liability of OverCo, the multimodal operator, in each case. Logically, the legal analysis must progress by first considering the basis of OverCo's responsibility (i.e., whether it should be held responsible for the missing machinery) before secondly, assessing the extent of its liability (i.e., how much compensation it is bound to pay). As a prerequisite to any question of liability of OverCo, however, TrucSA, the cargo claimant, must satisfactorily establish its loss.

Proof of Loss

Liability will depend on the cause and extent of loss. TrucSA claims two packages of machinery were damaged. Ordinarily the cargo claimant must prove the extent of its loss.[2] That is sufficiently done by presenting a clean transport document issued by the operator and providing evidence of the state of the described goods upon delivery.[3] This responsibility should not be difficult for TrucSA to perform in this Case. It has a clean Combined Transport Bill of Lading which describes the cargo as 28 packages of metal machinery and it can presumably bring forward a surveyor's report of the damage which would be made for insurance purposes. Traditionally this proof would be sufficient to establish a *prima facie* case, i.e., a good claim to answer.[4]

---

1   Sir M.J. Mustill & J.C.B. Gilman, *Arnould's Law of Marine Insurance and Average* (London: Stevens, 1981) at 1079, 1088.

2   See M. Clarke, 'Containers: Proof That Damage To Goods Occurred During Carriage' in C.M. Schmitthoff & R.M. Goode, *International carriage of goods: some legal problems and possible solutions* (London: Centre for Commercial Law Studies, 1988) at 64; W. Tetley, *Marine Cargo Claims* 3d ed. (Montreal: Yvon Blais) at 142.

3   See M. Clarke *ibid.*; R. Colinvaux, *Carver's Carriage by Sea* 13th ed. (London: Stevens, 1982) at 74; Sir A.A. Mocatta, Sir M.J. Mustill & S.C. Boyd, *Scrutton on Charterparties and Bills of Lading* 19th ed. (London: Sweet & Maxwell, 1984) at 115; W. Tetley *ibid.* at 299.

4   See ICC 1975 rule 9; MTC 1980 art. 10(a); UNCTAD/ICC 1992 rule 3.

The operator, however, never warrants in the transport document the actual condition of the cargo it receives, only that it is in *apparent* good condition. After all, the operator cannot see the goods themselves within their packing; only the condition of the packages can be observed. Containerization has complicated this situation by removing the goods even further from the operator's inspection. When, as is common, the shipper both packs the goods, and stuffs and seals the container, the operator can only observe, and report on the transport document, the condition of the container. As a result the undamaged condition of the goods at the beginning of the journey may be challenged by the operator.

Frequently the operator asserts that the goods were not packed in sufficiently strong materials or were not adequately braced against shifting when stuffed in the container to withstand the rigours of multimodal carriage. As a result, the cargo claimant may have to go further than simply producing the clean multimodal document to establish its claim. Thus TrucSA may have to provide affirmative proof of the manner it packed and stuffed the container.[5] This should not be difficult provided the container, once the damage to its contents is discovered, is left undisturbed until it can be independently surveyed. The cargo insurer may identify a local surveyor to assess the damage and the current state of the cargo, as well as to evaluate TrucSA's means of packing and securing the load in the container.[6]

Once TrucSA has made a good claim for OverCo to answer, it will fall to the latter to prove that the damage was not caused by anything done within its responsibility.[7] The only practical way to dispel this burden of proof is for the operator to establish the particular cause of the damage, which may be extremely difficult to do. Some kinds of inquiry, like water damage, can fairly readily be attributed. Wetting leaves tell-tale indicators on the injured goods, such as mould, rot, rust and water marks, depending on the character of the cargo. Samples of the water can also be tested to determine if it is sea, fresh, or rain water. But broken goods seldom bear any marks suggesting when and how they may have been so bumped, crushed, jammed, jolted or dropped to incur the damage in the long journey through many carriers' and cargo handlers' custody. The container that held the goods can also be inspected for damage or stress marks which may be subjected to forensic investigation, but quite likely the circumstances of their occurrence will not be discovered. Thus OverCo may find it practically impossible to prove the cause of the damage to TrucSA's machinery, and so it will be saddled with a claim for unattributable loss. The further discussion of OverCo's responsibilities proceeds on this assumption.

---

5   See M. Clarke, *supra* note 2; W. Tetley *supra* note 2 at 646.

6   The procedural details of handling a claim are discussed in Chapter 9.

7   See M. Clarke *supra* note 2; R. Colinvaux, *Carver's Carriage by Sea, supra* note 3, at 154; W. Tetley, *supra* note 2 at 143 and 361.

Basis of Liability for Unattributed Damage

If TrucSA can show that two packages of machinery were delivered damaged but OverCo cannot explain how the injury occurred, on what basis should the resulting commercial loss be allocated? In ordinary circumstances, OverCo will be presumed at fault and held responsible for the breakages unless it can provide an acceptable excuse. All three sets of Multimodal Rules invoke a presumption of fault as the general principle of liability.[8] It is enough to find liability that the packages were in OverCo's charge at the time they were damaged. OverCo will be held liable for their injury whether that was the result of its own acts or omissions, or those of its employees, agents or subcontractors, such as the actual carriers and cargo handlers,[9] until proven otherwise. The Rules differ, however, on the reasons which will excuse OverCo from liability. Some are quite specific; others express a more general principle of justification.

The ICC Rules 1975 particularize the available excuses in a lengthy list.[10] OverCo would have to show the loss occurred because of 1) the fault of the shipper,[11] 2) defective packing or marking, 3) inherent vice of the goods, 4) an unavoidable work stoppage, 5) a nuclear incident, or 6) any other cause which could not be avoided and whose consequences could not be prevented by the exercise of reasonable diligence. The MTC 1980 would permit OverCo to escape liability by proving it 'took all measures that could reasonably be required to avoid the occurrence and its consequences.'[12] The new UNCTAD/ICC Rules take a similarly principled approach. They would exempt OverCo from liability if it proved that 'no fault or neglect' of its own, its employees, or its sub-contractors 'caused or contributed' to the loss.[13] Though these formulations of the exemptions from liability differ widely, the spirit of all three sets of rules is very similar. OverCo will be excused by showing the loss was not its fault. The list of specific exemptions in the ICC Rules 1975 are merely examples of circumstances that would be beyond the control of OverCo and therefore not its fault. They are, in any case, largely redundant in light of the culminating clause excusing OverCo for any cause of the loss shown to be beyond its ability to avoid or prevent.

---

8   ICC 1975 rule 5(3); MTC 1980 art. 16; UNCTAD/ICC 1992 rules 5.1.

9   ICC 1975 rule 5(a)-(d); MTC 1980 arts. 15, 16; UNCTAD/ICC 1992 rules 4.2, 5.1. And see Chapter 8 under Application of the Multimodal Rules to the Operator's Agents.

10   ICC 1975 rule 12.

11   Or the consignee, but in this case since the goods were stuffed in the container by the exporter and shipped Ex Works, TrucSA had nothing to do with them before they were put in the charge of OverCo.

12   MTC 1980 art. 16(1).

13   UNCTAD/ICC 1992 rule 5(1).

In this case of unlocalized damage to cargo there is not much scope for a defence by OverCo. If it cannot discover the source of the loss, it probably will not be able to establish it took the necessary care of the cargo. Its only realistic hope may be to try and contradict TrucSA's proof of its claim. However, a consignee, such as TrucSA, is entitled to rely on the evidence of the transport document issued by the operator.[14] This rule is designed to protect the consignee because it typically has bought the goods sight unseen, and paid for them on the faith of their description in the transport document. Thus OverCo will be prevented from proving against TrucSA that the shipper was at fault by failing, in fact, to ship all 28 packages in apparently good condition.[15]

There is, however, some difference of expression between the Rules in the standard of fault avoidance which may be significant in other situations. Exercising 'reasonable diligence' (ICC Rules 1975) and taking 'measures ... reasonably ... required' (MTC 1980) are not particularly different standards of care, but acting with 'no fault or neglect' at all (UNCTAD/ICC Rules 1992) arguably raises that standard of conduct. Under the former, OverCo might actually be at fault but would still escape liability if it could demonstrate that it took reasonable precautions against the occurrence of the loss. Under the UNCTAD/ICC Rules 1992, taking reasonable precautions is not a sufficient justification; on a literal interpretation, if OverCo was at fault, the presumption of liability is irrebuttable.

However, the difference may only be semantic. It may be argued that if OverCo took all the precautions it reasonably could to care for TrucSA's shipment, it would not be considered to have committed any 'fault or neglect.'[16] To the extent there remains some doubt on this point, it is unfortunate the new Rules have abandoned the previous clarity in formulating the grounds for exemption from operator liability.

---

[14] ICC 1975 rule 9; MTC 1980 art. 10; UNCTAD/ICC 1992 rule 3.

[15] If OverCo is liable to TrucSA, it may yet pass the loss back to the shipper by making proof of a short or damaged shipment, for the shipper, in concluding the transport contract, is regarded as warranting the accuracy of the description of the goods handed over to the carrier or operator. Thus misdescription of the cargo or short shipment are equally faults of the shipper in breach of the transport contract for which the operator is entitled to an indemnity. See ICC 1975 rule 7; MTC 1980 arts. 12, 22; UNCTAD/ICC 1992 rule 8. And see Chapter 8 at note 9.

[16] The explanation of the Rules accompanying their publication by the ICC supports this interpretation for it states that the MTC 1980 was relied upon to set forth the general principle of liability. See ICC Publication No. 481, at 8.

Extent of Liability for Unattributed Loss

Assuming the operator, OverCo, is held responsible for the damage to the two packages of machinery, one may proceed to quantify the amount of compensation that is due to the consignee, TrucSA. The general principle of remedies for breach of contract is that the injured party should receive sufficient compensation to put it, so far as money can, in the same position it would have occupied had the agreement been properly performed.[17] This calculation involves assessing the kinds of loss suffered by TrucSA and valuing the extent of its injuries. In this Case TrucSA's claim is simply for the physical destruction of its property,[18] so the remaining concern is how to value that commercial loss.

Even so, the cargo owner may not be fully compensated by the operator because of the existence of limits to its liability. The Multimodal Rules have adopted an approach to imposing liability that began with the Hague Rules for sea carriage and spread through the other unimodal conventions. Each regime strikes a balance in the allocation of the risks of transportation by imposing minimum standards of cargo care on the carrier or operator in return for maximum limits of compensation to the cargo claimant for loss resulting from breach of those standards. Thus TrucSA may not recover the full value of its two damaged packages of machinery if they are worth more than the ceiling on compensation obliges the operator, OverCo, to pay.

This ceiling may be revised upwards by agreement between the parties. All the sets of rules recognize that if the shipper, when handing the goods over to the operator, declares a value for them that is higher than the limit of liability specified by the Rules, the operator must pay compensation for loss up to that elevated amount.[19] In practice, cargo owners do not often declare the value of their goods, perhaps because the higher transport charge the operator will then impose is likely to exceed the cost of alternative protection through insurance.

Valuation of losses, at least of physical cargo damage as in this Case, is relatively straightforward. Both the ICC Rules 1975 and the new UNCTAD/ICC Rules specify that the damage to goods shall be assessed by reference to the commodity exchange price, or failing that, the current market price of sound goods of the same kind at the place and time they

---

17 *Wertheim v. Chicoutimi Pulp Co.* [1911] A.C. 301 (P.C.). See H. McGregor, *McGregor on Damages* 15th ed. (London: Sweet & Maxwell, 1988) at 7-8; S.M. Waddams, *The Law of Damages* 2d ed. (Toronto: Canada Law Book, 1991 looseleaf) at 5-1-5-5.

18 Theft, delay, diminished profits and other kinds of consequential losses are discussed subsequently in the contexts of Cases 2, 3 and 4 in Chapters 5, 6 and 7 respectively.

19 See ICC 1975 rule 11(c); MTC 1980 art. 18(b); UNCTAD/ICC 1992 rule 6.1.

were or ought to have been delivered.[20] This is a restatement of the widely practised commercial and legal principle of arrived sound market valuation.[21] The MTC 1980 contains no comparable provision, but perhaps the omission only reflects the widespread application, and therefore assumption, of this principle. In any event, failing a provision in the Convention, local law is most likely to supply the rule of arrived sound market value. Thus TrucSA's packages of machinery will be valued for compensation according to the price for which they could be replaced in TrucSA's market area, i.e., in Belgium or Western Europe. From this TrucSA must deduct the residual value of the damaged machinery, if any, since it is bound to mitigate its losses by salvaging what it can from the casualty.[22]

The limits to the quantum of compensation are set in the Multimodal Rules in two ways, first as to individual items of loss and then as to the aggregate value of all kinds of losses. The Rules also specify the exceptional circumstances in which these ceilings on liability may be overreached and the cargo claimant's losses in excess of these limits must be fully compensated by the operator. In this Case, TrucSA is simply looking for compensation for the two packages of broken machinery, so aggregation of different kinds of losses is not an issue,[23] but the limits on itemized loss may be if the machinery is particularly valuable. Then TrucSA will also be concerned whether it can break the limit of liability and claim full compensation.

Limits of Liability for Unattributed Damage

In the event of unattributable cargo loss of the kind assumed in this Case, all three sets of multimodal rules set out clear principles for the calculation of maximum levels of liability. However, the different sets of rules assign different liability maxima per unit which, when multiplied out by the extent of cargo damage, can generate sizable variations in the total amount of compensation that must be paid.

---

[20] See ICC 1975 rule 11(a) & (b); and UNCTAD/ICC 1992 rule 5.5. Under the ICC Rules 1975 all considerations of localized damage are referred to the relevant unimodal rules. However, valuation of damage will, most likely, still be made according to the arrived sound market value of the goods because the unimodal conventions either specify this principle or leave it at large for local practice to determine.

[21] See Chapter 3, at note 4.

[22] See Chapter 3, at note 5.

[23] Limits to aggregated compensation for multiple kinds of loss are discussed in the context of Case 4 in Chapter 7.

Under the ICC Rules 1975 the limit of liability for cargo lost or damaged is set by weight at 30 Poincaré gold francs per kilogramme.[24] The gold franc is an outdated unit of account that has now been superseded in all other international transport regimes. The modern unit of account is the SDR or Special Drawing Right of the International Monetary Fund's creation.[25] One SDR is an immediately convertible, and thus easily applied, unit which at the beginning of August 1996 was approximately equal to US$1.48, C$2.00, £0.96, FF7.66.[26] The limit of 30 Poincaré gold francs per kilogramme set by the ICC Rules 1975 is roughly equivalent to 2 SDR per kilogramme.[27]

Under the MTC 1980 the limit is fixed alternatively at 920 SDR per package or shipping unit, or 2.75 SDR per kilogramme, whichever produces the higher level of compensation.[28] The MTC 1980 also recognizes the realities of container transportation by calculating the number of packages according to the count enumerated in the transport documentation, and treating the container itself, if not owned by the multimodal operator, as a separate additional unit for the purposes of compensation. To these rules in the MTC 1980 there is one exception. In the event the multimodal movement does not involve a sea leg, the limit of liability is set higher, by weight alone, at 8.33 SDR per kilogramme.[29] This variation reflects the practice in the unimodal conventional rules. While the limits for sea carriage are low (in the 2 SDR range), the limits by road are typically 8.33 SDR, though the ceiling for rail and air cargo is more like 17 SDR. The MTC 1980, therefore, strikes a very crude kind of compromise between these different unimodal practices.

The UNCTAD/ICC Rules 1992 take a similar approach to the MTC 1980 but with lower limits of liability. They set the ceiling of recovery at 666.67 SDR per package or unit, or 2 SDR per kilogramme, whichever produces the higher compensation, unless there is no sea leg in the movement, in which case the limit is fixed at 8.33 SDR per kilogramme. Why, it may be wondered, are the limits under the UNCTAD/ICC Rules 1992 set lower than those in the MTC 1980 when part of the movement is by sea? One may be forgiven for expecting that the continuing devaluation

---

[24] ICC 1975 rule 11(c). One Poincaré gold franc was established by French law in 1928 as 65.5 milligrammes of gold of millesimal fineness 900. See W. Tetley *supra* note 2, at 878.

[25] See S. Sorkin, *Goods in Transit* (New York: Matthew Bender, looseleaf) at para. 13.22[1].

[26] The currency values of 1 SDR are calculated daily and made available through the financial press and international banking centres.

[27] A similar limit of 30 gold francs per kilogramme found in the Hague/Visby Rules on carriage by sea was converted to 2 SDR per kilogramme by the Protocol of 1979. See Appendix 1, S. Sorkin *supra* note 25, at para. 13.22, and J.-L. Magdelénat, *Air Cargo Regulation and Claims* (Toronto: Butterworths, 1983) at 173.

[28] MTC 1980 art. 18.

[29] *Ibid.*

over time of all currencies, and thus also of the SDR, would have led to a higher, or at least equivalent, limit of liability in the UNCTAD/ICC Rules 1992 compared to the MTC 1980 of more than a decade ago. In fact the UNCTAD/ICC Rules 1992 have dropped the ceiling of a multimodal operator's liability to the extremely low limits of the Hague/Visby Rules of 1968[30] for unimodal sea carriage.

Since OverCo was engaged in the marine transportation of TrucSA's shipment, it will be able to take advantage of these low limits of liability. The calculation of its actual liability for the broken machinery will be made by comparing the arrived sound market value of the goods less their residual worth with the limit of liability computed under the Rules by multiplying the number of packages or the weight of the goods, as declared on the transport document, with the appropriate SDR value. OverCo will only have to pay full compensation for the damaged goods if that sum is less than the computed limit of liability. Consider the computations for this Case that are set out in Exhibit 4.1.

Exhibit 4.1:
Case 1—Limits of Liability for Unattributed Damage

Regime	Rate	SDR Limit	US$ Limit
ICC Rules 1975[1]	(2 SDR/kg.)	1,390.00	2,057.20
MTC 1980[2]	920 SDR/pkg. 2.75 SDR/kg.	1,840.00 1,911.25	2,723.20 2,828.65
UNCTAD/ICC 1992[3]	666.67 SDR/pkg. 2 SDR/kg.	1,333.34 1,390.00	1,973.34 2,057.20

Basis of calculations: Shipment of 28 packages of machinery weighing 19,460 kg. Hence the 2 damaged packages weigh 695 kg. each. 1 SDR approximately equals US$1.48.
Notes:
[1] Rule 11(c). The limit specified is 30 francs/kg., which is taken to be equivalent to 2 SDR/kg.
[2] Art. 18(1), (3).
[3] Rule 6.1 and 6.3.

The variation in these limits of liability is striking. There is more than 30 per cent difference in the maximum compensation payable between the highest and the lowest figures. The mass of this cargo is also significant. Machinery tends to be very heavy and thus the calculation of the limit of liability by weight works out to the advantage of the cargo claimant. But

---

[30] As converted into SDR in 1979. See Appendix 1.

high value merchandise, such as instrumentation and other hi-tech products, tends to weigh very little by comparison and so attracts lower levels of compensation. For instance, destruction of two cartons of photographic equipment weighing perhaps 50 kilogrammes. each would require the operator to pay under the new UNCTAD/ICC Rules up to US$1,973.34 on a package calculation and only US$296.00 on a weight computation. Even though the cargo claimant is entitled to the higher of these two limits, it is grossly below the value of such a cargo.

The widely differing range of computed limits by item and by weight would be of less consequence if the amounts were all high enough to cover the value of most, if not all, of the cargoes carried and potentially lost or damaged. But in fact the limits set by the Multimodal Rules are all scaled to those found in the regimes for carriage by sea, which are much lower than the ceilings of compensation established by international agreement in all the other modes.

It should also be remembered that the limits to liability spelled out in Exhibit 4.1 apply to OverCo regardless of whether the packages of machinery were damaged at sea or not. In other words, because these limits apply whenever the occasion of the loss cannot be attributed to a particular stage of the journey, OverCo will escape with a much lower burden of liability and TrucSA will receive much less compensation than would be the case were it possible to show that the injury took place on land. The result is possibly a windfall of avoided liability for OverCo.

One way for TrucSA to recover greater compensation is by over-reaching the limitation of liability. All the sets of rules admit that in certain situations the multimodal operator ought not to have the benefit of limiting its liability, but should be accountable for the full extent of the losses it has caused. Thus the Rules state that the operator is not entitled to limit its liability if the losses result from a personal act or omission which was done with intent to cause damage, or was committed recklessly with the knowledge that damage would probably result.[31]

The notion that the operator should be exposed to unlimited liability for the consequences of its wilful or reckless acts, as opposed to negligent ones, has the entirely laudable objective of deterring such conduct. As a practical consideration, however, this rule will not often help the cargo owner. In the present Case, TrucSA would have to establish its losses were the result of some act of OverCo itself, and not merely of its subcontractors, the actual carriers and cargo handlers. TrucSA would also have to show that OverCo's action was done deliberately or at least recklessly in disregard of the safety of TrucSA's shipment. Such conduct must be most unlikely in this situation or any other multimodal transaction involving a reputable operator. Moreover, TrucSA would face an extremely difficult burden of

---

31   ICC 1975 rule 17; MTC 1980 art. 21; UNCTAD/ICC 1992 rule 7.

proof since all the necessary evidence would likely be in the control of OverCo. Therefore, TrucSA should not expect to be able to break the limits of liability and recover any greater compensation from OverCo.

CHAPTER 5

Liability for Attributed Loss of Goods

Case 2: Attributed Loss of Goods

A 40' dry van container said to contain 28 packages of metal machinery weighing 19,460 kilogrammes and measuring 28.53 cubic metres was shipped on a Combined Transport Bill of Lading by Overseas Shipping Co. Limited (OverCo), a multimodal operator. The shipment, originating in Lansing, Michigan, was transported from the exporter's factory by Landfast Ltd., a trucking firm working on behalf of OverCo, to the rail yards at Detroit. From the rail terminal, the container was transported by Railfast Inc. to the Port of Montreal; it arrived at Speed Terminal 14 hours before OverCo's next sailing closed and was allocated a slot on the apron. The container was loaded and the ship sailed on an uneventful voyage to Rotterdam, where it was unloaded. After 6 hours in Rotterdam's European Container Terminal, the local road transport firm of van Lines b.v., under a contract to haul all of OverCo's cargoes through that port, picked up the container and carried it over the Belgian border to Turnhout. There it delivered the container to the warehouse of Trucs Belges de Turnhout S.A. (TrucSA), the consignee. When the container was opened, 2 packages of the 28 were missing. TrucSA, which had bought the goods on an Ex Works (EXW) basis, claims the packages were stolen. It has contacted OverCo and given notice of its claim.

Introduction

The second illustrative Case is substantially like the first one deliberately to permit comparison. The only significant factual difference is that TrucSA's two packages of machinery have disappeared in transit rather than being broken. TrucSA asserts that the lost packages were stolen. This factual variation alone would not necessarily make the legal analysis of the claim differ from the previous chapter concerning Case 1. That will depend upon whether the circumstances in which the packages of machinery disappeared can be localized and thus the responsibility for their loss may be attributed to a particular stage in the carriage. This determination will depend upon the evidence available to support the cargo owner's claim. Thus it is appropriate to proceed, as in the last chapter, to explore first the proof of loss and then the implications of localized injury on the operator's responsibility and financial liabilities.

Proof of Loss

TrucSA claims two packages of machinery were stolen. By this claim, TrucSA asserts both the magnitude and the cause of the loss. Ordinarily the cargo claimant must prove the extent of its loss, then the carrier or operator bears the burden of establishing the cause of the injury and some excuse from responsibility for that causative incident.[1] TrucSA should have little difficulty in making its proof. As explained in Chapter 4,[2] the cargo claimant only has to produce a clean transport document describing the cargo received by the operator and sufficient evidence of the disparity in the quantity and condition of the goods actually delivered.

TrucSA may face a small complication in establishing its claim as a result of the machinery being containerized. If the shipper stuffs and seals the container, the operator cannot be sure what goods it receives into its charge. The multimodal document is likely to state, as in this case, that the container is 'said to contain' the described cargo. In other words the operator does not warrant that it received exactly those goods because it has no way of verifying the accuracy of their enumeration and description by the shipper. As a result, if the shipper were to make a claim for missing goods, it would have to go further in affirmative proof than simply producing the clean multimodal document.[3] However, TrucSA, as the consignee, may assert the contents of the transport document against the operator, who signed and issued it, if TrucSA relied on it in paying for and acquiring rights to the cargo.[4]

---

[1] See M. Clarke, 'Containers: Proof That Damage to Goods Occurred During Carriage' in C.M. Schmitthoff & R.M. Goode, *International carriage of goods: some legal problems and possible solutions* (London: Centre for Commercial Law Studies, 1988) at 64; W. Tetley, *Marine Cargo Claims* 3d ed. (Montreal: Yvon Blais, 1988) at 142-143.

[2] See Chapter 4 under Proof of Loss.

[3] See ICC 1975 rule 9; MTC 1980 arts. 8, 9, 10(a); UNCTAD/ICC 1992 rule 3; M. Clarke, *supra* note 1 at 66; R. Colinvaux, *Carver's Carriage by Sea* 13th ed. (London: Stevens, 1982) at 74-76; W. Tetley, *supra* note 1 at 272-280.

[4] See ICC 1975 rule 9; MTC 1980 art. 10(b); UNCTAD/ICC 1992 rule 3; W. Tetley, *supra* note 1 at 283-286, 646-648. If the operator is forced to compensate the consignee even though there was an error in the enumeration of the goods in the transport document, it may seek an indemnity from the shipper for the consequences of any inaccuracy that the shipper originated. See the discussion in Chapter 8 under Form and Content of the Multimodal Contract.

Proof of the cause of loss is also necessary. The ability to establish the cause may affect the liability issues in two ways. First, where the incident occurred will affect which liability regime will govern the loss. If the place and moment of the incident can be determined, the law regulating the carrier or terminal on that stage of the movement may also establish the operator's liability in place of the multimodal rules.[5] The operator will also be in the favourable position of being able to pass the loss back to the culpable party. But if the occasion of the loss cannot be determined, the operator will bear liability according to the Multimodal Rules and will not be able to pass it on.

Second, how the loss was caused may affect the kind of defence to liability that the operator can assert. Theft of the goods, as asserted by TrucSA, is obviously a different cause from mislaying them, although the loss to the cargo owner may be the same. TrucSA does not care whether the packages of machinery were lost or stolen for the effect on its business is identical. But OverCo may be concerned for both practical and legal reasons. The legal regime governing the incident may grant the operator certain defences and deny others.[6] Theft by strangers is likely to be a good defence but loss through negligence of employees is not. As a practical matter, once it is established the goods were stolen, the operator will be relieved of suspicion of liability.[7] But if it is shown that the goods were mislaid, the operator will have to prove their loss was no fault of its employees, and proving the absence of negligent conduct can be very difficult.

Normal transport industry practices would demand an investigation into the cause of loss. In many instances the source of the injury can be pinpointed sooner or later. In this Case of alleged theft, the first move would be to examine the container for obvious damage. If the theft had been smaller, it might have been achieved through a small hole or intrusion into the container. Given the size of the packages stolen, the container's seal is the most obvious starting point for investigation as it would have to be broken to open the doors. The seal is typically applied by the shipper after stuffing the container and checked and rechecked by each party subsequently responsible for the cargo. A Container Interchange Receipt (CIR) or an Equipment Interchange Receipt (EIR), as it is called in Europe, is completed at each transhipment point. If the container's seal is broken by customs, a new seal and number will be issued and noted on the documents.

Assuming in this Case that the shipper properly affixed a seal to the container, TrucSA's employees who discovered the cargo loss upon delivery of the container should also have noted before opening it whether the

---

5   See *infra* under Basis of Liability for Attributed Loss.
6   *Ibid.*
7   Unless the theft was by its employees.

original seal was still intact, or had been broken or tampered with, or a new one affixed. OverCo should also be able to produce a series of CIRs or EIRs verifying the condition of the container at each point of intermodal exchange and customs frontier (e.g., Detroit, Montreal, Rotterdam subject to customs pre-clearance and in-bond movements). If the seal was intact at destination and the papers are all in order, the evidence suggests the missing packages were never shipped. If the seal was not secure but the papers are in order, the theft is evident but OverCo may have considerable difficulty in determining in which leg of the movement it occurred. If the seal was broken and the CIRs record this fact, a theft attributable to a particular segment of transport is established and an on-site investigation as to how it was allowed to happen may be made. Supposing in this case TrucSA's allegation that two packages were stolen is confirmed and the theft can be localized, consideration of the legal consequences for the operator's liability will be pursued in turn for each stage of the multimodal movement to which the loss might have been attributed.

Basis of Liability for Attributed Loss

Under the MTC 1980

If the cause of TrucSA's loss can be localized, the three sets of multimodal rules do not take the same approach to the operator's liability. In the case of unattributed damage discussed in Chapter 4, the common approach of the Multimodal Rules is to presume the operator liable until it proves it was not at fault. Only the MTC 1980 applies this principle of presumed fault without regard to whether the loss can be localized or not.[8] Thus, OverCo would be held responsible unless it could prove it took all reasonable precautionary measures to preclude the loss of the machinery.

Suppose, for instance, it is discovered that the container was tampered with and the packages of machinery were stolen in Montreal, the port of loading onto OverCo's ship. To escape liability OverCo would have to demonstrate that it had put in place a proper system for receiving shipments at the terminal, that the system was reasonably capable of preventing theft amongst other risks to the cargo, and that its own staff were competent and careful in operating this system.[9] OverCo would also have to show that its shipping agents, the terminal operators, the stevedoring company and its employees and anyone else to whom it

---

[8]   MTC 1980 art. 16. Compare art. 19 which concerns the limit rather than basis of liability.

[9]   Compare the obligation of the sea carrier under the Hague and Hague/Visby Rules, Appendix 1, art. III(2) to carry, keep and care for the cargo 'properly and carefully.' See R. Colinvaux, *Carver's Carriage by Sea, supra* note 3 at 363; W. Tetley, *supra* note 1 at 551.

entrusted responsibility for the container at the point where the theft occurred also exercised reasonable precaution and care in handling the cargo.[10] This onus OverCo would find difficult to discharge. If its own security system or those of its subcontractors were inadequate, it would be liable for the loss. If the systems were judged secure, it is likely that the theft involved inside knowledge or assistance, i.e., the fault of an employee or subcontractor's employee, for which OverCo would also be held responsible. Probably OverCo could not escape liability.

Under the ICC Rules 1975

The simple and easily understood basis of liability provided in the MTC 1980 is obfuscated in the other two sets of rules by special provisions. The ICC Rules 1975 refer the matter of how to judge the operator's conduct to the underlying law of the stage in which the loss occurred.[11] That usually means the unimodal conventional rules as implemented by national legislation or, in their absence, the local law of the place of loss. Consequently, the standards of liability that might apply to a multimodal movement such as the Case under discussion could be numerous and varied. In this Case two unimodal international regimes will apply. The sea leg will be governed by the Hague/Visby Rules as a result of their implementation by Canada, the place of loading.[12] The final road delivery from Rotterdam over the Belgian border to TrucSA's warehouse will be regulated by the rules in the CMR Convention.[13] The other trans-frontier movement from Detroit, USA, to Montreal, Canada, is not controlled by an international regime. There is an international rail carriage convention[14] but it applies almost solely in Europe. Since neither the United States nor Canada are parties, the initial rail leg of the movement will be governed by the local law of origin, in this case U.S. federal law.[15]

In addition to these transborder phases of the movement, there are a number of local and essential connections. Initially the container of machinery was hauled by truck from Lansing to Detroit. This is an intra-

---

[10] See MTC 1980 arts. 15 & 16, and the discussion in Chapter 8 under Application of the Multimodal Rules to the Operator's Agents.

[11] ICC 1975 rule 13.

[12] Canada is not a party to the Brussels Convention of 1924 and Protocols of 1968 and 1979, which create the Hague/Visby Rules but it has adopted all of them by statute. See the *Carriage of Goods by Water Act*, S.C. 1993, c. 21.

[13] See Appendix 1.

[14] *Ibid.*

[15] Federal, not state, law is applicable because the commerce is international.

state movement which will be regulated by Michigan state trucking laws.[16] The container was also transhipped through terminals at the rail yards in Detroit and in the ports of Montreal and Rotterdam. In each place cargo handlers and terminal operators would have care and custody of the container. Even though transhipment is typically completed quickly and the terminals have charge of most containers only for a very short period, more incidents of loss and damage seem to occur at these points than during carriage.

If the activities of cargo handlers and terminal operators on behalf of the immediate carrier fall within the scope of the regime regulating that phase of carriage, they may be subject to its rules and standards as well. But if they are acting beyond the scope of that regime, they will be governed by separate and probably different laws and standards. For instance, once OverCo received the container in the Port of Montreal, it accepted responsibility for it according to the standards in the Hague/Visby Rules.[17] Hence, the liability for any loss occasioned by the terminal operators in loading OverCo's vessel would be determined according to these Rules.[18] But before OverCo accepted the container, while standing in the terminal it was in the independent care and control of Speed Terminal. The moment when a carrier takes charge of cargo depends on the arrangements in each port and place of transhipment. Often carriers use the terminal operator as their agent to receive cargoes as they arrive at the terminal. But in those situations in which the carrier only receives cargo at some later time in the terminal, the law governing the terminal operator's independent responsibilities for goods put in its charge will have to be determined.

To bridge this gap in the continuity between different modes of existing carriage regimes, the international community has established the *United Nations Convention on the Liability of Operators of Transport Terminals in International Trade*.[19] This convention is modeled on the Hamburg Rules[20] on sea carriage so as to accord as nearly as possible with modern unimodal carriage regimes, but it has not yet come into force and effect. Pending that event, one has to fall back on the local law of the place where the terminal is situated to determine the extent of its responsibilities. Hence in this Case, if Speed Terminal in Montreal had any independent control of the container in question, its responsibilities would be governed by the law obtaining in

---

[16] Unless the transfer from the warehouse to the rail siding is treated as a pick-up of a container on flatcar (COFC) and therefore an extension of the rail movement and subject to federal law.

[17] Pursuant to their Canadian implementation, *supra* note 12.

[18] This addresses the cargo owner's claim. Other rules, notably of contractual origin, will determine whether OverCo has a right to indemnity from the terminal operators for their misdoings.

[19] Done 19 April 1991, 30 I.L.M. 1503.

[20] See Appendix 1.

Canada, which might be federal maritime law or Quebec civil law.[21] A similar inquiry into the circumstances and thus the governing law at all the other points of transhipment in this movement would also have to be made.

It is obvious that the catalogue of legal regimes which might apply to a loss by reason of the reference in the ICC 1975 Rules can be very numerous even in a straightforward multimodal movement. Fortunately only one of the possible regimes matters, i.e., the law applicable at the place of the incident. Thus, by pinpointing the cause of loss, the choice of applicable law is also determined.[22] But that still means the cargo may be exposed to a great variety of different legal standards of liability, depending upon which particular regime is relevant. Fortunately there is very widespread application of the principle of liability based on the carrier's presumed fault in both unimodal conventions and national legal systems. It is impossible in the compass of this review of the Multimodal Rules to investigate the national legal regimes, but the international conventions will be briefly discussed here.[23]

The Hague, Hague/Visby and Hamburg Rules on Carriage by Sea

The central segment of the multimodal movement in this Case is the transport by sea. This mode of transport is subject to both the oldest and the newest international regimes in force. The Hague Rules were agreed at Brussels in 1924[24] but have since been revised and replaced. In 1968 amendments were made by the Visby Rules[25] chiefly to alter the limits of liability rather than change the basis of responsibility. In 1978 a United Nations conference concluded a completely new regime, known as the Hamburg Rules.[26] Although these Rules came into force in November 1993

---

[21] These alternatives result from the Canadian constitutional division of federal and provincial jurisdiction. The choice of appropriate law will likely turn on whether the activities of Speed Terminal under scrutiny are more closely related to sea carriage or to land based operations. See *ITO-International Terminal Operators Ltd. v. Miida Electronics Inc.* [1986] 1 S.C.R. 752; 1986 A.M.C. 2580.

[22] Carriers and multimodal operators frequently try to avoid these legal complexities by choosing and stating in their transport documents what law shall govern. While courts will usually respect such choice of law clauses, it is still necessary to determine what legal regime would otherwise apply in case it contains obligatory rules which override the selected governing law.

[23] Sea, road and rail conventions are specifically relevant to this case, but the air transport convention will also be discussed for comparison.

[24] See Appendix 1.

[25] *Ibid.*

[26] *Ibid.*

they have so far been adopted by only 23 countries[27] that are not significant participants in world trade and transportation. The majority of states, including the United States, continue to apply the Hague Rules, although most of the major trading nations have moved to the Hague/Visby Rules.[28]

Under the Hague Rules the basis of carrier liability is the now well recognized principle of presumed fault. However, this principle is subject to a large number of exceptions, in other words the sea carrier is afforded a great many excuses and defences. The principle and its exceptions are spelled out in rather elaborate and complex language. This complexity surrounding the principle of presumed fault of the carrier has resulted in some uncertainty regarding its application and much litigation about its interpretation.

Articles III(1) and IV(1) of the Hague Rules[29] require the carrier to exercise 'due diligence' to provide a seaworthy ship. A vessel is seaworthy if its hull and other structures are staunch against the perils likely to be encountered on the contemplated voyage, if it is properly crewed, supplied and equipped, and if its holds are fit and safe for the particular cargo to be carried.[30] The main point of these provisions in this context is that the sea carrier does not warrant its ship is absolutely seaworthy in the face of all hazards; it is only liable in the event of its lack of diligence to try and make the vessel seaworthy. However, this standard of fault is presumed to have been broken by the carrier in the event of a loss due to unseaworthiness unless, as Article IV (1) expressly requires, the carrier can prove it exercised the requisite diligence.

Article III (2)[31] of the Hague Rules extends the sea carrier's responsibilities beyond the condition of the ship to the actual protection of the cargo. The carrier must 'properly and carefully load, handle, stow, carry, keep, care for, and discharge the goods carried.' In other words, the carrier ought to protect and preserve the cargo in all its dealings with it. To do so 'properly and carefully,' the carrier must set up sound systems of cargo handling and operate and maintain them efficiently.[32] Once again, therefore, the carrier is not liable for every injury to the cargo, but only for those that occur through its fault in failing to provide the requisite degree of care. Whether the carrier will be presumed to be at fault when goods are

---

[27] As of the beginning of 1996: United Nations, *Multilateral Treaties Deposited with the Secretary General* UN Doc. ST/LEG/SER.E14 (1996).

[28] See U.S. Department of State, *Treaties in Force* (1995) at 381, and W. Tetley, *supra* note 1 at 1130, 1138.

[29] See Exhibit 5.1 for the full text of the Hague Rules arts. III(1) & (2) and IV(1) & 2.

[30] see R. Colinvaux, *Carver's Carriage By Sea*, *supra* note 3 at 350-360; W. Tetley, *supra* note 1 at 369-396.

[31] See Exhibit 5.1.

[32] See *Albacora S.R.L. v. Westcott & Laurance Line, Ltd.*, [1966] 2 Lloyd's Rep. 53 at 58, 64 (H.L.) and the references in note 9.

damaged through lack of care, as it will when they are injured through lack of diligence to put up a seaworthy ship, is less obvious. The matter continues uncertain because of the different way that these two obligations regarding the carrying vessel and the cargo are made subject to a further article that sets out the carrier's grounds of exemption from liability.

Exhibit 5.1:
Hague Rules on Carriage by Sea, Articles III(1), (2) & IV(1), (2)

Article III
Responsibilities and Liabilities

1. The carrier shall be bound, before and at the beginning of the voyage, to exercise due diligence to
   (a) make the ship seaworthy;
   (b) properly man, equip and supply the ship;
   (c) make the holds, refrigerating and cool chambers, and all other parts of the ship in which goods are carried, fit and safe for their reception, carriage and preservation.

2. Subject to the provisions of Article IV, the carrier shall properly and carefully load, handle, stow, carry, keep, care for and discharge the goods carried

Article IV
Rights and Immunities

1. Neither the carrier nor the ship shall be liable for loss or damage arising or resulting from unseaworthiness unless caused by want of due diligence on the part of the carrier to make the ship seaworthy, and to secure that the ship is properly manned, equipped and supplied, and to make the holds, refrigerating and cool chambers and all other parts of the ship in which goods are carried fit and safe for their reception, carriage and preservation in accordance with the provisions of paragraph 1 of Article III.

Whenever loss or damage has resulted from unseaworthiness, the burden of proving the exercise of due diligence shall be on the carrier or other person claiming exemption under this article.

2. Neither the carrier nor the ship shall be responsible for loss or damage arising or resulting from

continued on next page

Exhibit 5.1 (continued)

(a) act, neglect, or default of the master, mariner, pilot or the servants of the carrier in the navigation or in the management of the ship;
(b) fire, unless caused by the actual fault or privity of the carrier;
(c) perils, dangers and accidents of the sea or other navigable waters;
(d) act of God;
(e) act of war;
(f) act of public enemies;
(g) arrest or restraint of princes, rulers or people, or seizure under legal process;
(h) quarantine restrictions;
(i) act or omission of the shipper or owner of the goods, his agent or representative;
(j) strikes or lock-outs or stoppage or restraint of labour from whatever cause, whether partial or general;
(k) riots and civil commotions;
(l) saving or attempting to save life or property at sea;
(m) wastage in bulk or weight or any other loss or damage arising from inherent defect, quality or vice of the goods;
(n) insufficiency of packing;
(o) insufficiency or inadequacy of marks;
(p) latent defects not discoverable by due diligence;
(q) any other cause arising without the actual fault and privity of the carrier, or without the fault or neglect of the agents or servants of the carrier, but the burden of proof shall be on the person claiming the benefit of this exception to show that neither the actual fault or privity of the carrier nor the fault or neglect of the agents or servants of the carrier contributed to the loss or damage. ...

In addition to trying to prove it exercised due diligence towards its ship and properly and carefully treated the cargo, the carrier may also seek to avoid liability by asserting one or more of the long list of express exceptions enumerated in Article IV (2).[33] These exceptions may be raised by the carrier against allegations of breach of either of its obligations under Article III, that is unseaworthiness under paragraph (1) or lack of cargo care under paragraph (2). But apart from clause (q) which expressly places the presumption of fault on the carrier unless and until it proves to the contrary, it is not obvious how the exemptions in Article IV (2) are meant to take effect. In particular, it is not clear which party—the cargo claimant or the carrier—is expected to go forward with evidence to substantiate an

---

[33] See Exhibit 5.1.

70

exception. Should the cargo claimant have to disprove the application of the relevant exception, or should the carrier be required to establish its exemption, at the risk that if it does not, it will be presumed to be at fault?

It might be assumed that the carrier, as the party wishing to rely on an exception, would bear the burden of proving its application. However, the manner in which Article III is related to Article IV does not confirm this assumption. Article III paragraph (1), in establishing the carrier's responsibility for the seaworthiness of its ship, does not mention the exceptions in Article IV (2). In determining their relationship, the courts have interpreted these articles consistently with the assumption that the carrier should prove its lack of fault.[34] Article III (1) is treated as an overriding obligation upon the carrier[35] who must prove affirmatively that it exercised due diligence to make the carrying vessel seaworthy before it may assert any of the excepting protections in Article IV (2).

But Article III (2), concerning the carrier's liability for care of the cargo, is expressly made subject to the provisions of Article IV. This difference in wording between paragraphs (1) and (2) of Article III is noticeable. It invites a different legal interpretation in the effect of paragraph (2). In particular, carriers are happy to argue that they may assert an excuse from liability under Article IV (2) without having first to disprove their lack of care for the cargo.[36] In other words, they try to make the cargo claimant establish the claimed exception is not applicable by proving affirmatively that the loss was caused through want of due care. In this way the carrier is held responsible for its acts and omissions, but only after it has been shown by the cargo owner to have displayed inadequate care and not on a presumption of fault.

The correctness of this interpretation of Article III (2) depends in part on the particular wording of each individual exception in Article IV (2). That is too particular a matter to be pursued further in this examination of the Multimodal Rules.[37] Suffice it to say that the detailed enumeration of carriers' exemptions from liability found in the Hague Rules has caused a residual uncertainty that the basis of responsibility in sea carriage is always presumed fault.

The scope of the exceptions enumerated in Article IV (2) also requires brief attention. Most of the excepted perils could not be caused by the

---

[34] See R. Colinvaux, *Carver's Carriage by Sea, supra* note 3 at 351; Sir A.A. Mocatta, Sir M.J. Mustill & S.C. Boyd, *Scrutton on Charterparties and Bills of Lading* 18th ed. (London: Sweet & Maxwell, 1984) at 448; W. Tetley, *supra* note 1 at 372.

[35] See *Maxine Footwear Co. Ltd. v. Can. Govt. Merchant Marine Ltd.* [1959] A.C. 589 at 602-603 (P.C.).

[36] R. Colinvaux, *Carver's Carriage by Sea, supra* note 3 at 362; D.A. Glass & C. Cashmore, *Introduction to the Law of Carriage of Goods* (London: Sweet & Maxwell, 1989) at 180.

[37] See generally D.A. Glass & C. Cashmore, *ibid.*; W. Tetley, *supra* note 1 at 400, 413, 434, 456, 480, 494, 510, 516.

carrier and therefore may not be its fault. Some, however, protect the carrier even in the event of its default. Perils of the sea and the weather (paragraphs (c) and (d)) and the acts of officials and other members of the public who are not party to the carriage contract (paragraphs (e), (f), (g), (h), (j) and (k)) obviously are not attributable to the carrier. Similarly, the carrier cannot be imputed with the faults of the cargo owner (paragraph (i)) or the defects in the cargo or the way it is readied for carriage (paragraphs (m), (n) and (o)). That leaves three exceptions which expressly are made subject to the absence of fault by the carrier: fire, 'unless caused by the actual fault' of the carrier (paragraph (b)), latent defects in the ship 'not discoverable by due diligence' (paragraph (p)), and 'any other cause [of loss] arising without the ... fault' of the carrier or its employees and agents (paragraph (q)). These provisions excuse the operator of liability when the event is not attributable to it. The difference between these three and the previous exemptions is only in the onus and degree of proof of the carrier's disassociation from the cause of loss. In essence they are all specific situations illustrating the principle that the carrier is not liable when it is not at fault.

There remains the infamous provision in paragraph (a), which is a genuine exception to the principle of presumed fault. The carrier is allowed to excuse itself from liability for a loss that resulted from the negligence or default of its employees or its crew in the navigation or in the management of the ship. Normally an employer is vicariously liable for the acts and omissions of its employees.[38] In other words, the employer is attributed with the faults and negligence of its employees committed in the course of their employment on its business. Contrary to this usual commercial principle, the sea carrier is permitted to plead the fault of its employees as a defence to its own liability. Not surprisingly the courts have tended to interpret this liberty strictly by limitative application of the qualifying references to the navigation and management of the ship. It is said that 'if the cause of the damage is solely, or even primarily, a neglect to take reasonable care of the cargo, the ship is liable, but if the cause of the damage is a neglect to take reasonable care of the ship, or some part of it, as distinct from the cargo, the ship is relieved of liability.'[39] Thus, if the negligence of the crew primarily concerned the management of the ship, even though it also resulted in injury to the cargo, the sea carrier may successfully plead this defence. This distinction is often not easy to draw in practice, and it still means that an outright lack of care that results in damage to the cargo remains a crass fault for which the carrier may be excused from liability.

---

[38] See the discussion in Chapter 8 under Application of the Multimodal Rules to the Operator's Agents.

[39] *Gosse Millerd v. Canadian Govt. Merchant Marine* (1927), 29 Ll.L.Rep. 190, at 200 (C.A.) per Greer L.J. whose dissent was approved by the House of Lords in [1929] A.C. 223. See also R. Colinvaux, *Carver's Carriage by Sea, supra* note 3 at 147-153; W. Tetley, *supra* note 1 at 397-410.

The basis of liability in the Hague/Visby Rules is not different from the Hague Rules. In short, the Visby Amendments did not alter this aspect of the Hague Rules. The Hamburg Rules, however, express the basis of the carrier's liability in an entirely fresh and much simpler manner. The carrier is liable for losses incurred while the goods are in its charge 'unless the carrier proves that he, his servants or agents took all measures that could reasonably be required' to avoid the incident that caused the loss and its consequences.[40] This phraseology is similar to other unimodal conventions as well as the Multimodal Rules.[41] The provision straightforwardly states the carrier is liable on the basis of its custody of the goods which is assumed to be faulty, until the carrier proves it is not attributable with any neglectful conduct.

Unlike the Hague and Hague/Visby Rules, the generality of this principle of liability is not augmented by a long list of specific exceptions. Only one comparable qualification is expressed — loss resulting from fire or subsequent firefighting measures. However, it is mentioned only to reverse the burden of proof and require the cargo claimant to establish the faulty or neglectful conduct of the carrier in preventing or controlling the fire.[42] In other words, the carrier will be held to account for fire damage, but only on proof, not a presumption, of fault.

To TrucSA's claim in this Case it is the Hague/Visby Rules and not the Hamburg Rules that would apply to the sea leg of the multimodal movement. The governing law is typically the law of the place of loading, which was the Canadian port of Montreal, and Canada currently enforces the Hague/Visby Rules.[43] Although the theft of machinery from the container may be shown to have taken place in the port, in reality it is extremely unlikely that it would have occurred after the moment when the Hague/Visby Rules began to apply to the cargo, i.e., upon loading.[44] But supposing this was the case, then obviously the carrier is in breach of its duty in Article III(2) to keep and care for the missing packages of machinery, unless it can show that it 'properly and carefully' loaded them. The carrier is unlikely to do so since the presumption of fault in the event of theft is very strong and thus it will face particular difficulty in disproving the assumption of its lack of care. Nor will the carrier gain any relief from the exceptions to liability in Article IV(2). This is not a case of perils of the sea, accident, shipper's fault, official action, strike or public commotion. A thief is not a 'public enemy' in the sense used in paragraph (f). The carrier cannot even plead the negligence of its ship's crew or cargo supervisory

---

40 Hamburg Rules, Appendix 1, art. 5(1). See also Annex II.
41 See Chapter 4 under Basis of Liability for Unattributed Damage.
42 Hamburg Rules, Appendix 1, art. 5(4).
43 See the *Carriage of Goods by Water Act*, S.C. 1993, c. 21.
44 Hague/Visby Rules, Appendix 1, art. 1(e).

staff under paragraph (a) because the loss purely involves mistreatment of the cargo, and has nothing to do with the navigation and management of the ship to which that exception from liability is limited.[45]

Were the Hamburg Rules applicable, a similar holding of carrier liability would result for similar reasons. The theft would raise the presumption of liability against the carrier from the moment of taking charge of the goods in the port of Montreal[46] (i.e., somewhat earlier than the time of loading referred to under the Hague/Visby Rules). The carrier would only escape this liability if it were able to prove it took 'all measures that could reasonably be required' to prevent the theft or to recover the missing machinery. Although this standard has not yet been interpreted by the courts, the wording, especially the reference to 'all measures,' suggests it will be difficult for the carrier to make a convincing case of reasonable care against the theft.[47]

The CMR Convention on Carriage by Road

Once the container of machinery had been discharged at Rotterdam, it was picked up by a local road haulier for the final leg of the movement over land to the consignee in Belgium. This segment would be subject to the Convention on the Contract for the International Carriage of Goods by Road or CMR.[48] It specifies as the basis of the carrier's liability the now familiar presumption of fault but, like the Hague Rules, it also details some of the grounds of excuse from liability.[49] Thus Article 17 states:

> 1.   The carrier shall be liable for the total or partial loss of the goods and for damage thereto occurring between the time when he takes over the goods and the time of delivery, ...
>
> 2.   The carrier shall however be relieved of liability if the loss, damage or delay was caused ... through circumstances which the carrier could not avoid and the consequences of which he was unable to prevent.

---

45   *Supra* note 39.

46   Hamburg Rules, Appendix 1, art. 4.

47   Tetley calls the obligation under the Hague Rules 'a stringent one' and suggests the Hamburg Rules may demand 'a slightly lighter degree of care.' W. Tetley, *supra* note 1 at 553, 560.

48   See Appendix 1. The convention is in force in both the Netherlands and Belgium.

49   See Exhibit 5.2 for the full text of the CMR Convention arts. 17 and 18.

Exhibit 5.2:
CMR Convention on Carriage by Road, Articles 17 & 18

Article 17

1.   The carrier shall be liable for the total or partial loss of the goods and for damage thereto occurring between the time when he takes over the goods and the time of delivery, as well as for any delay in delivery.

2.   The carrier shall however be relieved of liability if the loss, damage or delay was caused by the wrongful act or neglect of the claimant, by the instructions of the claimant given otherwise than as the result of a wrongful act or neglect on the part of the carrier, by inherent vice of the goods or through circumstances which the carrier could not avoid and the consequences of which he was unable to prevent.

3.   The carrier shall not be relieved of liability by reason of the defective condition of the vehicle used by him in order to perform the carriage, or by reason of the wrongful act or neglect of the person from whom he may have hired the vehicle or of the agents or servants of the latter.

4.   Subject to article 18, paragraphs 2 to 5, the carrier shall be relieved of liability when the loss or damage arises from the special risks inherent in one or more of the following circumstances:
(a) Use of open unsheeted vehicles, when their use has been expressly agreed and specified in the consignment note;
(b) The lack of, or defective condition of packing in the case of goods which, by their nature, are liable to wastage or to be damaged when not packed or when not properly packed;
(c) Handling, loading, stowage or unloading of the goods by the sender, the consignee or persons acting on behalf of the sender or the consignee;
(d) The nature of certain kinds of goods which particularly exposes them to total or partial loss or to damage, especially through breakage, rust, decay, desiccation, leakage, normal wastage, or the action of moth or vermin;
(e) Insufficiency or inadequacy of marks or numbers on the packages;
(f) The carriage of livestock.

5.   Where under this article the carrier is not under any liability in respect of some of the factors causing the loss, damage or delay, he shall only be liable to the extent that those factors for which he is liable under this article have contributed to the loss, damage or delay.

continued on next page

Exhibit 5.2 (continued)

Article 18

1.   The burden of proving that loss, damage or delay was due to one of the causes specified in article 17, paragraph 2, shall rest upon the carrier.

2.   When the carrier establishes that in the circumstances of the case, the loss or damage could be attributed to one or more of the special risks referred to in article 17, paragraph 4, it shall be presumed that it was so caused. The claimant shall however be entitled to prove that the loss or damage was not, in fact, attributable either wholly or partly to one of these risks.

3.   This presumption shall not apply in the circumstances set out in article 17, paragraph 4 (a), if there has been an abnormal shortage, or a loss of any package.

4.   If the carriage is performed in vehicles specially equipped to protect the goods from the effects of heat, cold, variations in temperature or the humidity of the air, the carrier shall not be entitled to claim the benefit of article 17, paragraph 4 (d), unless he proves that all steps incumbent on him in the circumstances with respect to the choice, maintenance and use of such equipment were taken and that he complied with any special instructions issued to him.

5.   The carrier shall not be entitled to claim the benefit of article 17, paragraph 4 (f), unless he proves that all steps normally incumbent on him in the circumstances were taken and that he complied with any special instructions issued to him.

Article 18, paragraph 1 adds that the burden of proof rests on the carrier to show that it falls within conditions for relief from liability in Article 17, paragraph 2.[50] Thus the carrier will be liable for a loss of the goods while in its charge unless it proves it was unable to avoid the incident or to prevent the consequences. This appears to be a hard standard for the carrier to meet because the degree of fault is not expressly conditioned upon due diligence or reasonable care; it is stated in strict terms. However, there has been considerable controversy over the interpretation and application of this standard. It appears to have been developed from the concept of *force majeure* and therefore some commentators consider it substantially requires the road haulier to show that the damage to the cargo was incurred without its fault. Others argue that a showing of appropriate efforts to safekeep the

---

[50] *Ibid.*

cargo is sufficient, though the standard of safekeeping is said to be greater than the ordinary measure of reasonable care, probably more like utmost care.[51]

It is agreed by all that the road carrier would not be liable for losses through circumstances that were not its fault, some of which are specified in Article 17 as special risks.[52] Obvious ones include the faults of the cargo owner and the defects in the goods themselves or their packaging and marking. In the circumstances of the immediate Case, supposing the pilferage of the machinery had been pinpointed to the final stage of delivery by land, the road carrier would probably be liable for the loss, since it would likely be unable to show that the theft could not have been prevented.[53]

The CIM Uniform Rules on Carriage by Rail

The first international segment of this multimodal movement is overland from Detroit, U.S. to Montreal, Canada, by rail. Accordingly, the possibly relevant unimodal convention would be the Convention concerning International Carriage by Rail, or COTIF,[54] which contains in Appendix B the Uniform Rules concerning the Contract for International Carriage of Goods by Rail, known in abbreviated form as the CIM Uniform Rules. However, neither the United States nor Canada are parties to this Convention, which is essentially an European arrangement for the highly interlinked national railway systems on that continent. Thus the accusation of theft on the North American rail stage of the movement will fall for determination in accordance with the local law, which in this instance will likely be U.S. federal law, in the absence of any express choice by the parties of another legal regime. But supposing the CIM Uniform Rules were the law of reference, it is useful to compare their provisions with the other unimodal regimes.

---

[51] Compare M.A. Clarke, *International Carriage of Goods by Road: CMR* (London: Stevens, 1982) at 109; R. De Wit, *Multimodal Transport, Carrier Liability and Documentation* (London: Lloyd's of London Press, 1995) at 96; D.A. Glass & C. Cashmore, *supra* note 36 at 112; D.J. Hill & M.D. Messent, *CMR: Contracts for the International Carriage of Goods by Road* (London: Lloyd's of London Press, 1984) at 76; J. Libouton, 'Liability of the CMR Carrier in Belgium Case Law' in J. Theunis, ed., *International Carriage of Goods by Road* (London: Lloyd's of London Press, 1987) at 82.

[52] And carry a less onerous burden of proof: see art. 18(2)-(5).

[53] See D.J. Hill & M.D. Messent, *supra* note 51 at 80; J. Libouton, *supra* note 51 at 84.

[54] See Appendix 1. COTIF established the Intergovernmental Organisation for International Carriage by Rail and consolidated and replaced the earlier independent CIM Convention and CIV (passenger and luggage) Convention.

Exhibit 5.3:
CIM Uniform Rules on Carriage by Rail, Articles 36 & 37

Article 36
Extent of Liability

§1. The railway shall be liable for loss or damage resulting from the total or partial loss of, or damage to, the goods between the time of acceptance for carriage and the time of delivery and for the loss or damage resulting from the transit period being exceeded.

§2. The railway shall be relieved of such liability if the loss or damage or the exceeding of the transit period was caused by a fault on the part of the person entitled, by an order given by the person entitled other than as a result of a fault on the part of the railway, by inherent vice of the goods (decay, wastage, etc.) or by circumstances which the railway could not avoid and the consequences of which it was unable to prevent.

§3. The railway shall be relieved of such liability when the loss or damage arises from the special risks inherent in one or more of the following circumstances:

(a) carriage in open wagons under the conditions applicable thereto or under an agreement made between the consignor and the railway and referred to in the consignment note;

(b) absence or inadequacy of packing in the case of goods which by their nature are liable to loss or damage when not packed or when not properly packed;

(c) loading operations carried out by the consignor or unloading operations carried out by the consignee under the provisions applicable thereto or under an agreement made between the consignor and the railway and referred to in the consignment note, or under an agreement between the consignee and the railway;

(d) defective loading, when loading has been carried out by the consignor under the provisions applicable thereto or under an agreement made between the consignor and the railway and referred to in the consignment note;

(e) completion by the consignor, the consignee or an agent of either, of the formalities required by Customs or other administrative authorities;

continued next page

Exhibit 5.3 (continued)

(f) the nature of certain goods which renders them inherently liable to total or partial loss or damage, especially through breakage, rust, interior and spontaneous decay, desiccation or wastage;

(g) irregular, incorrect or incomplete description of articles not acceptable for carriage or acceptable subject to conditions, or failure on the part of the consignor to observe the prescribed precautions in respect of articles acceptable subject to conditions;

(h) carriage of live animals;

(i) carriage which, under the provisions applicable or under an agreement made between the consignor and the railway and referred to in the consignment note, must be accompanied by an attendant, if the loss or damage results from any risk which the attendant was intended to avert.

Article 37
Burden of Proof

§1. The burden of proving that the loss, the damage or the exceeding of the transit period was due to one of the causes specified in Article 36, §2 shall rest upon the railway.

§2. When the railway establishes that, having regard to the circumstances of a particular case, the loss or damage could have arisen from one or more of the special risks referred to in Article 36, §3, it shall be presumed that it did so arise. The person entitled shall, however, have the right to prove that the loss or damage was not attributable either wholly or partly to one of those risks.

The carrier's responsibility for the goods under the CIM Uniform Rules is expressed in language very similar to the CMR Convention on road haulage.[55] Thus Article 36 states:

1. The railway shall be liable for loss or damage resulting from the total or partial loss of, or damage to, the goods between the time of acceptance for carriage and the time of delivery... .

2. The railway shall be relieved of such liability if the loss or damage ... was caused ... by circumstances which the railway could not avoid and the consequences of which it was unable to prevent.

---

[55] See Exhibit 5.3 for the full text of the CIM Uniform Rules arts. 36 and 37.

By Article 37, paragraph 1, when relief from liability is asserted on these grounds, the burden of proof of fault, or rather its absence, is placed on the railway.[56] Thus the rail carrier appears to face the same high standard of presumed liability for the goods in its charge as the road carrier under the CMR.[57] Similarly, a number of specific and more numerous exceptions from liability, when the railway is not at fault, are set out in these articles.[58] Once again these 'special risks' centre on defaults of the goods' owner and defects in the goods themselves which are beyond the control of the railway. The theft of the machinery in this case, however, falls squarely within the rail carrier's duty of care for the goods, which it will have great difficulty in proving it did not breach.

The Warsaw Convention on Carriage by Air

There was no air carriage involved in the movement in this Case, but had there been, the Warsaw Convention[59] would be the governing unimodal agreement. This convention has been very widely adopted—more widely than any other international transport agreement—including by all the countries involved in this case. The basis of liability expressed in the Warsaw Convention is very similar to the two land transport agreements. Article 18 states:[60]

> 1. The carrier is liable for damage sustained in the event of the destruction or loss of, or of damage to, any registered luggage or any goods, if the occurrence which caused the damage so sustained took place during the carriage by air. ...

This custodial liability is qualified in Article 20:[61]

> 1. The carrier is not liable if he proves that he and his agents have taken all necessary measures to avoid the damage or that it was impossible for him or them to take such measures.

---

56 *Ibid.*

57 See R. De Wit *supra* note 51 at 117; D.A. Glass & C. Cashmore, *supra* note 36 at 147.

58 The burden of proof is also altered: see art. 37(2). See also arts. 19 and 20.

59 See Appendix 1.

60 Subject to amendment by the 1971 Guatemala Convention, *ibid.*, art. V, not yet in force, and the 1975 Montreal Additional Protocol IV, *ibid.*, art. IV, not yet in force.

61 Subject to amendment by the 1971 Guatemala Convention, *supra* note 59, art. VI, not yet in force, and the 1975 Montreal Additional Protocol IV, *supra* note 59, art. V, not yet in force.

Thus the air carrier is also liable on the familiar standard of presumed default in the safekeeping of the cargo in its charge. It may only escape this liability by proving that it took 'all necessary measures' of prevention possible. This appears to be a stringent standard to which the original Warsaw Convention makes no express exceptions. However, different interpretations of this standard have been applied in practice, especially between common law and civil law countries. Common law courts seem ready to exonerate the air carrier if it can show that it took all measures necessary with a reasonable degree of skill and care. Civil law courts appear to require a stricter standard of conduct, something akin to proof that the cargo damage was beyond the air carrier's control.[62]

If the Montreal Additional Protocol IV[63] should come into force, the Warsaw Convention will be amended and air carriers will clearly become subject to a regime of strict liability. The carrier will automatically be held liable for any loss or damage suffered by the cargo while in its charge, subject to four specific exceptions.[64] These are well known defences, namely inherent vice of the cargo, defective packing by the shipper, armed conflict, and acts of public authorities.

In substance, these incidents are all impossible for the air carrier to prevent and so they may also be regarded as grounds for excuse from liability under the general language of the Warsaw Convention presently in force. Theft of cargo, as occurred to TrucSA's machinery, is not of this nature. Were it to have occurred during air carriage, the carrier would find it extraordinarily difficult to establish that it took 'all necessary measures' to avoid the damage sustained by TrucSA.

Summary of Basis of Liability in Unimodal Conventions

The conclusion to be drawn from this brief exploration of the unimodal conventions is that the general principle on which the responsibility of the carrier is based is much the same. Thus under the ICC Rules 1975 whenever a loss can be attributed to a particular stage of the multimodal movement so as to invoke by reference the application of the international regime governing that mode of carriage, the operator will be deemed to be liable until it rebuts the presumption of fault. However, the unifying effect of this principle is moderated by the differences in the specified grounds for excuse from liability and in the standard of care demanded of the carrier. Even so, the unimodal conventions for air, rail and road transport and the Hamburg Rules for sea carriage probably all excuse the carrier, and thus the

---

[62] See G. Miller, *Liability in International Air Transport* (Deventer: Kluwer, 1977) at 161-167.
[63] See Appendix 1.
[64] *Ibid.*, art. IV.

multimodal operator, OverCo in this Case, if it made highly conscientious efforts to prevent or avoid the loss.[65] Only under the Hague and Hague/Visby Rules in the marine mode are there special and more generous exemptions from liability.

Under the UNCTAD/ICC Rules 1992

The UNCTAD/ICC Rules 1992 take an approach to the operator's liability for localized loss and damage that partially reflects the practice of both the previous sets of rules. Like the MTC 1980, the UNCTAD/ICC Rules 1992 apply the principle of presumed fault and do not refer to the underlying unimodal laws.[66] Thus OverCo will be held responsible unless it can show that the loss occurred without its fault or neglect, regardless of where the incident occurred. However, in one respect the UNCTAD/ICC Rules 1992 are comparable to the ICC Rules 1975 in that they make special provision for loss that is attributed to sea carriage. Extra defences against liability are granted in the event the casualty occurred on the sea leg. In these circumstances the operator is excused if the cargo loss resulted from the specific incidents of negligence in the navigation or management of the carrying vessel, or fire, if caused without its fault or privity.[67]

These excuses are a throwback to the two most contentious exceptions to liability found in the unimodal rules for sea carriage.[68] Moreover, they considerably complicate the liability regime governing multimodal transport. This is unfortunate, but explainable. The multimodal operator would not be able to recover an indemnity from the actual carrier on the sea leg in these circumstances, so why, it may be reasoned, should it have to take responsibility for the excusable faults of its subcontractors?[69] Therefore, under the UNCTAD/ICC Rules 1992, if OverCo cannot successfully establish that the loss of the machinery occurred without fault or negligence, it will be held liable. However, it may be excused if it can pinpoint the source of the problem to some negligent act of the ship's crew during the

---

[65] Compare R. Rodière, 'Introduction to Transport Law and Combined Transports' in *International Encyclopedia of Comparative Law*, Vol. XII (Tübingen: J.C.B. Mohr (Paul Siebeck)) at 31-32.

[66] UNCTAD/ICC 1992 rule 5(1).

[67] UNCTAD/ICC 1992 rule 5(4), provided the operator, OverCo, can prove it exercised due diligence to make its vessel seaworthy before the voyage.

[68] Namely the Hague and Hague/Visby Rules; see Appendix 1. The Hamburg Rules, in force but not widespread use, only contain a modified version of the fire exception. See the previous discussion of these Rules in this chapter after note 23.

[69] As opposed to its vicarious liability for their inexcusable faults; see UNCTAD/ICC 1992 rules 4.2, 5.1 and Chapter 8 under Application of the Multimodal Rules to the Operator's Agents.

sea leg of the movement.[70] Even so, such negligence is only excusable when it is committed in relation to the navigation or management of the ship.[71] Inadequate care and supervision of the container of machinery so as to prevent theft, as alleged in this Case, is not within the exemption from liability for negligent navigation.

Extent of Liability for Attributed Loss

Once the operator, OverCo, has been found responsible for the loss of the machinery, it is necessary to calculate the extent of its liability to compensate TrucSA. This calculation is governed first by the extent of TrucSA's commercial loss and then by the limits of OverCo's liability. Since the factual circumstances of Case 1 in Chapter 4 and Case 2 here are so similar, the quantification of TrucSA's loss will follow the same lines. In both cases, TrucSA was deprived of two packages of machinery, in the one by breakage and in the other by theft, but this difference in the cause of the injury does not affect the extent of the commercial loss.

Hence, following the analysis in Chapter 4,[72] TrucSA's claim is for the physical loss of two packages of its machinery, which will be calculated according to the arrived sound market value in Belgium for such products. TrucSA's concern will then be whether it can recover the full extent of its commercial loss from OverCo. The Multimodal Rules permit an operator, such as OverCo, to limit its liability in most situations, as outlined in Chapter 4.[73] But the manner of calculating the limit is a great deal more complicated where, as in this Case, the incident that caused the loss has been attributed to a particular carrier or cargo handler. Further, if the applicable limit of OverCo's liability is less than the value of the stolen machinery, TrucSA will want to try and set aside that ceiling in order to claim full compensation.

Limits of Liability for Attributed Loss

The different sets of multimodal rules are unanimous that, if the loss or damage to the cargo can be attributed to a particular stage of the movement, the appropriate rules for that mode should govern the limit of the

---

[70] The operator may also assert the fire exception where appropriate, but that defence seems hardly relevant in a case of theft, as opposed to an incident causing damage.

[71] As discussed in relation to the Hague Rules at note 39.

[72] See Chapter 4 under Extent of Liability for Unattributed Loss.

[73] *Ibid.*

multimodal operator's liability.[74] As a result, the multimodal operator will generally bear the same liability as if it had contracted as a unimodal carrier for each leg of the journey itself. The effect of this principle is to establish even greater variations in the limits of liability than the differences under the Multimodal Rules themselves for unattributable loss and damage. This is because the unimodal conventions make widely differing provisions for compensation. The variation in liability limits for unattributed loss under the Multimodal Rules, when a sea leg is involved in the movement, is from 2 to 2.75 SDR per kilogramme as displayed in Exhibit 4.1 in Chapter 4. For comparison, the table in Exhibit 5.4 provides a view of the full extent of divergence in liability limits when the unimodal regimes are brought into operation from 2 SDR per kilogramme for sea carriage under the Hague/Visby Rules up to 17 SDR per kilogramme for carriage by rail and potentially for air transport as well.

It is very noticeable from Exhibit 5.4 that the limits of liability for unattributed losses under all three sets of multimodal rules settle as a group close to the maximum rates of compensation payable for loss and damage at sea. The conclusion is inescapable that the limits under the Multimodal Rules have been set by reference to the lowest measure of liability under the separate unimodal regimes. This conclusion is reinforced by the provision in the MTC 1980 and the UNCTAD/ICC Rules 1992 that when there is no sea leg in the movement, the limit of liability rises to a figure equivalent to the next lowest maximum rate of compensation under the unimodal conventions, that is for transportation by road. As a result, the multimodal operator is afforded the protection that generally it will never have to pay more compensation for an unattributed loss than it would if the cause of the loss could be localized. The cargo claimant, on the other hand, is exposed to the risk that the cause of the loss cannot be localized and thus must forego possibly a very substantially higher sum of compensation. As Exhibit 5.4 displays, the maximum recovery for cargo injury by road is more than four times higher than for a loss at sea. In the case of rail or air transport, the recovery may exceed eight times the rate for loss by sea.

---

[74] ICC 1975 rule 13; MTC 1980 art. 19; UNCTAD/ICC 1992 rule 6.4.

Exhibit 5.4:Comparable Limits of Liability under Unimodal and Multimodal Regimes in Ascending Order of Magnitude

Regime	Limit by Weight	Limit by Item
Sea Carriage—Hague Rules[1]	n/a	U.S. $500/pkg($\cong$ 338 SDR/pkg)
– Hague/Visby Rules[2]	2.00 SDR/kg	666.67 SDR/pkg
– Hamburg Rules[3]	2.50 SDR/kg	835 SDR/pkg
ICC Rules 1975[4]	30 francs/kg ($\cong$2 SDR/kg)	n/a
UNCTAD/ICC Rules 1992[5] – but if no sea leg	2.00 SDR/kg 8.33 SDR/kg	666.67 SDR/pkg
MTC 1980[6] – but if no sea leg	2.75 SDR/kg 8.33 SDR/kg	920 SDR/pkg
Road Carriage—CMR[7]	8.33 SDR/kg	n/a
Rail Carriage—CIM Uniform Rules[8]	17.00 SDR/kg	n/a
Air Carriage—Warsaw Convention[9]	17.00 SDR/kg	n/a

Notes: Full references to the unimodal conventions appear in Appendix 1.

[1] Arts. IV(5) and IX. The limit was originally fixed at £100 gold value but the Hague Rules permit implementing states to translate this sum into their own currency, which most have done. The U.S. 'equivalent' (found in U.S. Carriage of Goods by Sea Act, 1936, 46 U.S.C. App. §1315, s. 4(5)) is given because the United States is the most important state still applying the Hague Rules. US$500 is converted at the rate of US$1.48 = 1 SDR (as of August 1996). The United Kingdom has moved from the Hague Rules and £ sterling values to the Hague/Visby Rules and SDR limits.

[2] Art. IV (5).

[3] Art. 6.

[4] Rule 11(c). 2 SDR/kg. is the unofficial conversion of 30 Poincaré gold francs: see Chapter 4, note 27.

[5] Rules 6.1 and 6.3.

[6] Art. 18(1), (3).

[7] Art. 23.

[8] Arts. 7, 40 and 42.

[9] Art. 22(2), which quotes a rate of 250 Poincaré gold francs/kg 17 SDR/kg will be the converted equivalent rate when the amending Montreal Protocols take effect.

In the application of the unimodal regimes by reference within the Multimodal Rules there is one small but significant variation. Unlike the ICC Rules 1975 and the UNCTAD/ICC Rules 1992, the MTC 1980 defers to the relevant unimodal rules only if they provide a higher limit of liability.[75] As Exhibit 5.4 shows, only in the case of loss during the ocean stage of a movement would this approach affect the limit of compensation. Hence, if the loss of the two packages of machinery in this Case were to be attributed to the sea stage of carriage by OverCo itself, the MTC 1980 would provide an advantage to TrucSA over the other sets of rules. The extent of this advantage is shown in Exhibit 5.5.

Exhibit 5.5: Case 2, Comparable Limits of Liability under the Marine Regimes and the MTC 1980

Regime	Rate[1]	SDR Limit	US$ Limit
Hague Rules	U.S. $500/pkg ($\cong$ 338 SDR/pkg)	-- 676	1,000.00
Hague/Visby Rules	666.67 SDR/pkg 2.00 SDR/kg	1,333.34 1,390	1,973.34 2,057.20
Hamburg Rules	835 SDR/pkg 2.50 SDR/kg	1,670 1,737.50	2,471.60 2,571.50
MTC 1980	920 SDR/pkg 2.75 SDR/kg	1,840 1,911.25	2,723.20 2,826.65

Note: [1] Per Exhibit 5.4. Basis of calculations: Shipment of 28 packages of machinery weighing 19,460 kg. Hence the 2 missing packages each weigh 695 kg. 1 SDR approximately equals US$1.48 (as of August 1996).

Since the limits of liability under the MTC 1980 are greater than under any of the three existing regimes for sea carriage, TrucSA may claim the benefit of the higher ceilings under the MTC. And since the MTC 1980 itself requires the multimodal operator to pay compensation at a rate per package or per kilogramme 'whichever is the higher,'[76] TrucSA can take advantage of the heaviness of its machinery to recover up to US$2,826.65. Were the

---

[75] MTC 1980 art. 19.
[76] MTC 1980 art. 18(1).

movement subject to the ICC Rules 1975 or the UNCTAD/ICC Rules 1992, TrucSA would be forced to accept compensation at a rate fixed by the particular marine regime applicable to that movement. In this Case, since the cargo was shipped out of Montreal to Europe, the Canadian law imposing the Hague/Visby Rules would apply.[77] Thus TrucSA would have to be satisfied with a maximum compensation, per Exhibit 5.5, of US$2,057.20.[78]

The application of the Hague/Visby Rules is coincidental to this movement. Any one of the three marine regimes might apply. If, for instance, the machinery had been shipped not from Montreal, but out of New York, the unamended Hague Rules, as implemented by U.S. legislation,[79] would be indicated. In that case the limit of OverCo's liability, per Exhibit 5.5, would be U.S. $1,000.00. This multiplicity of conventions and limits of liability for carriage by sea are not conducive to certainty or simplicity in the regulation of responsibility of the multimodal operator for attributed loss. Even so, the differences among the sea carriage conventions are insignificant in comparison with the liability limits in other modes.

If TrucSA's machinery had been stolen on the road or rail stages of the movement or in a terminal during transhipment, rather than on the sea leg, other much higher limits of compensation might apply. Exhibit 5.6 amply shows the magnitude of the differences in liability maxima that would fall upon OverCo in this Case under the appropriate conventions.

As it happens, the CIM Uniform Rules on rail carriage do not apply in this instance because the United States and Canada, where the rail journey occurred in this movement, are not parties to them. The vagaries in the limits of liability are thus exacerbated by the lack of universal adoption of the otherwise uniform modal conventions. Where the relevant unimodal convention is not applicable, the local national law will determine the extent of the multimodal operator's liability, and the possibility of any international uniformity is a matter of pure chance. Local law, typically made for good local reasons without reference to the needs of multimodal international transportation, may range from one extreme of requiring the operator to pay the full amount of the loss, without any right of limitation, to allowing it to disclaim all responsibility.[80]

---

[77] See Can. *Carriage of Goods by Water Act*, S.C. 1993, c. 21.

[78] The Hague/Visby Rules, Appendix 1, art. IV (5)(a), also permit the cargo owner to recover per package or per kilogramme, whichever rate produces the higher compensation.

[79] U.S. *Carriage of Goods by Sea Act, 1936*, 46 U.S.C. App. §1315.

[80] In this Case the relevant regime is probably the U.S. federal law since the rail movement originated in the United States before crossing an international frontier into Canada.

Exhibit 5.6:
Case 2, Limits of Liability for Attributed Theft of Machinery

Mode/Regime	Limit by Weight	SDR Limit	US$ Limit[4]
Sea Carriage[1] – Hague/Visby Rules (when ICC 1975 and UNCTAD/ICC 1992 Rules apply)	2.00 SDR/kg	1,390.00	2,057.20
– MTC 1980	2.75 SDR/kg	1,911.25	2,826.65
Road Carriage - CMR[2]	8.33 SDR/kg	5,789.35	8,568.24
Rail Carriage—CIM[2] Uniform Rules	17.00 SDR/kg	11,815.00	17,486.20
Air Carriage[3]—Warsaw Convention[2]	17.00 SDR/kg	11,815.00	17,486.20

Notes:
[1] Per Exhibit 5.5.
[2] Per Exhibit 5.4.
[3] Included for comparison, though not part of Case 2.
[4] 1 SDR approximately equals US$1.48 (as of August 1996).

In the event, TrucSA may not be satisfied with the amount of compensation it will receive for the two missing packages, as calculated in accordance with the applicable limit of liability, because their value exceeds this sum. Hence it will want to circumvent the ceiling on compensation in order to hold OverCo liable for the full extent of its loss. But, as explained in Chapter 4,[81] the Multimodal Rules set the exclusive grounds on which the limits of liability may be overreached. The operator will lose its right to limit its liability only if it committed a personal act or omission that was done either with the intent to cause the loss incurred, or recklessly with the knowledge that such loss would probably be incurred.[82] Consequently TrucSA will have practically no chance of breaking the limits of liability in this case. It is extremely unlikely that OverCo would be personally implicated in the theft of the machinery, unless it could be shown to have been recklessly careless in its methods of safekeeping cargoes from theft.

---

81 See Chapter 4 at note 31.
82 ICC 1975 rule 17; MTC 1980 art. 21; UNCTAD/ICC 1992 rule 7.

CHAPTER 6

Liability for Delayed Delivery of Goods

Case 3: Delayed Delivery of Goods

The Fascinating Toy Company (FTC) of Barking, Essex, in the United Kingdom makes a robotic Santa Claus which laughs and hugs children. The toy, called Happy Santa, is very popular with parents of children aged 3-4 as a Christmas or pre-Christmas present. The demand for the toy is seasonal, with sales between 25 December and 1 October being almost nil. Last year FTC's Happy Santa was selling remarkably well in stores in Vancouver, British Columbia, and so the Superior Department Store (SuperStore), which has 8 outlets in that city, placed an additional order with FTC on 1 November to restock its rapidly depleting shelves with more Happy Santas. The order from SuperStore indicated to FTC that the toys must be delivered on or before 10 December. The agreed price for the toys was £3,456 (C$6,912) and the stated terms of the purchase were CIP, i.e., carriage and insurance paid to SuperStore's warehouse in Vancouver, with payment on open account net 45 days.

FTC, assured by the Multi-Modal Company representative that there would be no difficulty meeting the 10 December deadline for delivery, booked a door-to-warehouse (Vancouver) move with a 8 December delivery date for 6 pallets of Happy Santas weighing 180 kilogrammes per pallet. The rate quoted for the move was £1,150 (C$2,300). Multi-Modal, which acts as a consolidator for a number of forwarding agents, set to work seeking other goods to add to FTC's LCL shipment. It ultimately dispatched a full container of packages weighing a total of 15,267 kilogrammes for a total freight of C$4,376. Multi-Modal subcontracted the sea carriage across the Atlantic to Halifax, Nova Scotia, to Overseas Shipping Co. Ltd. (OverCo) and the rail onward transport to Vancouver to Atlantic Canada Pacific Railways Ltd. (ACP Rail).

continued next page

Case 3 (continued)

> Unfortunately, Multi-Modal failed to meet the delivery date. The ocean carrying vessel suffered engine trouble and so docked 2 days later than scheduled in Halifax. On the rail journey across Canada, the car carrying the container was shunted onto a siding in Montreal, Quebec, and overlooked for a week. It was held up further by bad weather and snow that temporarily blocked the track through the Rocky Mountains in British Columbia. As a result, the Happy Santas were delivered 15 days late and SuperStore refused to accept them. Consequently FTC had to arrange to dispose of the toys at a fire sale price in Vancouver. It now claims from Multi-Modal Co. the whole benefit of the transaction lost by reason of the delay.

Introduction

The loss of business on account of delayed delivery, illustrated by this Case, is an increasingly frequent occurrence as manufacturers, assemblers and other producers and distributors have cut their inventories and capital costs and moved to just-in-time and similar logistically refined systems of scheduling their operations. In this Case, the date of delivery was crucial to the contract, as SuperStore made clear to FTC, and therefore Superstore was entitled to reject the toys for breach of this obligation.[1] But FTC has suffered a financial loss simply because its shipment was delayed in carriage. Naturally FTC will expect to recoup that loss from Multi-Modal with whom it contracted for delivery. However, breach of the delivery contract by delay differs significantly from breach by damage or destruction of the goods. Generally it is not a source of physical injury to the shipment and therefore does not result in permanent deprivation of the goods by their owner.[2] Delay only causes temporary loss of use of the goods which are otherwise delivered whole. Hence delay is not itself a measurable loss in the way that damage to goods can be quantified by reference to the value of the goods themselves. Delay in delivery causes purely economic, or financial, loss, if it causes any loss at all, and the extent of that loss will vary not by reference to the value of the goods but by reference to the reasons for moving them.

---

[1] See P.S. Atiyah, *The Sale of Goods* 8th ed. (London: Pitman, 1990) at 109; A.G. Guest, gen. ed., *Benjamin's Sale of Goods* 3d ed. (London: Sweet & Maxwell, 1987) at 345; A.G. Guest, gen. ed., *Chitty on Contracts* 27th ed., Vol. 2 (London: Sweet & Maxwell, 1994) at 1121.

[2] Unless the delay causes damage to the goods (e.g., perishable goods which are held up so long that they decay) in which case their owner essentially has a damage claim. Compare R. De Wit, *Multimodal Transport, Carrier Liability and Documentation* (London: Lloyds of London Press, 1995) at 216-217.

Hence different bases for ascribing responsibility to the multimodal operator and for measuring the extent of its liability have to be applied to claims founded on delay.

Proof of Loss

Like the cargo owner who has suffered physical loss or damage to goods, the claimant, FTC, bears the initial responsibility of proving it has suffered loss by delay.[3] This task may be more difficult than establishing a *prima facie* case of damage to goods. The usual practice of producing a clean transport document and a survey of the goods upon receipt will not disclose delay. FTC will have to go forward with affirmative proof that the shipment of Happy Santas was delivered late and that their untimely delivery was the cause of its financial loss. These are two separate matters: 1) the fact of delay, and 2) the cause of the loss. They must both be satisfactorily established to found a successful claim.

It is clear in this Case that the Happy Santas arrived several days after the consignee, SuperStore, wanted and expected them. But the fact the shipment was late under the contract of sale by FTC to SuperStore is not proof of delay by the carrier, Multi-Modal. The crucial question is whether FTC agreed on a date or time for delivery with Multi-Modal. In this Case, it is clear that the representative of Multi-Modal assured FTC that its desired December deadline for delivery would be met. Thus Multi-Modal can be shown to know of the need for, and to have agreed to, delivery of the shipment on or before 8 December.

If there had not been such a clear understanding between the shipper and the multimodal operator, as there often is not, the shipper would have a more complex task to prove delay. Absent an agreed date of delivery, the claimant cannot simply assert delay by showing the goods arrived later than it desired or expected them. Thus the fact that a liner vessel or a train falls behind the carrier's published schedule may not be sufficient proof of delay by the cargo claimant. In fact, carriers frequently declare in their schedules or in their transport documents that they are not bound by their timetables, which are merely indicative. When there is no fixed date for delivery, the cargo owner must show that the length of time it took to deliver the goods was unreasonable.[4] It becomes a question of fact, therefore, what would be

---

3 See M. Ganado and H.M. Kindred, *Marine Cargo Delays* (London: Lloyd's of London Press, 1990) at 77.

4 *Ibid.* See also MTC 1980 art. 16(2) which states: 'Delay in deliver occurs when the goods have not been delivered within the time expressly agreed upon or, in the absence of such agreement, within the time which it would be reasonable to require of a diligent multimodal transport operator, having regard to the circumstances of the case.' A practically identical definition of delay is expressed in UNCTAD/ICC 1992 rule 5.2.

regarded as the normal amount of time required for comparable movements to the one that was allegedly delayed. On this point the schedules of the particular carrier involved, as well as its competitors on the same route, are helpful, for they provide evidence, perhaps the best evidence, of what, in the practical experience of that trade, is a reasonable time for transit and delivery.

Once the cargo claimant has established how long the carriage reasonably should have taken and that it took longer, it has made a sufficient case for delay. It does not have to go further into the circumstances of the delay; that will be for the carrier or operator to argue in trying to refute its liability for the delay. But the cargo claimant must go on to prove that the delay caused the losses it claims to have suffered. That should not be difficult for FTC in this Case since the character of the goods is so evidently seasonal that the financial failure of the transaction can easily be ascribed to the loss of the Christmas market as a result of late delivery. But in other instances concerning non-seasonal and non-perishable goods the connection between the loss of market opportunity and delayed delivery will require more affirmative proof.[5] Once the cargo claimant has made a case of loss by delay, the question of the operator's liability for that loss comes forward.

Basis of Liability for Delay

Liability for delay is the area in which the international rules differ in approach most sharply. Each has its own basis of liability, which represents different attitudes to the issue of carrier responsibility for delayed delivery. The different standards of liability are immediately apparent upon reading the individual rules set out below. The difference in effect for a multimodal operator will become clear by discussing the application of each standard to FTC's claim in this Case.

Under the ICC Rules 1997[5], the operator 'is liable to pay compensation for delay only when the stage of transport where a delay occurred is known, and to the extent that there is liability under any [compulsorily applicable] international Convention or national law, the provisions of which ... would have applied if the claimant had made a separate and direct contract with the [multimodal operator] as operator of that stage of transport... .'[6] Thus the issue of delay in the multimodal movement is referred to the underlying unimodal rules and laws.

The MTC 1980 makes the operator 'liable for loss resulting from loss of or damage to the goods, as well as from delay in delivery, if the occurrence

---

5 As to the complexities of causation of loss through delay, see Ganado and Kindred, *supra* note 3 at 23-25 and 59-69.

6 ICC 1975 rule 14. See also rule 5(b), (c) and (f).

which caused the ... delay in delivery took place while the goods were in his charge ... unless [he] proves that he ... took all measures that could reasonably be required to avoid the occurrence and its consequences.'[7] Hence the basis of liability for delay under the MTC 1980 is the same principle of presumed fault that applies to claims of physical loss and damage to goods.

The UNCTAD/ICC Rules 1992 similarly apply the same principles to a claim of loss by delay as they do to claims for lost or damaged goods. Those principles also invoke the presumed fault of the operator but are subject to more defences and exceptions than the MTC 1980.[8] In addition, the UNCTAD/ICC Rules 1992 also state that the operator 'shall not be liable for loss following from delay in delivery unless the consignor has made a declaration of interest in timely delivery which has been accepted by the [operator].'[9] Thus the UNCTAD/ICC Rules require a prior agreement for timely delivery before the operator may be held liable for delay.

One subsidiary principle regarding delay is common to all three sets of rules. This is the principle that after 90 days of delay in delivery and in the absence of evidence otherwise, the shipper may treat the goods as lost.[10] This principle permits the shipper to bring a claim without having to wait for delivery forever. More importantly, it allows the shipper to convert its claim from delay in delivery to physical loss of its shipment. Thus the basis and extent of the MTO's liability will be assessed, probably to the advantage of the cargo claimant, in accordance with the principles for loss and damage to goods discussed in Chapters 4 and 5, and not further under the principles of delay in this chapter.

Under the MTC 1980

Consideration of the impact of the different approaches to responsibility for delay will proceed from the simplest to the most complex. The MTC 1980 poses least difficulty and uncertainty since it applies the familiar principle of presumed fault in a uniform way to all kinds of losses, both physical and financial. As discussed in Chapter 4 in respect of damage to goods,[11] the multimodal operator will be held liable for delay incurred as a result of both its own acts or omissions and those of its employees, agents and

---

7   MTC 1980 art. 16(1).
8   See the discussion in Chapter 5 under Basis of Liability for Attributed Loss under the UNCTAD/ICC Rules 1992.
9   UNCTAD/ICC 1992 rule 5.1.
10 ICC 1975 rule 15; MTC 1980 art. 16(3); UNCTAD/ICC 1992 rule 5.3.
11 See Chapter 4 under Basis of Liability for Unattributed Damage.

subcontractors.[12] This liability is assumed until the operator can demonstrate that it, and all the other carriers and cargo handlers into whose charge it placed the goods, took all measures that could reasonably be expected to prevent and limit the delay. Thus the operator's liability depends upon the collective responsibility of the performing carriers, terminals and other cargo handlers, as well as its own conduct.

This approach of collective responsibility is significant in this Case where there appears to have been three incidents that contributed to the ultimate delay of 15 days. The carrying ship suffered engine trouble and so fell behind schedule. The railway company parked the container in Montreal for a week and then its train was held up in the Rocky Mountains by bad weather. It does not seem to matter how much each incident contributed to the ultimate delay in delivery so much as whether each carrier took reasonable care to avoid delaying the movement of the goods. The operator, Multi-Modal, will be liable to FTC for all the consequences of the delay if any one of its subcontracted carriers did not act reasonably, for there is no suggestion in the MTC 1980 that the responsibility may be divided and attributed among them.[13]

It is necessary, however, to investigate each incident that contributed to the resulting delay to determine whether it could have been prevented or avoided by reasonable efforts by the carrier at the time, or was not its fault. Taking the incidents chronologically, the first to consider was the delay at sea said to be caused by engine trouble suffered by OverCo's ship. Without more details, it is impossible to say whether the engine failures could have been foreseen and prevented or their consequences avoided. The important point is there would have to be an investigation into the diligence of the master during the voyage and of the shipowner, OverCo, in preparing the vessel for sailing. Thus if the delay resulted from the vessel running out of bunker fuel or from an engine breakdown caused by lack of maintenance according to industry standards, OverCo would not have discharged its burden of reasonable diligence. In that event, Multi-Modal could not escape its liability for the resulting delay. If, however, OverCo could show that its ship was the victim of some unforeseeable and unpreventable mishap— perhaps that it suffered unforecast and unseasonably heavy weather—it could not be blamed for being late in arriving at Halifax, and therefore Multi-Modal would have established it was not liable for the delay to FTC's shipment on account of this incident.

The conduct of OverCo and its master and crew will be judged by the standards for carriage by sea, that is according to either the Hague,

---

12 MTC 1980 art. 16(1).

13 Whether an operator, such as Multi-Modal, can recover an indemnity from its subcontracting carriers depends upon their own contracts, which frequently severely limit or exclude responsibility for delay.

Hague/Visby or Hamburg Rules.[14] As a result, it is possible that OverCo may have an excuse for misconduct which it may assert against Multi-Modal but which Multi-Modal may not rely on to defeat the claim of FTC. For instance, in certain circumstances a shipowner is excused from liability when the relevant misconduct was negligence in the navigation of the ship.[15] But if OverCo were able to rely on this defence to its breach of contract by delay, Multi-Modal could not *vis-à-vis* FTC because its conduct is not judged by the same regime. Indeed the proof of negligent navigation by OverCo as an excuse for itself would at the same time condemn Multi-Modal for breach of its responsibilities under the MTC 1980. All measures that could reasonably be required of Multi-Modal and its subcontractors were not taken if there was negligence in the navigation of the carrying vessel on the sea leg of the movement. In these circumstances, Multi-Modal would bear liability for delay towards FTC which it could not pass back to the defaulting carrier, OverCo.

A similar kind of inquiry would also have to be undertaken into the other two incidents causing delay during the rail movement across Canada. At first glance it seems apparent that ACP Rail ought to be held responsible for sidelining FTC's consolidated shipment for a whole week in its Montreal yards but should not be liable for lost time when its track through the Rocky Mountains was blocked by snow. But Multi-Modal has the duty to prove that ACP Rail could not have avoided these delays by reasonable efforts if it (Multi-Modal) is to escape liability. Hence each incident will require a closer investigation into the methods of ACP Rail's operations compared to the alternative ways it might reasonably have been expected to conduct its business, according to accepted railway industry practices, so as to prevent, avoid or minimize the delays that it incurred.

It is possible that good railroad practices would justify a holdover of goods at Montreal for a week, but the evidence would have to be strong to demonstrate that this was not only normal, but also reasonable, business conduct by ACP Rail in order to overcome the implication that it had simply lost track of FTC's shipment of Happy Santas. It is also possible that good railroad practices might suggest that alternative arrangements or routing should be established against the foreseeable risk of snow blocking the railroad, but ACP Rail would have a much easier task of showing it did not act unreasonably in failing to evade the delay in light of the implication that the incident was an Act of God or *force majeure*, i.e., an event beyond its control.

Thus the level of proof of reasonable business conduct will vary according to the circumstances of the incidents causing delay. Further, the

---

14 These rules are cited in Appendix 1 and discussed in Chapter 5 under Basis of Liability for Attributed Loss after note 23.

15 *Ibid.* especially at note 38.

test of whether the operator, Multi-Modal, is liable for delay depends upon, in addition to its own conduct, the reasonableness of each of its subcontracted carriers throughout the movement. In this Case, whatever the circumstances of OverCo's difficulties at sea and ACP Rail's problems in the Rocky Mountains, it is unlikely that ACP Rail will be able to establish that it took all reasonable measures to avoid delaying FTC's shipment of toys at Montreal. Hence Multi-Modal probably will not escape its presumed liability for their delayed delivery in Vancouver.

Under the UNCTAD/ICC Rules 1992

Since the approach of the UNCTAD/ICC Rules 1992 to the issue of liability for delay is the same as the MTC 1980, a similar analysis of Multi-Modal's responsibility would be made. Consequently Multi-Modal will be presumed liable for the delayed delivery in Vancouver until it can demonstrate that all its subcontracted carriers and cargo handlers, as well as its own staff and employees, acted without fault or neglect throughout the movement.[16] Thus the conduct of OverCo and of ACP Rail and its ship and train crews would be scrutinized, particularly concerning the three incidents that appear to have contributed to the ultimate delay. But in addition to the similarities in the inquiries to those that would be made under the MTC 1980, the UNCTAD/ICC Rules 1992 also require two further matters to be considered before Multi-Modal's presumed liability may be upheld.

First, the shipper may not claim for loss resulting from delay unless it had made clear to the operator at the time they agreed upon the movement that delivery on time was important. The rider to the rule of presumed liability for delay states:

> However, the MTO shall not be liable for loss following from delay in delivery unless the consignor [i.e., the shipper] has made a declaration of interest in timely delivery which has been accepted by the MTO.[17]

Thus one prerequisite to a successful claim for delay is that the shipper made the multimodal operator aware of its concern for timely delivery. But although the provision indicates this concern of the shipper must have been 'accepted by the MTO,' it does not seem to require their agreement on any

---

16 See UNCTAD/ICC 1992 rules 5.1 and 4.2. On the significance in the variation of the wording of the operator's responsibilities between the MTC 1980 ('measurers ... reasonably ... required') and the UNCTAD/ICC Rules 1992 ('no fault or neglect') see the discussion in Chapter 4 under Basis of Liability for Unattributed Damage after note 15.

17 UNCTAD/ICC 1992 rule 5.1.

particular period of transit or time of delivery. It is enough if the shipper communicates its interest in timely delivery and the operator, knowing that, does not refuse to accept the goods or to disclaim responsibility. This interpretation is supported by the next rule, which defines delay in delivery:

> Delay in delivery occurs when the goods have not been delivered within the time expressly agreed upon, or, in the absence of such agreement, within the time which it would be reasonable to require of a diligent MTO, having regard to the circumstances of the case.[18]

In the Case at hand, FTC would readily satisfy this prerequisite to its claim since it received an assurance from Multi-Modal that there would be no difficulty in meeting its declared deadline for delivery by December 10. In fact, Multi-Modal agreed to the delivery date of December 8.

The second difference between the UNCTAD/ICC Rules 1992 and the MTC 1980 in regard to claims for delayed delivery is that the operator is granted a complete defence for delay incurred by certain defined actions and events during sea carriage. Thus Multi-Modal would not be liable for the delay if it resulted solely from:

- act, neglect, or default of the master, marincr, pilot or the servanto of the carrier in the navigation or in the management of the ship;
- fire, unless caused by the actual fault or privity of the carrier.[19]

These are exceptions to the principle of the presumed fault of the operator. They have undoubtedly been drawn from the Hague and Hague/Visby Rules governing marine transportation[20] to provide excuses from liability for the operator in those situations where it would not have any recourse against the defaulting subcontracted sea carrier. In so doing, they favour the operator at the expense of the cargo owner. They resolve the operator's problem under the MTC 1980 of a lack of indemnity[21] by removing the need for one. Instead they leave the consequences of the delay to fall on the cargo owner uncompensated.

In the present Case, the first exception may assist the operator. Multi-Modal may escape liability for the delay occasioned by the engine trouble on OverCo's ship during the sea stage of the movement by establishing either that OverCo and its employees took all reasonable measures that prudent industry practices would demand, or that its crew members were negligent in the navigation of the vessel. When a ship suffers engine trouble

---

[18] *Ibid*. rule 5.2.
[19] UNCTAD/ICC 1992 rule 5.4.
[20] *Supra* note 14.
[21] Discussed *supra* at note 15.

at sea, the master and crew are almost completely in control and hence the operator's liability depends upon their conduct. Since the operator may escape liability whether the crew are reasonable or negligent in the navigation of the ship, Multi-Modal could claim the same benefit in respect of the delay incurred at sea.

There is a possibility that Multi-Modal may continue to be presumed liable for delay during the sea stage on account of the failure of OverCo to provide a seaworthy ship for the voyage. The exceptional defence of negligence in navigation[22] is subject to a proviso that:

> whenever loss or damage has resulted from unseaworthiness of the ship, the MTO can prove that due diligence has been exercised to make the ship seaworthy at the commencement of the voyage.[23]

Thus, before Multi-Modal can take advantage of the defence of negligent navigation by OverCo's crew members, it might have to prove, as a prerequisite, that OverCo itself acted diligently in preparing the ship for the voyage. This requirement is uncertain, however, because a close reading of the text of the rule discloses a difference of phraseology in its various parts. When introducing the exceptions for negligent navigation and fire, the rule speaks of 'loss, damage or delay,' but the subsequent proviso about seaworthiness only concerns 'loss or damage.' On a literal interpretation of the rule, the omission of 'delay' from the proviso suggests that the operator does not have to establish the due diligence of the shipowner to make its ship seaworthy in order to take advantage of the exception for the crew's negligence.[24] Such an interpretation runs counter to the general principle of the operator's liability that it shall prove the absence of fault and neglect by all persons who handle the cargo on its account. Since the protection afforded to the operator in the event of neglect in the navigation of the carrying ship by its crew is a special exception to the principle of fault liability, there is not requirement to enlarge it.[25]

---

22 And the fire exception too.

23 UNCTAD/ICC 1992 rule 5.4.

24 As in so many areas of uncertainty in multimodal transport, no known litigation has decided the point. In the Hague and Hague/Visby Rules of the marine mode, from which these exceptional provisions are drawn, the shipowner has an overriding obligation of due diligence in preparing a seaworthy ship before it may claim the benefit of the exception for negligent navigation: see the discussion in Chapter 5 under Basis of Liability for Attributed Loss, especially at note 37.

25 Perhaps the clause 'loss or damage has resulted from unseaworthiness' may be read as referring to the economic injuries caused by the physical 'loss, damage or delay in delivery with respect to goods.' Then the MTO would have to prove the diligence of the shipowner in preparing its ship before it could allege a defence based on the crew's negligence in navigation whether the cargo was lost, damaged or delayed.

Under the ICC Rules 1975

Delay is dealt with in the ICC Rules 1975 by deferring it to the underlying unimodal rules or, in their absence, local national law. No claim for delay is entertainable unless it is localized and attributed to a particular stage of the multimodal movement. If that can be done, the basis of responsibility for delay is governed by the law of that stage. This approach creates large conceptual and practical difficulties.

Although it is often, but not always, possible to point to particular incidents during a movement which contributed to the ultimate delay in delivery, it is not possible to determine whether delay has occurred until delivery. Unlike physical loss or damage to cargo, which occurs at a particular moment and location in its geographical transit, the time taken to move goods is a fluid and continuous undertaking that encompasses the whole of the transit. One cannot tell whether there has been a delay in delivery until the journey is over. The multimodal operator's undertaking to deliver on time begins as soon as the movement is agreed with the shipper and may be affected by its actions even before it receives the shipment. Thus the operator's decisions about which means of carriage and which carriers to employ will materially influence the speed of performance of the movement. But whether some segments of the carriage go faster or slower than might be expected, there is no accounting of lateness before the goods reach their destination. Thus delay in delivery is a cumulative breach of obligation by the operator.[26]

Given this particular character, liability for delay may be very difficult for the operator to pass back to the performing carriers and cargo handlers who are ultimately responsible for it. But this is quite an insufficient reason to deny the cargo claimant a remedy for the breach and compensation for its financial loss. Whether this was the reason that the ICC Rules 1975 allowed multimodal operators to avoid taking responsibility for delayed delivery, the fact is that by treating the obligation only as a localizable incident of carriage they have effectively done so.

There are also practical objections to this standard of responsibility for delay. In particular, how shall the liability of the performing carriers be apportioned and that of the multimodal operator be aggregated if there are contributing incidents in more than one stage of the movement? Suppose the first carrier is very tardy but the second moves with despatch and makes up some of the lost time of the first, so that the third carrier delivers the shipment late but not so delayed as might have been expected had the second carrier not performed so well. Should the operator (and the first

---

[26] See Ganado and Kindred, *supra* note 3 at 19 and 70. Compare R. De Wit, *supra* note 2 at 215.

carrier) receive the benefit of reduced liability *gratis* the second carrier?[27] In the instant Case, supposing both the sea carrier, OverCo, and the railway, ACP Rail, defaulted in the timely performance of their portion of carriage, how shall Multi-Modal's overall responsibility for the movement be determined? No single unimodal convention or local law can resolve this multimodal problem.

Even though the approach of the ICC Rules 1975 is unsound, an attempt will be made to explain the impact of the unimodal rules that affect each of the performing carriers if only to show the diversity of their approaches to delay and hence the increased complexity they create at the multimodal level. In this Case the first stage on which delay was incurred was the sea leg from the United Kingdom to Halifax, Canada, which would be governed by the international Hague/Visby Rules.[28] Unfortunately, these Rules contain no express provisions about delay. Yet they speak of 'loss or damage' and since delay is a cause of financial loss, it is presumably included. In particular, they impose on the carrier an obligation to 'properly and carefully load, handle ... [and] carry' the goods,[29] which may be breached by their delayed delivery as much as by their physical injury.[30]

Inclusion of delay within the ordinary principles of loss or damage under the Hague/Visby Rules means that the familiar principle of presumed fault of the carrier will apply so soon as the cargo owner has substantiated a claim of delay. In this Case, as previously discussed,[31] FTC and Multi-Modal had agreed upon delivery by a fixed date (December 8) which was missed. Thus it will fall to OverCo, the sea carrier, to explain why its apparent, contributing delay due to engine trouble should be excused. In this task, OverCo may try and assert any of the multiple justifications found in the Hague/Visby Rules[32] and discussed in connection with physical injury to cargo in Chapter 5.[33] This could be difficult because OverCo will have to demonstrate that the engine trouble encountered on the voyage was not due to a lack of due diligence to make the ship seaworthy, in addition to establishing an exculpating excuse. The most obvious excuse available to OverCo under the Hague/Visby Rules is the infamous exclusion of liability for the acts, neglects or defaults of the master and crew

---

[27] See also the examples discussed in K. Grönfors, 'Liability for Delay in Combined Transport' (1974) 5 J. Maritime Law & Commerce 483, at 486, and R. De Wit, *supra* note 2 at 140.

[28] Both England and Canada have implemented the Hague/Visby Rules by compulsory legislation, although Canada has also enacted the Hamburg Rules to replace the Hague/Visby Rules at some future time by government order. See *Carriage of Goods by Sea Act 1971*, U.K. 1971, c. 19 and *Carriage of Goods by Water Act*, S.C. 1993, c. 21.

[29] Art. III(2).

[30] See further the discussion in Ganado and Kindred, *supra* note 3 at 20.

[31] *Supra* under Proof of Loss.

[32] Art. IV(2) in particular.

[33] See Chapter 5 under Basis of Liability for Attributed Loss after note 23.

in the navigation of the ship. This is the same exemption as found in the UNCTAD/ICC Rules 1992; indeed it is surely the source of the provision there.[34] As previously discussed in that context, OverCo, and thus Multi-Modal, would probably be excused of liability if OverCo could show it had exercised due diligence to make its ship seaworthy for the voyage.[35]

Were the alternative and more recent Hamburg Rules[36] to apply to this sea voyage, the determination of liability for delay would be much simpler since those Rules contain explicit provisions on the subject. Delay is expressly included in the general clause imposing liability on the basis of presumed fault.[37] Indeed, the language of the clause closely matches the provisions for delay in the MTC 1980,[38] which was based on the Hamburg Rules. The criterion is whether OverCo took all measures that could reasonably be expected of it to avoid delay. No excuse for negligent navigation of the ship by OverCo's employees would be permitted. But a diligent effort to ready the ship and its engines for the voyage would have to be proved by OverCo as part of its demonstration that it took appropriate and reasonable measures. To this extent the determination of the sea carrier's liability for delay under the Hamburg Rules would parallel the previous discussion of the practical aspects of its responsibility under the MTC 1980.[39]

The other incidents giving rise to delay occurred during the rail journey of FTC's shipment of Happy Santas across Canada. There is no international railway convention in force in Canada, so the issue of delay would be decided by local law, i.e., federal Canadian law. But, had the CIM Uniform Rules[40] been applicable, quite different provisions from the Hague/Visby Rules on the sea leg would operate. The CIM Uniform Rules apply the same principles of liability to delay as to loss and damage to the goods. As explained in Chapter 5, where the relevant provisions are set out,[41] the carrier is liable 'for the loss or damage resulting from the transit period being exceeded' unless it proves the delay was 'caused by circumstances which the railway could not avoid and the consequences of which it was unable to prevent.'

Uniquely among the unimodal conventions, the speed of transit is fixed in the CIM Uniform Rules themselves. The shipper selects transport by

---

[34] For the reasons explained *supra* at notes 15 and 21.

[35] *Supra* at note 23.

[36] See Appendix 1. The status of the Hamburg Rules is discussed in Chapter 5 at note 27.

[37] *Ibid.* art. 5.

[38] And reported previously at note 7.

[39] *Supra* after note 13.

[40] See Appendix 1.

[41] See Chapter 5, Exhibit 5.3.

grande or *petite vitesse*.[42] Under *grande vitesse* for wagon load consignments, the railway is allowed no more than 12 hours for despatch and 24 hours for each 400 kilometres of the intended journey. Under *petite vitesse* the corresponding transit periods are 24 hours for dispatch and 24 hours for each 300 kilometres of travel.[43] Hence, whether goods are delayed in delivery by rail can be easily determined: the question is not whether the time taken was unreasonably long but simply whether the defined transit period was exceeded.

Coupled to this clarity in the time for delivery is a high standard of justification for any delay. Reasonable efforts to avoid or prevent delay are not sufficient. The rail carrier seems to be strictly liable for any delay unless it 'could not avoid' it[44] because, for instance, it was caused by some act of the shipper such as giving misdirections. In this Case, ACP Rail would have a great deal of difficulty in justifying the hold-up in its Montreal yards. It might have a much stronger claim to be excused of responsibility for delay in the Rocky Mountains since it had no control over the fall of snow that blocked the track. It was an Act of God.

There are no road or air stages in the movement in this Case, but to appreciate the full diversity of approaches to problems of delay it is worth noting the provisions in the other unimodal conventions. The CMR convention on road transport[45] treats delay along with physical loss and damage. It states:

> The carrier shall be liable for the total or partial loss of the goods and for damage thereto ... as well as for any delay in delivery.[46]

At first sight, this standard of responsibility appears as strict as the CIM Uniform Rules for rail carriage. There is relief from liability only in specified circumstances. The road haulier will be excused for delay resulting from errors of the shipper and an enumerated group of 'special risks' and for late delivery that he proves[47] he 'could not avoid and the consequences of which he was unable to prevent.'[48] In practice the unavoidability of the

---

[42] CIM Uniform Rules, Appendix 1, art. 12.

[43] *Ibid.* art. 27. The shipper and the railway may agree to speedier transit. Similar transit periods are also established for less than wagon load consignments.

[44] Grönfors states the excuse is 'restrictively constructed as meaning a kind of *force majeure*' as compared to similar language in road transportation which is 'understood in a milder way as referring to a liability with a reversed burden of proof as far as negligence is concerned': see K. Grönfors, *supra* note 27 at 489.

[45] See Appendix 1.

[46] *Ibid.* art. 17(1). See also arts. 19 (defining delay in delivery) and 20 (converting a claim for delay into a claim for total loss of the goods after 30 days delay).

[47] Art. 18.

[48] Art. 17(2). Articles 17 and 18 are set out in full in Chapter 5 in Exhibit 5.2.

delay has not always been pressed strictly against the carrier. However, more than reasonable precaution to avoid and prevent delay is required.[49]

In the event of delay by air transport, the Warsaw Convention[50] asserts baldly:

> The carrier is liable for damage occasioned by delay in the carriage by air of passengers, luggage or goods.[51]

This assertion of carrier liability is qualified by the very next article:

> The carrier is not liable if he proves that he and his agents have taken all necessary measures to avoid the damage or that it was impossible for him or them to take such measures.[52]

Thus the standard of the air carrier's liability for delay is its presumed culpability unless it can demonstrate it took 'all necessary measures' of prevention. Clearly this standard is not as stringent as to require proof that the delay was unavoidable, but it still appears to demand quite a high level of conduct. The reference to 'all necessary' measures suggests that more than reasonable measures of precaution are required.[53] In any event, the air carrier certainly will be excused if it can prove the incident causing delay was beyond its control.[54]

The variety, even vagaries, in the approaches to problems of delay in different modes of transport are summed up for comparative purposes in

---

[49] See the discussion in D.A. Glass & C. Cashmore, *Introduction to the Law of Carriage of Goods* (London: Sweet & Maxwell, 1989) at 112. Compare M.A. Clarke, *International Carriage of Goods by Road: CMR* (London: Stevens, 1982) at 109; K. Grönfors, *supra* note 44; D.J. Hill & M.D. Messent, *CMR: Contracts for the International Carriage of Goods by Road* (London: Lloyd's of London Press, 1984) at 76.

[50] See Appendix 1.

[51] *Ibid.* art. 19.

[52] Art. 20(1). Subject to clarifying amendments in the 1971 Guatemala Convention, article VI, not yet in force, and the 1975 Montreal Additional Protocol IV, article V, not yet in force: see Appendix 1.

[53] In fact it has been interpreted less rigorously as 'all measures which a reasonable man would deem necessary.' See D.A. Glass & C. Cashmore, *supra* note 49 at 226-227.

[54] The airlines largely avoid the problem by not agreeing to fixed delivery times and by declaring that their published timetables are not guaranteed. Thus the issue of liability is converted into the antecedent question of whether there has been any delay at all. In the absence of a fixed time of delivery, only an unreasonably long time in delivery will constitute delay. Hence the standard for scrutiny of the air carrier's service is, in effect, the reasonableness of its conduct in all the circumstances of the case. Consider I.H.Ph. Diederiks-Verschoor, *An Introduction to Air Law*, 5th rev. ed. (Deventer: Kluwer Law & Taxation, 1993) at 74; J.-L. Magdelénat, *Air Cargo Regulation and Claims* (Toronto: Butterworths, 1983) at 84.

Exhibit 8.1. It displays the starkly different standards of responsibility that may be applied to carriers from strict liability to excuse on account of negligent conduct of employees. For the purposes of applying a basis of responsibility for delay that operates continuously throughout a multimodal movement governed by the ICC Rules 1975, the unimodal rules are irreconcilable.

Exhibit 6.1:
Bases of Carrier Liability for Delay in Unimodal Conventions

Mode	Basis of Liability–Carrier is liable unless it proves:
Sea–Hague/Visby	Due diligence was exercised to make the ship seaworthy, and a proper and careful cargo system was established, but then excused if delay caused by crew's negligent navigation.
Sea–Hamburg	All reasonable measures of avoidance were taken.
Air–Warsaw	All necessary measures of avoidance were taken.
Road–CMR	Delay was unavoidable.
Rail–CIM Rules	Delay was unavoidable.

Note: Full references to the unimodal conventions appear in Appendix 1.

Extent of Liability for Delay

Quantifying the compensation payable by a multimodal operator who is held responsible for delayed delivery involves the same two steps that remedying loss or damage to cargo requires. The cargo claimant must demonstrate the extent of its losses and then the operator may assert the relevant limits to its liability. But the nature of a claim for delay is so very different from a claim for loss or damage to goods that its measurement proceeds in a very different way. In addition, the limits of operator and carrier liability for delay are generally very much more severe from the claimant's perspective than the ceilings on recovery for lost or damaged goods.

When goods are lost or damaged, the measure of immediate injury to their owner is determined by their value had they been whole at their destination.[55] Injury due to delay cannot be measured this way because the goods reach their destination in whole condition.[56] The relevant inquiry is into the economic consequences of being delivered whole but late. From the point of view of the importing cargo owner, which may have supply contracts to fill or a production schedule to keep, delayed delivery of the goods can be as damaging financially as their total loss or destruction. On the other hand, their late delivery may matter little to the cargo owner if it has no immediate need or use for them. Thus the cargo claimant must demonstrate the extent of its injury by quantifying the loss of intended use of the delayed goods.[57]

In the current Case, FTC lost the benefit of its sale of the Happy Santas because they were rejected by its buyer, SuperStore, as was its right when the shipment was so greatly delayed. Hence FTC's loss of use of the Happy Santas is very clear and the extent of that loss can easily be quantified. It is the delivered price FTC would have been paid for the toys, less the price it actually received when it was forced to sell them off as best it could at their destination in Vancouver.[58] Supposing their 'fire sale price' was no more than 25 per cent of their invoice value, which was quoted as £3,456 (C$6,912) CIP Vancouver, FTC would be looking to Multi-Modal for C$5,184 in compensation (C$6,912 x 75%).

But accounting the extent of financial loss is not sufficient for the cargo owner to substantiate its claim. In addition to proving the delay in delivery caused this loss,[59] the cargo claimant must also show that the kind of use it intended to make of the goods was reasonably to be expected by the operator. Contract law imposes a double requirement of causation and foreseeability of the injury suffered.[60] In consensual transactions it is evidently sensible that the losses which are compensable must have been within the contemplation of both parties, not just the injured claimant. Thus the cargo owner's quantified losses will not be compensated beyond the injuries about which the multimodal operator was previously informed, or was capable of anticipating, would be the consequences of delaying delivery.

---

[55] See the discussion of valuation in Chapter 4 under Extent of Liability for Unattributed Loss.

[56] Delay resulting also in damage to the goods will ordinarily be treated as a damage claim. *Supra* note 2.

[57] See the discussion of categories of injury on account of delayed delivery in Ganado and Kindred, *supra* note 3 at 126, and H. McGregor, *McGregor on Damages* 15th ed. (London: Sweet & Maxwell, 1988) at 691.

[58] Claimants of loss by delay, as in other breaches of contract, must always try to mitigate their injuries. See Ganado and Kindred, *supra* note 3 at 122.

[59] Discussed previously in this chapter under Proof of Loss.

[60] See the discussion of measure of damages for delay in Ganado and Kindred, *supra* note 3 at 116, and H. McGregor, *supra* note 57 at 696.

Quite frequently the cargo owner's claim stumbles at this point because the operator is told little and knows less about the shipper's business or purposes for the cargo. However, as the transportation industry becomes more specialized, the expertise of carriers will continue to rise and they may be increasingly expected to anticipate the injurious effects of delay. Meanwhile the spread of just-in-time and similar supply and production scheduling systems among merchants is leading to greater concern for, and insistence upon, timely delivery. Obviously the best protection for the cargo owner is to inform the operator in advance why timely performance of the movement is important.[61]

In this Case FTC received an assurance from Multi-Modal of delivery by 8 December and thus there was mutual understanding of the importance of avoiding delay. But it is less clear whether Multi-Modal was told about the consequences of delay. However, since it did know the nature of the goods by their description, it ought to have realized they only had seasonal retail use and value. Hence FTC would be able to substantiate the full extent of its quantified claim of C$5,184.

In response, Multi-Modal would assert its right to limit liability which for claims of delay is generally rated in multiples of the freight, i.e., the cost of transportation. Why a different system of limiting liability is applied in the event of delayed delivery is not obvious.[62] The per kilogramme or per package approach to limiting liability for physical loss or damage to goods could just as readily be applied to delayed goods.[63] A common approach would be consistent with the mutual method of measuring the cargo claimant's economic injury which is the value of the loss of use of the goods, whether permanent in the case of their destruction, or temporary in the instance of delay. A common approach would also be simpler and more uniform to administer, particularly in claims for both physical damage and delay.

Whatever the wisdom of limiting the operator's liability for delay by reference to freight, the method is employed differently in each set of multimodal rules. The ICC Rules 1975 are the most complex because, as previously discussed,[64] losses due to delay are only compensable in accordance with the legal regime governing the modal stage in which the delay is said to have been incurred. Their provision on delay[65] subjects both

---

[61] Discussed by Ganado and Kindred, *ibid.* at 140.

[62] Except that the Multimodal Rules have followed the practice of most of the unimodal conventions.

[63] As it is under the Warsaw Convention for air transport, see Exhibit 6.2 *infra*, and J.-L. Magdelénat, *supra* note 54 at 90.

[64] See under Basis of Liability for Delay Under the ICC Rules 1975.

[65] Reproduced *supra* at note 6.

the basis and extent of liability to the relevant unimodal regime. In addition it imposes an overall limitation:

> However, the amount of such compensation shall not exceed the amount of the freight for that stage, provided that this limitation is not contrary to any applicable international Convention or national law.[66]

It is therefore necessary first to calculate the limit of liability for delay under the relevant unimodal regime and then to compare that amount with the freight for that stage. The lesser figure will be the operable limit of the operator's liability, provided it is not contrary to the relevant mandatory unimodal regime.

The limits of liability for delay established by the unimodal conventions are most diverse both as to amounts and as to the methods of calculation. The limits are variously expressed by weight, by package and by freight and the levels of compensation vary from 2 to 17 SDR per kilogramme and from 1 to 3 times total freight. A comparative perspective of these variations is displayed in Exhibit 6.2. In addition, each convention has particular rules about the circumstances in which the limit of liability may exceptionally be exceeded, usually on account of wilful or reckless delay by the carrier. Further, the shipper is generally permitted to agree with the carrier about a higher level of compensation by declaring an interest in timely delivery and paying extra freight.

The calculations of the multimodal operator's liability based on the incidents of delay caused by the performing carriers and subject to the unimodal regimes can quickly become complex. In this Case, for instance, separate calculations presumably would have to be made for the incidents of delay on the sea leg and the rail stage. But how shall they be combined? Is it intended that there should be some kind of apportionment between the modes? By reference to what—the relative lengths of the different incidents of delay, or the proportions of the whole movement in each mode, or the proportions of the total freight by mode perhaps? These questions are likely to become the focus of settlement negotiations in the absence of clear legal principles.[67]

Further, the overall limit established by reference to freight for the stage in which the incident causing delay occurred is no more easy to ascertain. Where, as in this Case, the delay resulted from incidents in two stages, it is unclear whether the overall limit is the sum of the freight for both stages, or some proportionate combination of the two. Moreover, it may be difficult to ascertain 'the freight for that stage' where the operator

---

[66] ICC 1975 rule 14, last para.
[67] See K. Grönfors, *supra* note 27 at 488.

quotes the shipper a through rate for the whole movement. In this Case, Multi-Modal offered to move FTC's LCL shipment door-to-door for C$2,300. It then consolidated the shipment with others to make up a full container which was delivered for a total cost of C$4,376. It might be possible, therefore, to apportion the freight for each stage of transportation of FTC's goods by the fraction the quote (C$2,300) bears to the whole cost (C$4,376) provided that can be broken out by modal and terminal charges. Yet even if this is possible, Multi-Modal's pricing of its quote to FTC may have borne little relation to the charges it ultimately incurred for the FCL movement. All in all, the system of assessing the operator's limit of liability for delay under the ICC Rules 1975 is far too complex, to the point of being unworkable.

Exhibit 6.2: Comparable Limits of Liability for Delay under Unimodal Conventions

Regime	Limit by Weight	Other Limit
Sea Carriage – Hague/Visby Rules[1] – Hamburg Rules[2]	2.00 SDR/kg. n/a	666.67 SDR/package, whichever is higher 2.5 x freight for goods delayed, to a maximum of total freight
Road Carriage—CMR[3]	n/a	total freight
Rail Carriage—CIM Uniform Rules[4]	n/a	3 x total freight
Air Carriage—Warsaw Convention[5]	17 SDR/kg.	n/a

Notes: Full references to the unimodal conventions appear in Appendix 1.
[1] Art. IV(5). And see Ganado and Kindred, *supra* note 3, at 147 fwd.
[2] Art. 6(1)(b).
[3] Art. 23(5).
[4] Art. 43, subject to art. 45 (lower limits for exceptional tariffs).
[5] Art. 22(2). The original provision of 250 Poincaré gold francs/kg. is still in force. 17 SDR/kg. represents a rough equivalent and is the substituted limit set down in Montreal Protocol IV, which is used here for ease of comparison. On the method of conversion of Poincaré gold francs into national currency, see J.-L. Magdelénat, *supra* note 54 at 173.

By comparison, the limits of liability for delay in the other two sets of rules are simple to ascertain. The limit is fixed in the MTC 1980 at 'an amount equivalent to two and a half times the freight payable for the goods delayed, but not exceeding the total freight payable under the multimodal transport contract.'[68] This approach still requires a double calculation but at least it is by reference to the freight as a whole in the multimodal contract. It is unlikely that part of a shipment only is delayed. A container of goods is either delayed as a whole or delivered on time. But it is possible that a LCL is not consolidated in one container or part of it is temporarily mislaid. Alternatively, the shipment might consist of two FCLs and one container is held back. Then under the MTC 1980 the limit of liability calculated against that container, i.e., 50 per cent of the shipment would be 50 per cent x 2.5 total freight or the equivalent of 125 per cent of the total freight. Immediately the overall limit of liability for delay under the MTC 1980 would operate to strike this sum down to a maximum of 100 per cent of total freight. Indeed a quick calculation shows that total freight will be the absolute limit of compensation whenever 40 per cent or more of the cargo is delayed. When a smaller proportion of the cargo is late, the effective limit will be 2.5 times the freight for that portion.

FTC, in this Case, has suffered delay of the whole of its shipment and hence the absolute limit of total freight will apply. Thus FTC is entitled to just C$2,300, being the cost of transportation quoted by Multi-Modal for FTC's LCL shipment.

The UNCTAD/ICC Rules 1992 straightforwardly set the ceiling on compensation for delay at the total freight for the movement.[69] Therefore, whether there is delay in delivery of a part or the whole of the cargo is irrelevant. This is a sensible way to proceed for often a delay of part of the goods will prevent the cargo owner using the rest that are received on time but incomplete. For example, in this Case, SuperStore would be within its contractual rights to reject all the Happy Santas had they been delivered in two lots, one on time and the other late, just as much as when they were all delayed in delivery. SuperStore is entitled to full performance of its contract with FTC.[70] As it turned out in this Case, the whole shipment of Happy Santas was delayed and rejected, and so FTC's maximum recovery under the UNCTAD/ICC Rules 1992, as under the MTC 1980, would be limited to the total freight for the movement, that is C$2,300.

The net result of these diverse provisions about the consequences of delay is that under the ICC Rules 1975 the exact amount of compensation payable would have to be finally settled by negotiation, but under the MTC 1980 and the UNCTAD/ICC Rules 1992 the limit of FTC's recovery would be the freight it paid, namely C$2,300. This sum compares poorly with FTC's substantiated claim for C$5,184. In addition, the shipment of Happy

---

68   MCTC 1980 art. 18(4).

69   UNCTAD/ICC 1992 rule 6.5.

70   See M.G. Bridge, *Sale of Goods* (Toronto: Butterworths, 1988) at 371; A.G. Guest, gen. ed., *Benjamin's Sale of Goods, supra* note 1 at 279.

Santas was also small and the freight was a relatively high percentage of the delivered value of the goods. In other shipments, the value of the cargo could be very much greater than the freight, and so the ceiling on compensation for delay would be an even smaller proportion of the financial loss sustained by the cargo owner. In the current global trend towards just-in-time production and freer trade, the volume of high value products moving multimodally has grown dramatically. As a result, the value:freight ratio has also grown and, therefore, the value of freight increasingly fails to grant adequate compensation in the event of delay.

CHAPTER 7

Liability for Consequential Business Losses

Case 4: Consequential Business Losses

The Excellent Manufacturing Company (EMCO) has carefully refined its stock requirements for component parts feeding into its consumer appliance manufacturing facility in Hamilton, Ontario. EMCO acquires identical parts from 3 different manufacturers in 3 different global locations in order to diversify its sourcing risk, as well as risk from transport strikes, carrier bankruptcies, and so on. EMCO plans regular shipments from each source and these are directed to the plant on a timed delivery basis to reduce EMCO's need for warehousing to only 4 days of buffer stock. Without such an inventory control system, EMCO believes its products would not be competitive in the global market, given the lower wage levels available to competitors producing similar products in Taiwan and South Korea. Because of this, EMCO has a stringent monitoring system for assessing the performance of the carriers it uses. Sealane Shipping handles one-third of EMCO's shipments from its UK supplier in Manchester on a FCL basis, with all shipments purchased by EMCO ex-works (EXW). As part of EMCO's continuing carrier performance monitoring programme, EMCO instructed Sealane's Commercial Department about the consequences for the company of any delays or damage en route. A typical shipment is three 20' containers per week, each containing 9 pallets with a total weight of 15,867 kilogrammes, volume 11.67 cubic metres and a container load value of C$123,100. (Because of the delicacy of the components, EMCO does not stack the pallets and therefore does not use the full space available.) The freight paid per container, inclusive of all terminal and carriage charges, totals C$1,666. Sealane acts as a multimodal operator, subcontracting the land transport at both ends of the movement. When the last shipment arrived at the EMCO manufacturing plant, the contents of one of three containers showed clear stress fractures, as if a heavy weight had jarred the container, rendering the components unusable. Nor could EMCO use the sound contents of the other two containers because they were interdependent component parts. EMCO had insufficient stock to stay open and 5 day later the plant shut down, laying off 120 workers for 5 days. EMCO is now claiming that the layoff caused it to lose a contract worth C$6.5 million which its Taiwanese competitor acquired in its place from a major multinational retailer.

Introduction

Physical loss, damage and delay are the events that cause injury in the delivery of goods and give rise to the liability of the multimodal operator. But there are many more ways in which the cargo claimant may suffer financial loss as a result. Case 4 presents a situation in which EMCO, the cargo owner, suffers multiple losses. They include the physical loss of one of three containers full of components, the loss of use of the whole shipment, loss of plant production, and loss of a major business opportunity. The rules of multimodal transport treat these claims of loss separately and differently. They also regulate how such losses may be aggregated and what the maximum total allowable recovery shall be.

The purpose of this chapter is not to repeat the discussion of the incidence of damage, loss and delay already made in Chapters 4, 5 and 6 respectively. It is to explain the consequences of multiple claims arising from a single shipment and to demonstrate the legal limits to their aggregation. The chapter will therefore proceed in the same pattern of analysis as previous ones but it will rely on them for explanation of individual incidents already discussed and will dwell upon the compounding effects of their occurrence in one movement.

Proof of Loss

The root cause of all of EMCO's claims of loss in this Case is the damage to the components in one container. Hence EMCO bears the usual burden of proving that damage was incurred while the components were in the charge of the multimodal operator, Sealane. This it will discharge in the usual way by producing the clean transport documents describing the goods received by Sealane and showing the extent of damage discovered upon delivery.[1]

The cause of this damage will also be sought, not least because Sealane will be most interested to attribute the fault to a particular carrier or cargo handler so as to minimize its liability. If the source of the damage to EMCO's shipment can be localized, Sealane should be able to pass all or most of its liability back to the defaulting party. Otherwise Sealane will sustain all the liability and will have to recompense EMCO by itself.

In many instances of cargo damage the source of injury can be pinpointed. In this case the destruction of the contents of one container occurred by being jarred. If the container had been crushed, such a readily apparent defective condition would make it easy to trace at what stage the damage occurred. The receipts or other documents that would have been made out when EMCO's shipment was transferred between carriers and

---

[1]   See further in Chapter 4 under Proof of Loss.

terminals along the route ought to reveal the condition of the containers at every point of transhipment.[2] In the absence of such external evidence of damage to goods, it may prove much more difficult to attribute the injury to one particular stage of the movement. Stress fractures in the components caused by jarring their container is the kind of concealed damage that might have been incurred in many ways in many places along the route.[3]

Basis of Liability

Whether the cause of the damage to EMCO's shipment can be localized will also affect the basis on which Sealane's responsibility to EMCO will be determined. If the source of the damage cannot be localized, Sealane will be held responsible in accordance with the standard within the Multimodal Rules themselves. In other words, Sealane will be presumed at fault and held responsible unless it can prove an acceptable excuse. As discussed fully in Chapter 4 on Liability for Unattributed Damage to Goods,[4] all three sets of Multimodal Rules invoke a presumption of fault as the general principle of responsibility, but they differ somewhat in the reasons which will excuse Sealane from liability. To overcome the presumption of responsibility Sealane must prove, in the case of the ICC Rules 1975, that the damage resulted from a 'cause or event which the [operator] could not avoid and the consequences of which he could not prevent by the exercise of reasonable diligence'[5] or, in the words of the MTC 1980, that Sealane 'took all measures that could reasonably be required to avoid the occurrence and its consequences,'[6] or, as the UNCTAD/ICC Rules 1992 require, that 'no fault or neglect' of Sealane 'has caused or contributed' to the loss or damage.[7]

In effect, Sealane would have to show that the damage sustained by the components was beyond its ability to avoid or prevent.[8] If, for instance, it was determined upon examination of the container that the damage resulted from inadequate bracing of the pallets of components by EMCO or its agents when stuffing the container, Sealane would not be liable. But Sealane has the burden of proving EMCO was to blame, which is often

---

2   See the discussion of this receipt system in Chapter 5 after note 7.
3   It is also the kind of damage for which the operator will attempt to avoid liability by trying to show that the goods were insufficiently packed in the container by the cargo owner.
4   See Chapter 4 under Basis of Liability for Unattributed Damage.
5   ICC Rules 1975 Rule 12 (f).
6   MTC 1980 Art. 16(1).
7   UNCTAD/ICC Rules 1992 Rule 5.1.
8   This responsibility extends to the conduct of all of Sealane's subcontracted carriers and terminals along the route. See Chapter 8 under Application of the Multimodal Rules to the Operator's Agents.

difficult to do in instances of concealed damage that cannot be attributed to any particular incident during the movement, and so probably Sealane will be held liable on the presumption of its fault.

When the cause of the damage to EMCO's components can be localized, the three sets of multimodal rules do not take the same approach to the operator's liability. Only the MTC 1980 applies the principle of presumed fault without regard to whether the damage can be localized or not.[9] Thus Sealane would be held responsible under the MTC 1980 unless it could prove it took all reasonable precautionary measures to prevent the damage to the container of components.

The other two sets of rules make reference to the regimes regulating the actual carriers and terminals in determining the multimodal operator's liability. As discussed fully in Chapter 5,[10] the ICC Rules 1975 refer the issue to the unimodal convention or the local law of the stage in which the damage occurred. The UNCTAD/ICC Rules 1992 do apply the principle of presumed fault of the operator but also add excuses found in the international regime for marine transportation when the multimodal movement includes carriage by sea. Fortunately, the unimodal rules also operate on the basis of the presumed fault of the operator so there is general unanimity about the basis of legal liability. But the unifying effect of this principle is attenuated by the differences in the grounds for excuse from liability that are found in the sea, road, rail and air conventions and laws.

Sealane may escape liability under any of these regimes if it made suitably conscientious efforts to prevent or avoid the damage. Proving the cause of the damage was EMCO's fault will always be a successful defence, though a difficult one to sustain. In addition, the unimodal regimes may afford Sealane other special and more generous exemptions from liability. In particular if the damage were to be localized to the sea leg, Sealane may be able to rely on the negligent navigation of the carrying vessel by its master and crew as a sufficient, though notorious, defence.[11]

Extent of Liability

Assuming Sealane is held responsible for the damage to EMCO's components, the next step is to quantify the amount of compensation that is due. This is the aspect in which Case 4 is particularly instructive. The general principle of contract law is that the injured party should receive compensation sufficient to wipe out its economic losses following from the breach it has suffered. In other words, EMCO should be put in the same

---

9   MTC 1980 art. 16.

10   See Chapter 5 under Basis of Liability for Attributed Loss.

11   See the discussion in Chapter 5 at note 38.

position, so far as money can do so, as it would have been if its agreement with Sealane had been properly performed.[12]

But the principle of compensation for breach of contract is not unlimited. Not every kind of economic loss is compensable. Even those that are may be subjected to legal limits of liability. EMCO, therefore, should not expect to recover fully for all its injuries.

Compensable Losses

None of the sets of multimodal rules controls what kinds of injuries should be recompensed. They only set outside limits on the amount of compensation. It is left to the local law of contract or obligations to fix which items of the total loss suffered should be accounted against the multimodal operator. As pointed out previously, EMCO has suffered multiple losses, including destruction of one container of components, loss of use of the whole shipment, interruption in plant production and consequent loss of sales' profits, and the loss of a major supply contract. The question is which of these consequences for EMCO can be attributed in law to Sealane.

The usual legal principle is that the contract breaker will be held liable to compensate the injured party for all those losses it could reasonably have been expected to have contemplated as likely to result in the particular circumstances.[13] On this criterion it is generally clear that the multimodal operator is responsible for the immediate physical injuries to the cargo, that is loss and damage,[14] as well as for the consequences of delay in some situations.[15] Other losses of the cargo owner are derivative because they depend upon the effects of the destruction or delayed delivery of the cargo. Recovery for these consequential losses is much less certain. Each type of claim will be individually scrutinized to see whether it passes the test of reasonable expectation. Whether it does will depend in each instance upon the extent of the operator's knowledge about the nature and uses of the cargo.

Hence Sealane will be accountable to EMCO only for the losses which it knew about or ought reasonably to have expected. Given the commercial relationship between Sealane and EMCO, Sealane must be taken to

---

[12] *Wertheim v. Chicoutimi Pulp Co.* [1911] A.C. 301 (P.C.). See H. McGregor, *McGregor on Damages* 15th ed. (London: Sweet & Maxwell, 1988) at 7-8; S.M. Waddams, *The Law of Damages* 2d ed. (Toronto: Canada Law Book, 1991 looseleaf) at 5-1 - 5-5.

[13] *Hadley v. Baxendale* (1854), 9 Exch. 341, 156 E.R. 145; *Victoria Laundry (Windsor) Ltd. v. Newman Indust. Ltd.* [1949] 2 K.B. 528 (C.A.); *Koufos v. C. Czarnikow Ltd. (The Heron II)* [1969] 1 A.C. 350 (H.L.). See also H. McGregor *ibid.* at 143-162; W. Tetley, *Marine Cargo Claims* 3d ed. (Montreal: Yvon Blais, 1988) at 319-322; S.M. Waddams, *ibid.* at 14-1 - 14-13.

[14] See Cases 1 and 2 in Chapters 4 and 5 respectively.

[15] See Case 3 in Chapter 6.

appreciate that the components would be damaged when the container was mishandled. The harder question is what Sealane could be expected to contemplate as the consequences of this physical damage. In the ordinary course of events Sealane must have foreseen that damage to one container of components would prevent EMCO from using them, but could it reasonably be expected to appreciate that all the rest of the shipment would be rendered useless too? Next, should Sealane have realized that as a result of the fact that the shipment of components could not be used by EMCO in the manufacturing process when intended, its plant would be shut down for five days causing lay-off costs and loss of production and sales? Ultimately, should Sealane have realized that, in addition to those production losses, EMCO would lose a particularly lucrative individual contract as a result of the plant being shut down and workers being laid off?

There is a logical link of cause and effect in these successive economic injuries. EMCO can establish that it has suffered all these losses as a result of Sealane's default. It will not realize the benefit of its contract unless it is compensated for all of them. On the other hand, the injuries become successively more distant and unrelated in kind from the error in carriage. Damage and delay to goods in carriage inevitably inhibits their use but does not necessarily create production stoppages, worker lay-offs, diminished sales, and loss of business opportunities. Hence contract law, as a matter of policy, imposes a limit on compensation for the consequential loss of business profits, whether they result from wasted expenses made in reliance of the contract or lost expectation of advantage from the contract.[16] In addition, contract law prohibits the claimant from running up its claim unnecessarily by requiring it to mitigate its losses.[17]

In applying the legal criterion of reasonable expectations to the consequences of the breach of contract in this Case, account must also be taken of what Sealane actually knew about EMCO's business situation. For example, it may be difficult to say that in the ordinary course of events a multimodal operator such as Sealane would reasonably foresee that damage to one container of goods would prevent the use of the rest or cause the closure of a whole manufacturing plant. The operator might reasonably point out that it had no way of knowing how the goods were to be used or that they were required for immediate use. It might suggest successfully in its defence that the cargo owner could reasonably be expected to have an inventory of other, like goods sufficient for its short term needs.

Such doubts about the foreseeability of EMCO's economic injuries and consequential losses would be set aside in the specific circumstances of this case. In the course of agreeing to the movement, Sealane was expressly

16 See H. McGregor, *supra* note 13 at 166-167 and 685-688; W. Tetley, *supra* note 1, at 333-338; S.M. Waddams, *supra* note 12 at 14-14.
17 See Chapter 3, note 5.

instructed by EMCO about the consequences of a default in performance. Hence Sealane actually knew that its performance was being monitored and that damage or delay to the shipment would interfere with EMCO's business activities. In light of this knowledge, it is not difficult to say that Sealane ought to have realized the likelihood of the plant closure and, as a result, the loss of some business profits.

The circumstances in this case may seem somewhat unusual since multimodal operators are generally disinterested and may not be told much about the nature or the purposes of the goods they are invited to move. However, manufacturers and other traders are becoming increasingly concerned about the economic inefficiencies associated with large inventories and unreliable or delayed deliveries. More and more businesses are operating on just-in-time and similar supply and production schedules. The enchanced efficiency of operations thus achieved places greater importance on scheduled deliveries promptly performed. Thus the transport industry faces increasing expectations for timely and reliable service. The kind of performance monitoring system employed by EMCO in this Case is typical of firms that operate on just-in-time schedules in competitive global industries. As the modern developments in logistics spread more widely, multimodal operators and transport service providers in general will be much more closely involved in their customers' business. With the knowledge thus gained, they will foresee, or will reasonably be expected to foresee, many of the economic injuries and consequent loss of business profits that default in delivery will induce.

But knowledge of the cargo owner's operations does not necessarily lead to foresight of all consequential business losses. The criterion is still what could reasonably be foreseen as likely to result in light of the actual state of the multimodal operator's knowledge. Thus, if the operator is told that the shipment to be moved contains components for immediate use in the cargo owner's assembly plant, the operator can readily foresee that damage to them will reduce production, resulting in a loss in the profits expected in the ordinary course of events. But the operator's foresight could not reasonably be expected to extend beyond the consequential loss of ordinary business profits without the cargo owner supplying further and more particular details of its activities. For example, in this Case, it is highly unlikely that Sealane will be held accountable to EMCO for the loss of the special, and highly valuable, supply contract to its Taiwanese competitor. This business opportunity is not an ordinary incident of the process of production. Without prior information about the impending contract, Sealane could hardly be expected to contemplate its loss.[18]

---

[18] Compare *Victory Laundry (Windsor) Ltd. v. Newman Indust. Ltd.*, *supra* note 13, and see the references cited there.

Having determined the scope of compensable losses, it is necessary to put a value on them. Valuation, at least for physical cargo damage, is relatively easily made. As previously discussed,[19] the extent of loss will be quantified by assessing the arrived sound market value of the goods and subtracting the actual value of the goods delivered in damaged condition. Thus EMCO's container load of damaged components will be valued for compensation according to the price for which they could be replaced in EMCO's market area in Southern Ontario. Against this amount, an allowance will be made for any residual value the damaged components may have, whether EMCO disposes of them or not. This reduction reflects EMCO's duty to mitigate its loss so far as it reasonably can.[20] EMCO's claimed consequential business losses will also have to be proved positively as far as they reasonably can be. Thus the manner of estimating the net loss of expected business profits and the reliability of the supporting records of past production, costs and sales from which the prediction is made must all be explained and may be exposed to a degree of judicial scrutiny.[21]

Limits of Liability for Damage to Cargo

While the international rules do not regulate what losses are compensable, they do set limits to the quantum of compensation. They do this in two ways, first as to individual items of loss and then as to the aggregate value of all losses. EMCO will face both methods of limitation of its recoverable losses. The limits of liability for itemized claims for loss, such as physical damage to cargo, also depend on whether the injurious event can be attributed to a particular stage of the movement. If it cannot, the Multimodal Rules themselves establish the limit of liability. If the damage to cargo can be localized, the question about the extent of the operator's liability will be referred to the relevant unimodal convention and local law.

In the event of unattributable damage to cargo, all three sets of rules set out clear principles for the calculation of maximum levels of liability. These are discussed in detail in Chapter 4. They were fixed by reference to the low limits under the unimodal rules for sea carriage. However, the different sets of multimodal rules assign different liability maxima per unit which vary from 2 SDR to 2.75 SDR per kilogramme or alternatively from 666.67 SDR to 920 SDR per package.[22] When multiplied out for EMCO's damaged cargo, these rates generate sizeable variations in the total amount

---

[19] See Chapter 3 at note 4.

[20] *Supra* note 17.

[21] See H. McGregor, *supra* note 12 at 1134; S.M. Waddams, *supra* note 12 at 5-41 - 5-44 and 13-3.

[22] See Exhibit 4.1 in Chapter 4. SDR refers to the Special Drawing Rights operated by the International Monetary Fund. Refer to Chapter 4 at note 25.

of compensation that must be paid. For example, for the components worth C$123,100, EMCO might be limited to compensation as low as C$12,000[23] or as high as C$87,268.50.[24] EMCO would only recover the full value of its components in the unlikely event it was able to break the limits of liability by establishing that Sealane acted wilfully with intent to cause the damage or recklessly with the knowledge that such damage would probably result.

If the damage to the cargo can be attributed to a particular stage of the movement, the different sets of multimodal rules are unanimous in referring the question of the multimodal operator's limit of liability to the governing regime for that stage.[25] As a result, the multimodal operator bears exactly the same liability as if it had contracted as an unimodal carrier or employed one to do the carrying for it.

The effect of this principle is to establish even wider variations in the limits of liability than the differences under the Multimodal Rules for unattributed damage. The extent of these variations from 2 SDR to 17 SDR per kilogramme is set out for all modes and regimes in Exhibit 5.4 in Chapter 5, where the application of the limits of liability for localized loss and damage are fully discussed. This network system is most advantageous to Sealane since it will never have to pay more in compensation for damage to the shipment of components than it can recover from the culpable carrier. But EMCO will be exposed to very variable rates of compensation depending on the moment in the movement when the injury happened to occur. However, it can never recover more than its actual loss, which in this case is one container load valued at C$123,100 less the salvage value of the damaged components, if any.

Liability for Consequential Loss

Consequential business losses have not received the same degree of attention in either the unimodal or the Multimodal Rules as cargo damage and delay. Perhaps the reason is because responsibility for losses beyond cargo damage have frequently not been imposed at all. In the past the operator has generally known too little about the goods it is moving to be able to contemplate the effects of depriving the owner of their use. In any event, neither the ICC Rules 1975 nor the MTC 1980 contain any express provision regarding liability for consequential loss in the case of unattributable damage. Nor do the unimodal conventions, which might

---

[23] Calculated from UNCTAD/ICC 1992 rule 6.1 as follows: 666.67 SDR/package x 9 pallets of components x C$2.00/SDR (as of August 1996).

[24] Calculated from MTC 1980 rule 18(1) as follows: 2.75 SDR/kg. x 15867 kg. x C$2.00/SDR (as of August 1996).

[25] ICC 1975 rule 13; MTC 1980 art. 19; UNCTAD/ICC 1992 rule 6.4.

apply when the incident giving rise to the losses can be localized, deal with consequential loss. An argument might be made that the general language limiting liability for physical damage impliedly governs recovery for consequential loss, but the provisions in the Multimodal Rules are not clear and have not been tested in litigation.

The ICC Rules 1975 require the operator 'to pay compensation in respect of loss of, or damage to the goods.'[26] This clause does not say that compensation shall be paid in the amount of the value of the lost or damaged goods. The phrase 'in respect of' is wide enough to include compensation for injury to the goods themselves and consequential business losses resulting from their unavailability for commercial use. The language in the MTC 1980 is more suggestive of this interpretation. The multimodal operator may assert the prescribed limitations when it 'is liable for loss resulting from loss of or damage to the goods.'[27] These words more clearly distinguish the economic loss flowing from the physical loss or damage to the cargo and therefore might be read to include consequential business injuries.

The difficulty with this approach to interpretation is that the limits are subsequently prescribed in terms of units of account per package or kilogramme of the physical goods. In other words, the limits are set in accordance with a rateable value for the lost or damaged goods themselves, so there is no opportunity for compensation for consequential business losses to be added. Thus even a generously wide reading of the ICC 1975 and MTC 1980 provisions to include consequential losses does not make much sense in the context of the detailed prescription of limits. It is more probable that consequential losses were not contemplated by the rule makers and they remain unregulated. In these situations, therefore, EMCO might expect to recover all its consequential losses for which it could hold Sealane accountable.[28]

The UNCTAD/ICC Rules 1992, on the other hand, do set a limit of liability for consequential business losses. The rule is expressed as a limit of total freight (i.e., transport costs).[29] In EMCO's Case, this is described as C$1,666 for each of three containers, or a total of C$4,998. This amount is derisory when compared with the value of the shipment (described as C$123,100 per container). It is only a tiny portion of the loss to EMCO of production and sales' profits, for which, as was earlier discussed, Sealane is likely in this Case to be held accountable. Why, one must wonder, is the limit of consequential loss tied to the freight? The value of the freight

---

26 ICC 1975 rules 11 and 13.

27 MTC 1980 art. 18(1).

28 Subject to a clause in the transport document or the operator's standard terms of trade that expressly limits or disclaims liability for consequential loss.

29 UNCTAD/ICC 1992 rule 6.5.

compared to the consequential losses, in those infrequent cases when they are compensable at all, will usually be so disproportionately small as to suggest recovery is not encouraged. If that was the intention, it would have been simpler, though not necessarily fair, to rule out all claims for consequential loss.

Limits of Aggregate Liability

Though the Multimodal Rules do not specifically regulate the compensation payable for all kinds of the cargo owner's loss individually, some of them do have a mechanism to control the total or aggregate amount that may be recovered. Since the ICC Rules 1975 do not entertain the point, presumably there is no limit on the aggregation of liability for cargo damage and consequential losses. In contrast, the MTC 1980 and the UNCTAD/ICC Rules 1992 express a principle that the aggregate compensation payable shall not exceed the limit of liability for the total loss of the cargo.[30] However, close reading of these provisions reveals a significant difference in their application. The aggregate liability of the operator under the MTC 1980 is expressly stated to be the sum of the compensation assessed for cargo loss and damage and for delay. Since the MTC 1980 makes no reference to consequential losses, presumably they are recoverable beyond the aggregate limit of liability for other kinds of losses. Indeed, as noted above, when an operator, such as Sealane, is responsible for consequential losses it may bear unlimited liability for them.

Under the new UNCTAD/ICC Rules 1992 there is no such exception: aggregate liability is clearly intended to be all inclusive. In other words, under these Rules, when the goods are completely destroyed in transit, the limit of liability for the total loss of the cargo is immediately engaged and no further losses are compensable. When, as in EMCO's case, only some of the goods are damaged, the compensation for them will be less than the limit of liability had the whole shipment suffered the casualty. Hence EMCO will be permitted to claim a margin of its consequential losses but only up to the outstanding portion of the limit of liability for a total loss of the shipment.

For example, supposing the damage to the container of components cannot be localized, the limits of Sealane's liability under the UNCTAD/ICC

---

[30] MTC 1980 art. 18(5); UNCTAD/ICC 1992 rule 6.6. This limitation does not affect the rule that the operator will bear unlimited liability for wilful or reckless cargo injury: see MTC 1980 art. 21; UNCTAD/ICC 1992 rule 7 and Chapter 4 at note 31. But the cargo owner may not circumvent the limit of aggregate liability by suing the operator and the defaulting carrier separately. This limitation does apply to the cumulation of compensation from the operator and all its employees, agents and subcontractors: see MTC 1980 art. 20(3); UNCTAD/ICC 1992 rule 12.

Rules 1992 will be calculated at a rate of 2 SDR per kilogramme.[31] Thus the limit of compensation payable to EMCO for the damaged components themselves is 2 SDR/kilogramme x 15,867 kilogrammes (1 container of components) x C$2.00 per SDR (as of August 1996) or C$63,468. The limit of aggregate liability, having been set at the limit of liability for the total loss of the shipment, i.e., 3 containers, would be 2 SDR/kilogramme x 15,867 kilogrammes x 3 containers x C$2.00 per SDR for a grand total of C$190,404. Therefore there is room for EMCO to claim consequential business losses only up to C$190,404 less C$63,468, that is C$126,936.

The measure of consequential losses that are potentially recoverable by EMCO compares poorly with the likely total value of its lost production and profits. Indeed, as the proportion of cargo that is damaged rises, the amount of compensation payable for consequential losses diminishes. The above example shows that the effect of the rule on aggregate liability in the UNCTAD/ICC Rules 1992 is to limit recovery for consequential losses severely, regardless of the specific provision concerning them. When that is taken into account, the position of the cargo owner may be even worse.

The stringency of the provision specifically about consequential loss will probably mean that in EMCO's case the actual aggregate compensation payable by Sealane will be less than the amount allowed by the express provision limiting aggregate liability. The actual aggregate liability is calculated by adding together the limit of compensation for the damaged components and the equivalent of total freight for the consequential loss of business and profits. Thus the maximum cumulative compensation that EMCO might be paid under the UNCTAD/ICC Rules 1992 is C$63,468 (the limit of liability for the damaged components)[32] plus C$4,998 (the total freight for the shipment of 3 containers)[33] for a total of C$68,466. This sum is barely more than one-third of the limit of aggregate liability calculated above as C$190,404.

It is worth noting, as a final point, the shifting effect on the aggregate limit of liability in the UNCTAD/ICC Rules 1992 as a result of expressing it by reference to the limit of liability for the total loss of the goods. As discussed previously,[34] that limit differs not only between the sets of multimodal rules but also very widely among the unimodal rules which may become operable when the cargo loss can be localized. Thus the computation of the aggregate limit of liability, it seems, will track the same

---

31 UNCTAD/ICC 1992 rule 6.1. See the table of limits of liability for unattributed damage in Exhibit 4.1 in Chapter 4. The alternative rate of 666.67 SDR/pkg. would produce a substantially lower ceiling of liability in this Case as the shipment was enumerated as 9 pallets in each container. According to the Rules, EMCO is entitled to claim the higher ceiling.

32 As calculated *supra* after note 31.

33 As calculated *supra* after note 29.

34 See under Limits of Liability for Damage to Cargo.

complicated pattern as the calculation of the limit of liability for physical cargo loss and damage.

CHAPTER 8

Other Legal Requirements of the Multimodal Rules

Introduction

When accidents befall cargo in multimodal operators' hands, cargo owners are wont to demand compensation. The international Multimodal Rules have been created in order to assist resolution of such incidents and disputes. They allocate the risks between the operator and the shipper so each knows the extent of its responsibilities and can take steps to protect itself.[1] They affix liability and set the rate of compensation payable when a casualty does occur. The previous four case studies show in detail how the Rules operate to determine the basis and extent of liability for both physical and financial loss. These are the core matters involved in the contractual partnership, and its breach, between the multimodal operator and the cargo owner. But when a question of liability arises, there are many other considerations that may affect its imposition or exclusion. Claims by cargo owners must satisfy procedural requirements in addition to having substantive bases in culpable damage. Defences for operators may be available on technical grounds in addition to proving the absence of fault. A number of these considerations exist in general law and so will not be dealt with further here. Others are specified in the Multimodal Rules themselves, generally in very similar terms and standards. Therefore, towards a complete understanding of the operation of the Multimodal Rules, their remaining provisions affecting the scope of liability, which have not been discussed elsewhere, are collected in this chapter.

The seven items of significance to be discussed here are: 1) the form and content of the multimodal contract; 2) the relation of the Multimodal Rules to other contractual terms; 3) the application of the Rules to the operator's employees and agents; 4) the period of responsibility of the operator; 5) notices of loss and claims; 6) time limitations on bringing actions; and 7) alternative actions for breach of contract or tort.

---

[1] Typically, but not exclusively, by insurance. See the discussion of the different perspectives of the parties to multimodal transport in Chapter 2.

Form and Content of the Multimodal Contract

Since the Multimodal Rules are voluntary regimes,[2] they must be brought into effect for a particular movement by agreement between the operator and the shipper. This is achieved by incorporating them by reference into the multimodal contract.[3] In addition, the Rules set out various requirements for the form and content of the multimodal contract. These provisions are not so much inhibitive as facilitative of the smooth application and operation of the Rules to a particular movement.

The operator is expected to provide the shipper with a signed multimodal contract which specifically applies the relevant set of rules, but this document may be in either negotiable or non-negotiable form.[4] The MTC 1980 and the UNCTAD/ICC Rules 1992 also permit the use of electronic signatures and messages so the multimodal contract is not restricted to the traditional documentary paper form.[5] The contents of the multimodal contract, so far as they are regulated at all by the Rules,[6] replicate in varying detail the ordinary practices of the transportation industry. Thus the Rules call for inclusion in the multimodal contract of such information as the names and addresses of the shipper, the consignee if known, and the operator, a description of the nature, marks, number, weight or quantity and apparent condition of the goods, as well as the place and date of receipt and delivery of the cargo.[7] This is all information that is necessary to execute the multimodal movement and to determine the scope of liability if a casualty should occur.

Since this information in the multimodal document will be used as evidence of the receipt and carriage of the cargo, it must be accurate.[8] The operator accepts its responsibility for the document and its contents when it signs and issues it. But usually most of the details about the goods are provided by the shipper. Since the consignee is entitled to rely on the information on the face of the multimodal document,[9] the operator may find itself in the difficult position of having to accept liability for the

---

2   See the discussion of the legal status of each set of rules in Chapter 3 at notes 9, 15 and 28.

3   ICC Rules 1975 rules 1(a) and 2(c); UNCTAD/ICC 1992 rule 1.1.

4   ICC Rules 1975 rule 2(c); MTC 1980 art. 5(1); UNCTAD/ICC 1992 rule 2.6.

5   MTC 1980 art. 5(2), (3); UNCTAD/ICC 1992 rule 2.6. This is true so long as electronic contracts are not inconsistent with local law.

6   The UNCTAD/ICC Rules 1992 do not contain any provisions regarding the contents of the multimodal agreement beyond their express incorporation.

7   See ICC Rules 1975 rules 3, 4, 9; MTC 1980 arts. 6-9, 11, 13.

8   See the discussion of the evidentiary effect of the multimodal document in Chapters 4 and 5 under Proof of Loss. In addition the MTC 1980 art. 11 imposes unlimited liability on the operator for the consequences of intentional misstatements about the cargo in the multimodal document.

9   *Ibid.* and ICC Rules 1975 rule 9; MTC 1980 art. 10(b); UNCTAD/ICC 1992 rule 3.

consequences of a misdescription of the goods that it made on the basis of the details supplied by the shipper. The operator cannot escape this liability but it may want, quite reasonably, to pass it back to the shipper who created the chain of misapprehensions in the first place. Such indemnification is permitted by all the sets of Multimodal Rules by deeming the shipper to have guaranteed the accuracy of the particulars about the goods that are furnished by it.[10] Thus the operator is able to hold the shipper liable and, if necessary, to sue the shipper for breach of this guarantee and so to recover whatever compensation it had to pay to the consignee.

Relationship between the Multimodal Rules and Other Contractual Terms

Since the Multimodal Rules are only brought into operation in any particular movement by incorporation into the contract between the multimodal operator and the shipper,[11] there is a chance that they will clash with other contractual terms agreed by the parties. Because the incorporation of the Multimodal Rules is as voluntary as the other agreed terms, it cannot be assumed that they will override any other terms they may happen to contradict. The courts see their task as giving effect, so far as they can, to the intentions of the parties gathered from all the terms of their contract.[12] Indeed, the canons of contractual interpretation would suggest that a specific term expressly agreed between the parties will override a conflicting stipulation of a general character introduced by reference to some external source or document.[13] This result reflects a judicial attitude that specific matters which have received the express attention of the parties are more likely to reflect their true intentions than incorporated terms which were not discussed and cannot be construed consistently with the rest of the contract. The operation and integrity of the Multimodal Rules are therefore put at risk by the process of incorporation and the chance of alteration.

Fortunately the Rules themselves have largely resolved this dilemma. The ICC Rules 1975 and the UNCTAD/ICC Rules 1992 both include provisions to make them supersede any additional terms of the multimodal

---

[10] ICC Rules 975 rule 7; MTC 1980 art. 12 reinforced by art. 22; UNCTAD/ICC 1992 rule 8. The shipper is also bound to notify the operator about any dangerous characteristics of the goods being moved and may be responsible, according to the relevant international conventions or national law, for the injuries they cause or incur. See the references in ICC Rules 1975 rule 8; MTC 1980 art. 12; UNCTAD/ICC1992 rule 8.

[11] See *supra* at note 3.

[12] See G.H.L. Fridman, *The Law of Contract in Canada*, 3d ed. (Scarborough, ON: Carswell, 1994) at 453-455 and 466-472; A.G. Guest, gen. ed., *Chitty on Contracts* 27th ed. (London: Sweet & Maxwell, 1994) at 580-595.

[13] G.H.L. Fridman, *ibid.* at 471-472; A.G. Guest, *ibid.* at 589.

contract with which they conflict, insofar as those terms derogate from the Rules.[14] In other words, the terms that are agreed to be incorporated into the multimodal contract by the operator and the shipper include a stipulation about the priority among all the terms of the contract. The parties have effectively expressed their intention that the set of multimodal rules they have incorporated shall take precedence over terms that would reduce the operator's liability. The court, seized with a disputed claim, is most likely to give effect to this expressed preference as best representing the intentions of the parties and so to set aside some other conflicting term.

The authors of the MTC 1980 did not have to cope with the risk that its provisions might be superseded because they were drafted as a convention that would take effect as compulsory law and so would automatically override any private contractual arrangements that disagreed with them. Since the rules within the MTC 1980 are currently only available for application by voluntary incorporation of the parties, they do not mandatorily supersede other agreed terms. However, the express intent of the MTC 1980 is to establish a uniform international regime from which derogations in liability may not be made,[15] so it is expected that a court would construe conflicting terms of the multimodal contract in this spirit.

Application of the Multimodal Rules to the Operator's Agents

The scope of the operator's responsibility is also intimately affected by the extent of liability it is bound to bear for the delinquencies of those who work for it. Businesses are usually said to be vicariously responsible for the acts of their employees, agents and subcontractors. This approach has long been applied in the transportation industry and has now been carried forward in the Multimodal Rules. As the UNCTAD/ICC Rules 1992 so clearly state:

> The multimodal transport operator shall be responsible for the acts and omissions of his servants or agents, when any such servant or agent is acting within the scope of his employment, or of any other person of whose services he makes use for the performance of the contract, as if such acts and omissions were his own.[16]

Thus the operator must take full responsibility for persons acting on its behalf. For instance, if the operator employs an agent to arrange for transhipment at some distant port, it must accept the blame for a failure to

---

[14] ICC Rules 1975 rule 1(c); UNCTAD/ICC 1992 rule 1.2.

[15] See MTC 1980 arts. 3 and 28.

[16] UNCTAD/ICC 1992 rule 4.2. See similarly ICC Rules 1975 rule 5(b), (c) and MTC 1980 art. 15.

do so. Similarly, if the operator engages carriers, terminals or cargo handlers to perform parts of the multimodal movement, it may be held liable for the errors in their subcontracted activities.

Even though the operator has to take responsibility for the acts of its employees, agents and subcontractors, those persons will also be concerned about the scope of their own liability for errors and omissions. When a casualty occurs, the cargo owner sometimes considers it advantageous to lay a claim not only with the operator but also against the defaulting subcontractor. Perhaps the operator is not a business with much financial substance compared to the defaulting carrier, who is consequently a more attractive defendant to the cargo owner. Maybe it is procedurally easier for the cargo claimant to sue or to secure the assets of the culpable party rather than the operator.

In the first place the liability of the operator's agents and sub-contractors will be governed by the terms of their own contracts with it and the governing local laws. These contracts typically include clauses that limit or exempt the particular cargo handler or carrier from personal liability for the cargo, to the extent they are not prohibited by compulsory law. Further, individual subcontracted carriers will be regulated by the existing unimodal conventions or national transportation laws. In addition, those engaged to execute the movement often try to extend their limits and protections from liability through the operator to the cargo owner.[17]

The Multimodal Rules deal with these concerns by including all the parties to the performance of the movement as subject to their operation.[18] Thus the operator's employees, agents and subcontractors may rely on the Rules for the same defences and limits of liability that are available to the operator itself whenever a claim is laid by the cargo owner. Thus the cargo owner cannot circumvent the limiting effects of the Multimodal Rules on its claim against the operator by pursuing the defaulting carrier, terminal or cargo handler.[19]

---

[17] For example, by circular indemnities and Himalaya type clauses agreed by the performing carriers and handlers with the operator to be included in the latter's contracts with cargo owners. See R. De Wit, *Multimodal Transport: Carrier Liability and Documentation* (London: Lloyds of London Press, 1995) at 483 fwd., W. Tetley, *Marine Cargo Claims* 3d ed. (Montreal: Yvon Blais, 1988) at 757-779; P. Todd, *Modern Bills of Lading* (London: Collins, 1986) at 113-123.

[18] ICC Rules 1975 rule 18 (the operator may include his agents and servants); MTC 1980 art. 20(2); UNCTAD/ICC 1992 rule 12.

[19] Some commentators consider that a wilfully or recklessly damaging act of the operator's subcontractors might not be imputed to the operator and so might expose them to unlimited liability without defeating the operator's right to limit its liability. See W.D. Driscoll & P.B. Larsen, 'The Convention on International Multimodal Transport of Goods' (1982) 57 Tulane Law Rev. 193, at 231. If this view is correct, it could be advantageous to the cargo claimant to pursue the defaulting subcontractor as well as the operator, subject to the invocation of a circular indemnity clause: *supra* note 17.

Period of Responsibility

The period during which the operator is responsible for the cargo owner's goods is another crucial element in allotting liability. Since the operator has custody and safekeeping of the goods even as it is moving them, it is generally expected to accept responsibility for the whole period it is in possession of them. Thus the Multimodal Rules all specify that the multimodal operator has responsibility for the goods between 'the time of taking them into his charge and the time of delivery.'[20]

Hence the operator is responsible for goods in its charge whether actually moving or merely storing them. The idea that someone in the carrying business might be liable for goods upon receipt but before loading or after reaching the destination but prior to actual delivery has occasioned some uncertainty. Thus some of the Rules have tried to clarify the legally effective moment at which the goods are said to be 'taken in charge' by the operator and when they are to be treated as 'delivered' to the consignee.[21] These provisions make appropriate allowance for the intervention of officials, such as Customs officers, by authority of the local law. The operator, for example, may fulfil its obligation to deliver the goods and thus terminate its responsibilities for them by handing them over to the consignee or to an authority designated for receipt compulsorily by the law at their destination.

Notice of Loss

In the unfortunate event of injury to the cargo, the owner is generally expected to give notice to the operator of the loss or damage sustained. If the cargo owner does not do so, then, especially where the damage is concealed, the operator will have no reason to suspect it has defaulted on the multimodal contract in the view of the cargo owner and may be subjected to a claim. In the practice of the transportation industry, while the cargo owner only has to present a *prima facie* case of default by the carrier, which then has to disprove its liability,[22] the cargo owner must give prompt notice of loss or damage, or the carrier will be deemed to have delivered the cargo in good order. Such a timely notice will afford the carrier reasonable opportunity to survey the damage, investigate the cause of the casualty, preserve the evidence of the incident and its effects, and generally seek to remedy the problem or defend against the claim.

---

[20] ICC Rules 1975 rule 5(e). See similarly MTC 1980 art. 14(1) and UNCTAD/ICC 1992 rule 4.1.

[21] MTC 1980 art. 14(2); UNCTAD/ICC 1992 rules 2.7, 2.8.

[22] See Chapter 4 under Proof of Loss.

The Multimodal Rules extend this approach to multimodal transport. The different sets of rules each establish short, and in that sense strict, time limits in which the cargo owner shall give notice of loss or damage to the operator. For obvious damage to the goods, the cargo claimant must give notice either at the time they are handed over to it (ICC Rules 1975 and UNCTAD/ICC Rules 1992) or by the following day (MTC 1980). When the damage is concealed, and thus there may be a delay before even the cargo owner discovers it, the cargo owner is allowed six (MTC 1980 and UNCTAD/ICC Rules 1992) or seven days (ICC Rules 1975) in which to give notice. In all cases the notice must be given to the operator in writing and must indicate the general nature of the loss or damage.[23]

The penalty for failing to give notice in time and in the correct form is that receipt of the goods by the cargo owner is *prima facie* evidence of delivery of them as described in the multimodal contract. In other words, the operator may rely on its delivery of the goods as full and complete performance of the agreed movement unless the cargo owner proves otherwise. The failure to give notice of loss or damage does not defeat the cargo owner's claim for compensation. It merely increases the burden of proof of that claim. This is not necessarily a much increased burden since the cargo owner always has to establish that the damage took place while the goods were in the charge of the operator.[24]

These rules about notice to the operator apply when physical loss and damage occur. They do not apply to claims of delay. The ICC Rules 1975 and the UNCTAD/ICC Rules 1992 are silent about the need for a notice in the event of delay. Perhaps one is not necessary to inform, and thus protect, the operator as it will always know when delivery is late. The MTC 1980, however, does require a notice. It states:

> No compensation shall be payable for loss resulting from delay in delivery unless notice has been given in writing to the multimodal transport operator within 60 consecutive days after the day when the goods were delivered... .[25]

By the terms of this provision, the function of this notice is different. The operator is surely alerted to the possibility of a claim but is not informed that delay has occurred (as the notice of damage informs about concealed injury to the cargo) for it already knows that. Rather, the lack of a

---

23 See ICC Rules 1975 rule 10; MTC 1980 art. 24; UNCTAD/ICC 1992 rule 9.

24 Compare the practice in sea carriage as discussed by R. Colinvaux, *Carver's Carriage by Sea* 13th ed. (London: Stevens, 1982) at 370; Sir A.A. Mocatta, Sir M.J. Mustill & S.C. Boyd, *Scrutton on Charterparties and Bills of Lading* (London: Sweet & Maxwell, 1984) at 440; W. Tetley, *supra* note 17 at 871.

25 MTC 1980 art. 24(5).

notice within the designated 60 days allows the operator to assume that the delay in delivery has not caused any loss to the cargo owner. In fact the operator is relieved of all liability for loss resulting from delay. Thus the singular provision in the MTC 1980 is not just an evidentiary burden like the other notice requirements, but a permanent restriction on the cargo owner's right to compensation for the consequences of delayed delivery. The cargo claimant who fails to give this notice loses its claim.

Limitation of Actions

In addition to the requirement to give the operator notice of loss or damage, there is also a time limit in which the cargo claimant may bring an action. Under the ICC Rules 1975 and the UNCTAD/ICC Rules 1992 the time allowed to institute an action is only nine months.[26] This is a short time compared to the limits established by the unimodal conventions[27] which govern transits that are likely simpler than multiparty multimodal movements to sort out. The penalty for failing to begin suit in time is severe: the action is time barred, the operator is discharged of all liability and thus the cargo owner's claim is defeated.

In light of the pressure that so short a time limit and so final a consequence induce, disputes about how exactly to measure the nine months are predictable. Fortunately, the Rules provide some guidance. The ICC Rules 1975 and the UNCTAD/ICC Rules 1992 both measure the time from the moment of delivery, or the date when the goods should have been delivered, or the date when failure to deliver them would give the cargo owner the right to treat the goods as lost.[28]

The main reason why the time limit on actions is so short is out of a concern for the multimodal operator's desire to seek an indemnity for localized loss or damage from the carrier to which it was attributed.[29] Having compensated the cargo owner for its loss under the multimodal contract, the operator has a right to recover from the defaulting carrier so much as it can for breach of their contract of carriage. But the extent of the operator's recovery will be regulated by the particular terms of the contract with that carrier, including any unimodal convention that is applicable to it. Hence the operator must bring its action for indemnity within the time limit for suits set by the relevant unimodal convention[30] or the defaulting carrier

---

26 ICC Rules 1975 rule 19; UNCTAD/ICC1992 rule 10.

27 The unimodal conventions allow either 1 or 2 years for suit and in some exceptional situations even longer. Refer to Appendix 1.

28 ICC Rules 1975 rules 15, 19; UNCTAD/ICC 1992 rules 5(3), 10.

29 See Driscoll & Larsen, *supra* note 19 at 239.

30 Or other compulsory national law.

will be discharged of liability and the operator will recover nothing. But until the operator is sued by the injured cargo owner, it has no reason to bring an action for indemnity.

The nine-month time limit on actions by the injured cargo owner is short enough to fall within the time bar for suit by the operator against the defaulting carrier.[31] Thus the operator is ensured of the opportunity to bring its own action for indemnity. This care for the rights of the operator is appropriate; however, its protection may be at the cost of the cargo claimant which is placed under great pressure, if not a risk of defeat, to bring its claim in very short order.

The MTC 1980 has found another way out of this difficulty which seems to be more equitable to both parties. It sets the time limit for the institution of a suit by the injured cargo owner at two years.[32] Thus the cargo claimant has a reasonable length of time to investigate all the circumstances of its injuries and losses and to try and negotiate a settlement of its claims with the operator and its representatives. There is little risk of the claims process being dragged out until the cargo claimant's right to sue is time barred. On the other hand, after two years the operator will have lost its opportunity to sue over against the defaulting actual carrier. To prevent this result, the MTC 1980 also requires the cargo claimant to give a written notice of its claim, stating enough particulars for the operator to understand the nature and extent of the suit it will have to answer if settlement is not achieved, within six months of the defective delivery.[33]

This notice is different from the notice of loss or damage discussed previously. That notice merely informed the operator that the cargo had been injured and thus afforded it the chance to survey the damage and investigate the cause of the loss. That notice and its consequences were merely procedural. This notice within six months later is a more formal statement by the cargo owner of its claim for compensation and involves substantive consequences. While this notice is not the institution of a legal suit as such (for that may be brought any time within two years after delivery), if it is not given in a timely and proper fashion, the cargo claimant's right to bring an action will be barred.[34] In other words, the cargo claimant must give written notice of its claim within six months in order to protect its right to sue the operator, if necessary, any time within two years.

---

31 *Supra* note 27.

32 MTC 1980 art. 25(1). By art. 25(2) the limitation period begins on the day after the goods were delivered or should have been delivered, i.e., it starts to run one day later than under the ICC Rules 1975 and the UNCTAD/ICC Rules 1992. See note 28. The MTC also sets some limits, in the interests of the cargo owner, on the range of places that a claim may be litigated or arbitrated. See MTC 1980 arts. 26 and 27.

33 Or where the goods have not been delivered, 6 months after the day on which they should have been. See MTC 1980 art. 25(1).

34 *Ibid.*

Meanwhile the operator receives sufficient notice of the nature and extent of the cargo owner's claim that it can take steps to pursue concurrently any rights it may have to institute a recourse action for possible indemnity.[35]

Alternative Action in Tort

Normally the cargo owner's claim is for breach of the multimodal contract, but occasionally it may be brought on some other basis of personal liability, such as tort. The most obvious situation is when the cargo owner wishes to pursue the particular carrier that had custody of the goods when they were damaged. This party to the multimodal movement is not in privity of contract with the cargo owner: they are separated by a string of two contracts, the cargo owner with the operator under the multimodal agreement and the operator with the carrier under the segmental carriage contract. The cargo owner cannot sue the carrier for breach of contract in the absence of a contract between them and so must frame its claim in the alternative action of tort.

The difference in the style of the cause of action can be significant to the resolution of the claim, especially in the amount of compensation payable. Actions for breach of contract are resolved in accordance with the terms of the agreement between the parties. These terms include the Multimodal Rules chosen for incorporation into their contract, including the principles and limits of liability found within them. An action in tort is not so limited since it is not based on agreement but on civil liability imposed by law. Hence it may be advantageous to the cargo claimant to sue in tort rather than in contract. But this choice of alternatives might allow the cargo owner to circumvent the effects of the Multimodal Rules which it has undertaken to respect. Such a consequence is an abuse of process against the operator and all those who work for it.

The Multimodal Rules do not try and prohibit actions in tort, which, being established by local law, they cannot contradict, but they all include a similar provision to equate the effects of suing either in contract or in tort. They state simply that the Rules shall apply to all claims relating to the performance of the multimodal contract whether they are founded in tort or contract.[36] Thus the cargo claimant is bound by the Multimodal Rules and their operation on the incident giving rise to loss, damage or delay however it frames its claim against the operator. The cargo owner's claim is similarly governed even when brought against the performing carriers and cargo

---

[35] The MTC 1980 grants the further liberality of an action for indemnity for at least 90 days, even after the time for suit has run out, provided no applicable unimodal convention or national law would thereby be broken. See MTC 1980 art. 25(4).

[36] ICC Rules 1975 rule 16; MTC 1980 art. 20; UNCTAD/ICC 1992 rule 11.

handlers who work for the operator since they are also entitled to the protections of the Multimodal Rules.[37] Thus the cargo owner is inhibited from gaining any advantage outside of its rights under the Multimodal Rules, however it chooses to present its claim.

This discussion completes the analysis of the provisions of the Multimodal Rules begun in Chapter 3 and extended in detail through Chapters 4-7. It is now possible to proceed in the next chapter to assess the impacts of the three sets of rules and to offer practical reasons for preferring one over another.

---

[37] See the prior discussion in this chapter under Application of the Multimodal Rules to the Operator's Agents.

CHAPTER 9

Evaluation of the Choice of Multimodal Rules

Introduction

The various business attitudes and practices of the major participants in multimodal transport were discussed in Chapter 2. Now that Chapters 3 to 8 have made clear the legal implications of the use of one set of Multimodal Rules over another, it is time to place this understanding within its commercial context. This chapter will offer an evaluation of the choice of Multimodal Rules against the business circumstances in which multimodal transport is provided. In order to do so, the chapter first reviews how a cargo claim for theft, damage, delay, and consequential or aggregated losses is likely to be handled. Once this process is appreciated, the pattern of claims is explored. A grasp of events which trigger a claim and of claims procedure builds the foundation for understanding the means by which the risks of transportation can be managed by the parties involved. The chapter concludes with a discussion of the impact of the choice of Multimodal Rules for each of the parties—cargo owners, carriers and third party logistic service firms—in order to evaluate the acceptability of the alternatives from a business risk point of view.

Handling a Claim[1]

When hidden damage occurs, it is normally the consignee of the cargo who discovers it and determines that a claim will be made. When damage is not hidden, the realization that a claim will be made may occur more obviously in transit. These situations will not necessarily be handled differently, however, as the first step in a claim is for the cargo owner to contact its insurance broker or the insurance company and arrange for the damage to

---

[1] The Institute of London Underwriters, *Notes for the Guidance of Settling Agents* (London 1987) provides a thorough and more definitive description of the duties of the survey agents than is provided here. Review Lloyd's Training Centre, *An Introduction to Lloyd's Market Procedures and Practices* (London 1987) for further understanding of insurance principles.

be surveyed.[2] If insurance has been arranged by the shipper, then the matter becomes its responsibility as the insured.[3]

A claim for cargo loss or damage filed after the container is stripped is less likely to be successful than one where the goods are left undisturbed until they can be examined by the insurer. If a claim for concealed damage uncovered during unpacking of the container is to be successful, it is important that the unpacking be discontinued from the moment the damage is noticed. Timely reporting is also a factor in the outcome of the claim. Most insurance policies and carriage contracts specify a time limit and procedure as to when and how a claim may be made. This time limit may vary depending on the contracts of insurance and transport; in other words, on the commercial terms and conditions under which insurers, carriers and operators provide their services. Three days is a common limit for giving notice of a claim,[4] which may be a problem in situations where the loss or damage is not immediately noticeable on delivery. The insured must notify all relevant parties of the loss or damage so as to keep open the insurer's right of subrogation.[5]

Upon notification, the insurance underwriter will appoint a settling agent who may or may not also be the cargo surveyor. (The settling agent may appoint an expert to act as surveyor.) The insured must contract for the survey and the survey certificate, agreeing to pay the associated fees, which will then be recoverable from the underwriter if there is an insured loss. If the surveyor, however, concludes that no loss has taken place, these fees are not recoverable and are borne by the insured.

The first act of the surveyor is to determine the contents of the container in order to identify whether the case involves goods subject to the International Maritime Dangerous Goods Code. If so, the next step is to ascertain whether an investigation will escalate the damage or have undesirable results. Once it is clear that it is safe to proceed with a physical examination of the cargo, it is normal practice to determine if the seal initially applied to the container is intact or if it has ever been tampered with, broken or replaced. It is customary to review and compare seal numbers and cargo receipts in trying to trace events.[6]

---

2 For a discussion of the legal right to bring a claim, refer to W. Tetley, 'Who May Claim or Sue for Cargo Loss or Damage' (1986) 17 Journal of Maritime Law and Commerce 407.

3 Most terms of trade identify the party charged with primary responsibility for arranging insurance. A thorough understanding of the risks and responsibilities implied in each trade term is a commercial necessity.

4 The time limit may also be controlled by the governing rules or law; see e.g., the impact of the Multimodal Rules discussed in Chapter 8 under Notice of Loss.

5 Subrogation is defined in Chapter 2, note 34. The Open Policy form and Certificate of Insurance require that the Insured take 'appropriate action' to preserve the insurer's ability to hold carriers liable for loss or damage.

6 Refer to the discussion on container security in Chapter 5 under Proof of Loss.

During examination of the shipment, it is the consignee's responsibility to separate the cargo in good condition from the damaged goods, in order that the surveyor may examine the damaged goods and make an assessment of the loss. The Institute of London Underwriters makes it quite clear to settling agents that it is not the responsibility of the surveyor to determine which goods are damaged.[7] This principle respects the fact that the cargo owner continues to own the goods and should act as if there were no insurance in order not to prejudice the outcome.

In the case of water damage, for example, the surveyor may take samples for chemical analysis to ascertain if the damage has been caused by condensation (a fault attributable to the shipper in packing for transport) or incursion of sea water (attributable to the ocean carrier). In the case of the latter, the surveyor will also be interested in whether the container was carried on deck, in which case it is treated differently than below-deck stowage for insurance purposes.[8] The loss may be determined by the surveyor to be only a partial loss if damaged goods have another use for which they can be sold, although they may not be of use to the owner. This investigation of the container contents can be as simple or as far-reaching as desired by the insurance company.

There are documentation requirements to fulfill in the filing of a claim including, but not restricted to, the original policy or certificate of insurance, the original contract of carriage and the shipping invoice, the survey report, the delivery receipt and any relevant correspondence.[9] Once the underwriter has all the necessary documentation in support of a claim and settles the claim with the insured party, the underwriter will seek a letter of subrogation from the insured in order to be able to seek recovery from those determined to be responsible for the loss.

The final outcome of the claim will depend on: (1) the type of insurance cover purchased, (2) the terms and conditions of the transport contract(s), and (3) the results of the survey agent's investigation. The first

---

7   The Institute of London Underwriters, *supra* note 1 at 1.

8   In research conducted for a study into the Hamburg Rules for Canada's Department of Transport, H. M. Kindred *et al.*, *The Future of Canadian Carriage of Goods by Water Law* (Halifax: Dalhousie Ocean Studies Programme 1982), a number of container carriers reported that it was customary to treat all containers, for insurance purposes, as if they were carried below deck for reasons of business expediency. This gives them greater flexibility in stowing a container on the vessel while the customer need not be concerned about its actual placement. Without this practice, all cargo owners would be seeking below-deck locations for their containers, because insurance premiums are lower and the risk of containers being washed overboard is reduced. As a result, vessel capacity would not be fully utilized, so most shipping lines have found this practice a preferable solution. The concept of a deck in container shipping is becoming legally irrelevant with modern configurations and hatchless, fully cellular designs.

9   For further understanding of the claims process, review R. H. Brown, *Marine Insurance— Volume 2: Cargo Practice* 2d ed. (London: Witherby & Co. 1973).

two factors set the rules by which the injury uncovered by the third will be ameliorated. The type of insurance purchased, and the terms and conditions of that cover as defined by the applicable contract, will be agreed by the party responsible for arranging the insurance, as defined by the contract of sale. The terms and conditions of the transport contract(s), including any listed exclusions to the operator's liability, will be established by the choice of contract and the clauses contained therein. Finally, the surveyor will determine, if possible, the type of loss and the party bearing responsibility for that loss. If the location and party responsible cannot be readily determined, there will likely be arbitration or litigation between the insurer, the cargo owner and the multimodal operator, who may join the participating carriers, to resolve the outstanding issues of attribution of loss, limits of liability and other issues as discussed in previous chapters.[10]

If the circumstances of the claim are clear and the documentation in order, timely compensation to the cargo owner for the loss is likely. (The insurance broker may not even wait for payment to come from the underwriter before paying out on the claim.) For the cargo owner, the level of satisfaction with the outcome of the claim will depend on its relationship with the insurance broker, the quality of the service provided by the broker (and often the professionalism of the settling agent and the surveyor) during this difficult time, and the speed with which the compensation is received.[11] Without prompt indemnification, the business risk held by the cargo owner becomes more uncertain, particularly given today's global markets and the volatility of currency fluctuation.[12]

For the operator and the underwriter, the result of the claim will differ depending on whether or not hidden damage can be attributed to a particular leg of the multimodal transport movement during the surveyor's investigation. In some cases, attribution is obvious, such as when a straddle carrier drops a container in a container yard and the bottles of wine inside break and spill their contents. Less readily apparent are cases of theft in transit, concealed damage and the like. The previous chapters have underlined the risks and financial implications for operators, third parties

---

[10] In addition to the limits of liability placed on operators and carriers, as discussed in this book, limits may also be imposed on insurance recoveries due to the incorporation of special clauses specific to the type of cargo within the insurance contract arranged.

[11] It is interesting to note that, in a recent study in Atlantic Canada, carriers are still perceived by shippers as providing poor service in the claims area with claims settlement ranked last of the 12 service elements examined (Atlantic Provinces Transportation Commission, *Tips and Topics* [October 1995] 35:10 at 4). Perhaps the carrier is receiving the blame for a process with a time line controlled by the insurance industry.

[12] The same may be said of the business risk of the one ultimately held liable for the loss but, in this case, the cost of capital tied up in uncompensated lost or damaged inventory is not part of the risk.

and cargo owners of the range of possible outcomes given the different Multimodal Rules which may be incorporated in the transport contract.

Once the basis of liability has been established and the limits of liability determined, the claim will be paid (or not) depending on the type of insurance cover purchased. There are two general types of insurance which may cover the claim depending on the insurance arrangements made by the operator, the shipper or consignee, and/or the third party service provider: cargo insurance and the carrier's Protection and Indemnity (P&I) insurance or the NVOC's Through Transit (TT) Club insurance.[13]

Except in cases of extremely low value, dense products, the insurance built into the transport contract (and paid for under the carrier's P&I insurance or the operator's TT Club insurance) simply will be inadequate to compensate the cargo owner in full in the event of loss or damage because of the low limits of liability. Therefore, in most cases, either the buyer or the seller will be required to purchase additional cargo insurance depending on the terms and conditions of the sale contract. It may be that both parties will purchase insurance for different stages of the transport, although this may pose problems later in the case of unattributed loss or damage. The simplest and most convenient arrangement is for the buyer and the seller in a multimodal transaction to agree to specify FCA (free carrier) or CIP (carriage paid to) terms of sale thus placing the responsibility for contracting and insuring the entire move on one of them. Whichever one accepts this responsibility should be aware of the pattern of claims likely to be faced.

Claims and Their Source

Of considerable importance in understanding the impact of the Multimodal Rules applying to multimodal transport is the transport industry's experience with marine insurance and the relative incidence of various types of claims. 'Marine insurance' is a ubiquitous term that includes all kinds of cargo cover, not just goods shipped by sea. Marine insurance claims arise from many sources, including land-based catastrophes. These claims vary widely from year to year, depending on the vagaries of weather, collisions, or simply upon substandard shipping practices and equipment.

There is no concerted worldwide effort to identify separate categories of cargo losses within marine insurance statistics. Furthermore, there is no unified approach to identifying multimodal claims as distinct from other types of cargo claims. Each insurance company guards its statistics closely

---

[13] Protection & Indemnity insurance provides shipowners with cover for a wide range of liabilities outside their hull and machinery insurance. Such coverage for third party liabilities obviously includes loss or damage to cargo. The Through Transit Club provides similar insurance to multimodal transport operators which are not carriers.

and very little data on claims and sources are published.[14] More generally, however, armed with some basic knowledge of claims and sources, operators can evaluate the terms they use on their contracts of carriage and shippers can examine the fine print of that contract knowledgeably. This section of the chapter will focus on what is publicly reported about cargo claims, so that a more informed discussion about the choice of Multimodal Rules may be made later in the chapter.

According to a 1995 article in *Lloyd's List*, nearly one-third of the claims faced by P&I clubs arise from loss of or damage to the cargo.[15] The article further notes that cargo claims, as a proportion of total P&I claims, has dropped due to the rise in personal accident and pollution claims. The United Kingdom Mutual Steam Ship Assurance Association reported 28 per cent of all claims by value related to cargo, but only 20 per cent of all those exceeding US$100,000 affected cargo.[16] Clearly, many cargo claims are for sums of less than US$100,000. The largest volume of claims arise from dry bulk goods, reflecting the vulnerability of these cargoes to hatch cover damage and water ingress. As dry bulk cargoes are seldom, if ever, moved multimodally, the share of claims arising from multimodal transport cannot be readily determined.

Some effort to tabulate the state of the insurance market from the premium purchase side was undertaken by *Seatrade Review*. Seven major insurance markets were examined and the share of premium income attributed to cargo as opposed to hull insurance was noted for each. The total premium volumes for 1992 for the seven markets came to US$8.5 billion, with hull insurance accounting for 43.5 per cent and transport/cargo insurance accounting for 56.5 per cent.[17] The largest of the cargo insurance markets was Japan, which alone had a cargo premium volume of US$1.5 billion.[18] Again, these data fail to segregate multimodal claims from other cargo claims.

The general view held by the insurance companies interviewed in the conduct of this research is that the majority of cargo losses are preventable.

---

[14] It is extremely difficult to get accurate information on the types of claims found in multimodal carriage. A large number of insurance companies and industry associations were contacted and almost all indicated that they do not track this type of information for multimodal transport. This is not surprising given the insurance industry's difficulty in evaluating the record for much larger marine casualty claims. Cargo claims are more numerous and smaller in value and therefore do not appear to be of as much interest. On the other hand, some insurers have indicated to the authors that they may keep their own sophisticated records but that not all do; most would not want these statistics revealed.

[15] J. Mulrenan, 'Keeping Tabs on Cargo Damage' [25 July 1995] Lloyd's List (Special Report: Marine Claims) 8.

[16] *Ibid*.

[17] Anonymous, 'Global Snapshots: A Roundup of Leading Marine Insurance Markets Worldwide' [December 1994] Seatrade Review at 53.

[18] *Ibid*.

The Canadian Board of Marine Underwriters reports that 83 per cent of worldwide cargo losses are preventable, while 33 per cent of total losses are due to the preventable causes of theft, pilferage and non-delivery.[19] One carrier interviewed estimated that shippers may be held accountable for approximately one-half of claims against that carrier.[20] One insurance company—CIGNA[21]—has published data showing that 39-45 per cent of cargo claims can be attributed to stowage and handling problems. (See Exhibit 9.1.) Experience indicates that 75 per cent of losses involving goods in transit can be prevented through careful attention to the basic principles and techniques of protective packaging, along with careful transport planning.[22]

Whichever estimate is considered, there is consensus that poor handling and stowage is the largest single cause of losses and that its incidence can be reduced by the exercise of greater care on the part of the shipper in packing the container for transport. Likewise, the shipper is in a position to decrease the potential for condensation during transport; appropriate selection of the container for the cargo and proper protection of the internal packages may limit losses due to condensation and minor leaks. Clearly, the shipper has significant opportunity to prevent the largest source of claims through careful planning and management of pre-shipment activity.

Checking the container's hinges, the means of securing the container, and tracking its movements may go some way to reducing the potential for theft and pilferage. Pilferage is even less likely in North America now that the use of doublestack containers has become commonplace. The configuration of the corner locks on doublestack rail cars makes opening the container's doors difficult if not impossible. However, it is clear that no amount of diligence on the part of the shipper will be able to overcome the pilferage that might take place during periods of inactivity. Although it is possible for pilferage to occur when a 6000'-long container train (of approximately 300-340 TEUs[23]) is halted for even 10 minutes on a dark siding to wait for another train to pass, it is more likely that theft will take place in smaller yards, or at origin or destination. The railway company needs to be vigilant, which may not be easy at all times.

---

[19] Canadian Board of Marine Underwriters, *Marine Insurance: The Silent Export* (1994) at 35. There is no source cited for these data.

[20] This confidential estimate was provided during an interview conducted for this book.

[21] Data appeared in B. M. Tarnef, 'Safeguarding Shipments When Going Global' [September 1993] Risk Management 20. This data set expanded a previously published data set by adding the years 1988-91 to the data published in External Affairs and International Trade Canada, *Safe Stowage* (Ottawa: Government of Canada 1990) at 3.

[22] B. M. Tarnef, *ibid.* at 22.

[23] A TEU is a Twenty-foot Equivalent Unit so that a 40' container accounts for 2 TEU.

Exhibit 9.1:
Types of Claims—One Insurer's Allocation

Year

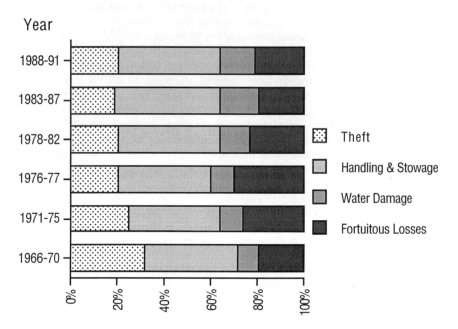

Definitions: Theft = theft, pilferage and non-delivery; handling and stowage = container damage including breakage, leakage and crushing, contact with oil and other cargo, contamination and infestation; water damage = fresh water, condensation and sea water; fortuitous losses = sinking, stranding, fire, collisions, and heavy weather.

Source: B. M. Tarnef, 'Safeguarding Shipments When Going Global' [September 1993] Risk Management 20 at 23. Reprinted with permission from Risk Management Magazine.

Theft is certainly not limited to the rail mode. The trade press reports the very serious problem of hijacking being experienced in the United States, particularly at major ports and distribution hubs.[24] One estimate of cargo theft and hijacking in the United States placed losses at several billion

---

[24] Cargo theft in the United States is responsible for annual losses totaling hundreds of millions of dollars, according to J. E. Mooney, 'The Perfect Crime of the 1990s: Cargo Theft' (1993) 41:11 Risk Management 58. He notes that the Cargo CAT (Criminal Apprehension Team) of the Los Angeles area reported 675 cargo thefts in 6 southern California counties in 1993 resulting in more than US$109 million dollars in wholesale dollar losses, a 35% increase over 1992. Cargo CATs note that most cargo is stolen while the truck is left unattended, according to R. Ceniceros, 'Cargo CATs Stalking Cargo Thieves' (1995) 29:39 Business Insurance 12.

dollars annually,[25] while the U.S. National Cargo Security Council has assessed them to be much higher at US$10 billion, noting that carriers do not report all thefts for fear of increased insurance rates.[26] Hijacking is not just a North American phenomenon. In the first six months of 1993, 740 trucks were reported as hijacked in and around London.[27]

Included in the losses experienced by the industry in recent years are losses from stock throughput policies. This type of coverage has been described as 'the "cradle to grave" cover that will not die.'[28] Stock throughput insurance is considered by the industry to be very risky as it extends to all activities from production to final sale and results in some marine insurers writing cover for non-transport activities. For example, the impact of the Northridge earthquake on warehouses in California resulted in up to US$70 million in 1994 quake-related losses—losses which should have fallen on other insurers.[29] In spite of a concerted effort by many to remove this type of cover from marine insurance business, it continues to distort the payout figures and to result in higher cargo premiums than would otherwise be assessed.

To conclude, information from a number of insurers in several countries leads to two conclusions. First, data are not available on the relative incidence of attributed (to a particular leg of the journey or mode or location) versus unattributed loss. Even if insurers track and record losses in this format, they do not see the need to report them publicly. Second, for a significant share of the claims, the shipper will be made to bear the risk for the loss as it will be deemed to have been preventable through adequate packaging and stowage.

Strategies for Managing Cargo Owner Risks

The importance of risk management in multimodal operations has grown in concert with the increasing penetration of containerization as a means of secure international transport and with the wider adoption of supply chain management by the business community. For many participants in international trade, however, the strategies to manage risk have not developed at the same pace.

---

25 R. Ceniceros, 'Cargo Theft Causing Loads of Problems' (1995) 29: 39 Business Insurance 3.

26 Anonymous, 'It's Ten O'Clock, Do You Know Where Your Freight Is?' (1996) 120:1 Purchasing 115.

27 J. Porter, 'Truckers Seek Ways to Combat Burgeoning Crime Rate in Europe' [20 August 1993] Journal of Commerce 2B.

28 A. Ladbury, 'Non-marine Losses Upset Cargo Insurers' (1994) 28: 40 Business Insurance 21.

29 *Ibid*.

Although theft and damage due to stowage may be readily attributed to a single stage in the logistics chain, and hence to the shipper or a single carrier or terminal, it must be clear from the Cases presented in earlier chapters that not all claims can be so attributed. Because both P&I and TT Club cover are limited, marine cargo insurance is a necessity of risk management for the cargo owner.

The purchase of basic marine insurance is only one risk reduction strategy available to the cargo owner. This section of the chapter reviews other means available to minimize the risks faced: the purchase of extended insurance cover, carrier selection and review strategies, document review and/or specification and, finally, loss prevention programmes.

Purchase of extended insurance cover

In addition to basic marine insurance for cargo loss and damage, it is possible for a cargo owner to purchase extended cover for additional economic losses and delay. According to the Canadian Bureau of Marine Underwriters, extended cover accounts for less than 1 per cent of policies issued as most shippers and consignees are not prepared to pay the costs of extended cover. The premium is high because 'cover for a $5 part could escalate into a claim for $50,000.'[30]

A 1989 study of the incidence of marine cargo delay experienced by Canadian shippers and consignees found that approximately 25 per cent of the Canadian companies participating in the study purchased delay insurance.[31] An alternative to marine insurance for delay is cover provided by trade associations and government agencies for delay due to political reasons. For example, U.S. firms may purchase Trade Disruption Insurance. This type of protection has been used by cargo owners to cover losses caused by delay due to the Tiananmen Square disruption of product manufacturing in China, or those due to documentation difficulties, JIT disruptions caused by a number of natural disasters, such as the Kobe earthquake and U.S. floods in 1993, and strikes.[32]

It is clear, however, from the relatively low use of extended cover (over and above that purchased for political risk) that many cargo owners have little interest in expending additional sums on insurance for delay or consequential economic loss. It may be that maintaining safety stock is a less

---

30 Telephone interview with Gerry Giroux of the Canadian Bureau of Marine Underwriters.

31 H. Kindred and M. R. Brooks, 'The Incidence and Effects of Marine Cargo Delays in Law and Commerce' (1990) 17 Maritime Policy and Management, 189. Of the 69 firms participating in the study, 17 reported purchasing cover for marine cargo delay (*ibid.*, at 193).

32 Reported in E. Canna, 'When the Supply Chain Snaps' [September 1995] American Shipper 48.

expensive alternative or that the incidence of delay is not regarded as sufficient to warrant the premiums for extended cover.

Carrier selection and review

Careful carrier selection is another means by which shippers can reduce transportation risks. In the early years of containerization, the selection of carriers was often a purchasing decision that involved few individuals, was made quickly and was held to be of little importance to the overall strategic objectives of the firm.[33] But that has all changed.

Over the last five to 10 years, the market for transport services has altered dramatically. Deregulation, time-based competition and the resulting focus by many transport users on JIT manufacturing strategies, along with globalized production and supply chain management, have turned the traditional buyer-seller transaction-based relationship between the cargo owner and the operator into what is now being reported by many manufacturers as a choice of partners.[34] It is anticipated that innovative contractual arrangements will continue to develop as many more firms, in the interests of improved competitiveness, pursue downsizing and outsourcing. The move by users of transport services towards time-defined or other forms of contracted logistics supply is often accompanied by a carrier reduction strategy, which focuses on selecting a few trusted carriers for longer-term use.[35]

Generally, loss and damage experience and claims response have not been perceived as important in a shipper's choice of carrier. Studies undertaken in 1982 and 1989 placed fast claims response as the 12th (of 17) and 11th (of 16) most important criterion in carrier selection, while past loss and damage experience was of even less importance at 13th and 14th respectively. In both studies, neither criterion was a determinant of choice.[36]

---

[33] M. R. Brooks, 'An Alternative Theoretical Approach to the Evaluation of Liner Shipping, Part I. Situational Factors' (1984) 11 Maritime Policy and Management 35.

[34] M. R. Brooks,'Understanding the Ocean Container Carrier Market—A Seven Country Study' (1995) 22 Maritime Policy and Management 39; B. J. Gibson, H. L. Sink & R. A. Mundy, 'Shipper-Carrier Relationships and Carrier Selection Criteria' (1993) 29 The Logistics and Transportation Review 371. This trend was discussed in greater detail in Chapter 2.

[35] K. A. O'Laughlin, J. Cooper & E. Cabocel, *Reconfiguring European Logistics Systems* (Oak Brook, IL: Council of Logistics Management 1993) at 9-10 report the leverage shippers gain through consolidation of the carrier base and negotiating deeper discounts on transport rates. Supplier consolidation is further noted by G. Backler, 'Co-Makership Relationships in European Distribution' (1991) 2:1 The International Journal of Logistics Management 48 at 49.

[36] These studies were reported in M. R. Brooks, 'An Alternative Theoretical Approach to the Evaluation of Liner Shipping, Part II. Choice Criteria' (1985) 12 Maritime Policy and Management 145 and M. R. Brooks, 'Ocean Carrier Selection Criteria in a New Environment'

Prior to the adoption of carrier reduction strategies by many transport buyers, the risk of contracting with a poor operator was spread by splitting the business over many suppliers. Now, other techniques of managing this risk are required and one of these is performance monitoring.

In a study of the North American manufacturing sector, a significant number of companies undertake some form of formal monitoring of transport supplier performance.[37] In keeping with the out-sourcing mood of the times, audits surfaced overwhelmingly as the preferred method. Two-thirds of the responding companies rely on audits while just over half use process reviews or inspections to ensure their requirements are being met. (See Exhibit 9.2.) Some companies also survey their customers to determine their level of satisfaction with the performance of a particular carrier or carriers. A performance-monitoring approach is one worth consideration by any firm which has grown too large for its institutional memory to continue to be effective.

Exhibit 9.2:
Methods Preferred for Carrier Performance Evaluation

Evaluation Method	Per Cent of Firms Using
Audits	65%
Process Reviews	55%
Inspections	52%
Certification	12%
Testing	9%
Other*	34%

Note: * This often included monitoring the temperature in refrigerated containers as a method of evaluating the supplier's ability to meet terms and conditions of hire in this special market.

Source: Unpublished data collected for the study reported in M. R. Brooks, 'Performance Evaluation in the North American Transport Industry' (1995) 1 Transportation Research Forum 37th Annual Conference Proceedings 226.

(1990) 26 The Logistics and Transportation Review 339. To be a determinant of choice, each criterion had to be important to the shipper and carriers had to be perceived by the shipper as having a significantly different performance on that 'importance' criterion. As 'fast claims response' and 'loss and damage experience' both failed to survive the first of these determinance tests, neither was examined for the second.

37 M. R. Brooks, 'Performance Evaluation in the North American Transport Industry' (1995) 1 Transportation Research Forum Annual Conference Proceedings 226.

Document review and specification

At the core of successful risk management in multimodal operations is a full understanding of the documents available for use. As noted in Chapter 2, shippers and consignees are not without influence on the terms and conditions of multimodal transport which will apply through their incorporation on the back of the operator's documents. National organizations and associations may also incorporate specific Multimodal Rules into bills of lading available for sale to members. For example, a recognized freight forwarding association may adopt the Negotiable FIATA Multimodal Transport Bill of Lading (FBL), which incorporates the UNCTAD/ICC Rules 1992. By specifying in a contract of sale that the movement must be made using the FBL, the shipper and the consignee are assured that the UNCTAD/ICC Rules 1992, if that is what they desire, will apply to their particular transaction and transport document.

The Canadian International Freight Forwarders Association (CIFFA) reports that about 50 per cent of its members have purchased its FBLs, which incorporate FIATA's FBL terms.[38] However, this only means that CIFFA members use them for those shipments requiring an FBL in either the terms of the letter of credit or the contract for sale of goods. The fact that members buy a box of FBL documents does not imply they are used, as members may only keep them on hand for those shipments when they are specifically requested. It is clear that many shippers and consignees are not aware of the terms in the fine print on the back of the document and so do not request FBLs. If, from a review of this book, a shipper or consignee determines it is in its best interests to use the UNCTAD/ICC Rules 1992, the establishment of a company policy to require the use of an FBL in all international sales agreements where a bill of lading (as opposed to a waybill) is desirable would be an appropriate risk reduction strategy.

Cargo owners can also reduce their risks by ensuring that the third-party service providers they use belong to a recognized standards organization. In Canada, CIFFA establishes uniform standards and practices for its members and these are incorporated in its forwarding contract. By dealing only with members of such recognized organizations, the risk of unusual contracts is reduced. This does not go as far as document review but is a step in the right direction.

As already explained in Chapter 2, there is a move towards greater outsourcing of logistical management. This development raises the concern that TPLs might not be professional and knowledgeable, or meet an acceptable minimum standard of practice and competence. There are TPLs who do not know the terms and conditions on the backs of their own

---

[38] Telephone interview with Marilyn Massaud of Canadian International Freight Forwarders Association.

documents. They rely completely on head office to take care of these details, and are unable to advise their customers which carrier(s) may offer the most advantageous and preferable terms on their transport contracts. As the cargo owner is the one that must live with the loss if it is not fully recoverable under insurance arrangements, it and not the third party logistics service provider must ultimately take responsibility for the terms and conditions of the transport contract.

Attention to detail is a key element of risk reduction by document review and specification. For example, a clear understanding of terms of trade should mean that shippers do not have unexpected surprises, like finding out that they do not have insurance when they expect that they do. A shipper may assume it has insurance cover on an FOB sale because the buyer is responsible for purchasing it, forgetting that the buyer's cover will not extend to the movement to the ship's rail. A shipper may also assume it has adequate cover (even under the operator's per package limitation) for a shipment it described as '480 boxes on 12 pallets in one 20 foot container'; however, its freight forwarder has reduced the claim against the carrier by describing the shipment as '1 20 foot container said to contain 12 pallets' on the transport document. The result is that the compensation paid for a total loss by the carrier's insurance is 1/40th of what was expected. When relying solely on the carrier's or operator's insurance cover, the cargo owner's personal vigilance over the transport documents is critical because the risk of loss falls onto the cargo owner even though responsibility for preparing the documentation may have been delegated to a third party. These may sound like small precautions but their impact can be significant.

Loss prevention programmes

If, as indicated previously, losses due to preventable causes account for a large percentage of total losses, the implementation of a loss prevention programme by the shipper may be a worthwhile consideration. Such programmes can include personnel training (in proper container stuffing), packaging redesign, container tracking, and a whole host of monitoring activities intended to reduce preventable loss. Such programmes can even include pre-shipment surveys by insurers. Savings are possible both by reducing losses and by seeking lower insurance premiums due to an improved claims record. Some carriers, to encourage shippers to embark on a loss prevention programme, have introduced 'safe shipper' awards. It is in the interests of both parties to participate in this type of risk reduction.

Cargo owners and operators alike, are seeking better control through cargo tracking or product-specific monitoring enhancements.[39] Tracking can be as simple as bar-code verification entry at various selected points in the move, or as complicated as satellite tracking. One new product (in the commercial development stage) has two-way satellite capability enabling the cargo owner to track the progress of an individual container, and to receive and send transmissions; for example, when the temperature changes within a refrigerated container, the product would transmit this information to the cargo owner who would communicate any desired corrections back, thereby adjusting the temperature of the container en route. The benefits of such technology in enabling the cargo owner to prevent damage to high value refrigerated products or to follow hijacked containers is obvious. With satellite tracking, the cargo owner also has access to the necessary proof of loss or delay of each container, thereby acquiring the additional facili- tatation of claims procedure.

It has been estimated that recoverable costs only account for 25 per cent of the economic loss incurred when sales, operations, administrative and training costs are included in the loss calculations.[40] Called by some 'the costs of service failure,' these costs can be significant. Many shippers are taking a closer look at loss prevention programsmes in order to minimize unrecoverable costs.

The Choice of Multimodal Rules

Now that it is apparent what part the selection of Multimodal Rules plays in the commercial relationship between the operator and the cargo owner, the choice itself may be addressed. Previous chapters have supplied the basis for preferring one set of Multimodal Rules over another in the course of answering two questions.[41] Chapters 3-8 made a detailed inquiry into the differences between the UNCTAD/ICC Rules 1992 and its predecessors. Chapter 2 investigated the commercial circumstances and viewpoints of the various parties to multimodal transport that will significantly affect the choice of Multimodal Rules. Together with the influences of claims experience and risk management opportunities discussed in this chapter, it is clear that the selection of Multimodal Rules is a heavily qualified choice.

---

[39] Temperature control monitoring equipment can be an important element in a loss prevention programme for a company shipping temperature-sensitive goods. Because many insurance policies contain a clause requiring the cargo owner to prove a breakdown for at least 24 hours before a claim will be paid out, this equipment affords the cargo owner the evidence in the event of a loss.

[40] J. Betz, 'The True Cost of Cargo Loss and Damage' [June 1990] Distribution 74.

[41] Specified in Chapter 1 under Choice of Multimodal Regimes and Structure of the Book.

The operator's interest is to limit its liability, a principle clearly established in the ICC Rules 1975. The subsequent sets of Multimodal Rules attempted to alter the allocation of the transport risks in favour of the cargo owner through adjustments, primarily in the operator's limits of liability. Strong carrier interests in many countries have prevented the MTC 1980 from finding sufficient support to bring it into effect. Now UNCTAD, in a further attempt to tip the balance of risks and responsibilities in the cargo owners' favour, has backtracked on its support for the MTC 1980 in the course of agreeing to an alternative—the UNCTAD/ICC Rules 1992. There are multiple viewpoints to be considered in assessing the choice of Multimodal Rules—cargo owner, TPL (as agent for the cargo owner or as operator) and carrier (as subcontractor or as operator). This section evaluates the alternatives, first from the carrying side and then in light of the cargo interests.

Operators' Preferences

TPLs (acting as multimodal operators) and carriers have the easier path to follow in their analysis of risk management. As both provide the documentation to the cargo owner, the choice of Multimodal Rules in all likelihood is already made to minimize their liabilities and reduce their obligations. Operators would like to limit their liability under all circumstances to no more than the value of the contract, i.e., the value of the freight. For simple instances of unattributed cargo loss and damage, it is quite clear from a direct comparison of potential outcomes[42] that the set of Multimodal Rules which best controls the liabilities faced by the operator is the ICC Rules 1975. The UNCTAD/ICC Rules 1992 fix a limit by weight no worse for the operator than the ICC Rules 1975, except when there is no sea leg in the movement. From the operator's point of view, the least preferable set of Multimodal Rules are those offered by the MTC 1980.

In general, the differences in impact between the Multimodal Rules when the cargo loss or damage can be localized are not so important as in cases of unattributed loss. All three sets of Multimodal Rules, in slightly different ways, refer claims of attributed loss for resolution according to the law of the stage in which the casualty occurred. Thus the same rule and level of liability should govern the loss whichever set of Multimodal Rules is applied in most cases of attributed cargo injuries. This conclusion may be explained in more detail in relation to the basis and extent of the operator's liability.

---

[42] Refer to Exhibit 4.1 in Chapter 4.

First, the basis of liability for attributed damage throughout the Multimodal Rules themselves and the unimodal conventions[43] is the principle of the presumed fault of the operator. Variation in this standard is only introduced by the express grounds of excuse granted to the operator[44] but, in general, they are not greater than the justifications allowed to the operator in the event of unattributed loss, namely exemption from liability for incidents beyond its reasonable ability to control.[45]

Second, the extent of liability for attributed losses is referred by all sets of Multimodal Rules to the law of the place of the incident. Thus, the limit of liability will usually be the same under the Multimodal Rules. The sole exception is found in the MTC 1980 which defers to the relevant modal limit of liability only when it is higher than the MTC 1980's own rule on compensation in the event of an unattributed loss. In effect, this means that the operator may have to pay more in compensation, in accordance with the MTC 1980's limit of liability, for cargo loss or damage on a sea leg than it would under the unimodal conventions on sea carriage. Claims for cargo losses by road, rail and air transport are compensated under the relevant unimodal conventions at rates which equal or exceed the limits of the MTC 1980 and will therefore take effect as fully as they do under the other two sets of Multimodal Rules. The slightly higher level of recovery by the cargo owner under the MTC 1980 for loss or damage by sea will not, however, exceed the compensation payable had the cause of the loss been incapable of attribution because the amount of compensation would be assessed in accordance with the MTC 1980's limit of liability for unattributed loss. Furthermore, even in this one situation (of cargo loss or damage attributed to the sea leg of a movement) when there may be any difference in the limit of the operator's liability between the MTC 1980 and the other two sets of Multimodal Rules, the variance in the compensation for attributed casualties will not be greater than that for unattributed casualties under the Multimodal Rules themselves.[46]

The advantage for the operator of the ICC Rules 1975 over the other two sets of Multimodal Rules in instances of simple loss and damage is not lost even when there are additional claims for compensation for delay and consequential business loss. Liability for delay is obscured[47] under the ICC

---

[43] Which are referred to for this purpose only by the ICC Rules 1975.

[44] See Exhibit 3.2 in Chapter 3 for a general comparison of the basis of operator liability for Attributed Damage. The specific exceptions are discussed in Chapter 5 after note 37 (sea carriage), at note 52 (road carriage), at note 58 (rail carriage), at note 64 (air carriage), and after note 66 (for the UNCTAD/ICC Rules 1992).

[45] Except the notorious exemption in sea carriage for the negligence of the master and crew in the navigation and management of the ship.

[46] See Exhibit 5.4 in Chapter 5 for a comparative table of limits of liability under the Multimodal Rules and unimodal conventions as they affect sea carriage.

[47] And so may be difficult to force against the operator.

Rules 1975 by referring it to the underlying law for each stage of the movement, while it is limited to the value of the freight under the UNCTAD/ICC Rules 1992. Once again the least preferable set of Multimodal Rules is the MTC 1980. Even so, the maximum exposure of the operator is only 2.5 times the freight.[48] Consequential losses are not tightly regulated by the Multimodal Rules. Where they are, as in the UNCTAD/ICC Rules 1992, compensation is again limited to the value of the freight. The absence of limits in the ICC Rules 1975 and the MTC 1980 potentially exposes the operator to unlimited liability for foreseeable consequential losses. This risk, however, can be avoided by the simple addition of a clause in the terms and conditions of the multimodal contract disclaiming responsibility for such losses. Nothing in any of the Multimodal Rules prevents the operator from presenting terms and conditions that relieve it of liability for risks that are not addressed by the Rules.

Indeed, the ability of operators to set the terms and conditions of the contract of carriage often controls the choice of Multimodal Rules. Absent the attempts of cargo owners to improve their lot, it is unlikely that either the MTC 1980 or the UNCTAD/ICC Rules 1992 would have been developed. If the cargo owner is inattentive or indifferent, the choice of Multimodal Rules is made by default and to the benefit of the operator.

Cargo Owners' Preferences

For the cargo owner, the choice of Multimodal Rules will clearly depend on the company's own particular business requirements and its claims history. Obviously, there is no sure means by which a cargo owner can predict whether the surveyor, in the investigation of a claim, will be able to attribute loss, damage or delay to a specific stage of the movement. Therefore, in examining the impact of the choice of Multimodal Rules, the cargo owner must undertake a situation analysis[49] in order to identify its own best interests prior to deciding upon its preferred set of Rules. In doing so, three sets of questions may be posed:

(1) What is the firm's claims history with respect to loss/ damage and delay, and what is the extent of multimodal usage within its overall claims record? Are there particular carriers or operators that have incurred a less than acceptable record of casualties or uncompensated claims?

---

[48] Refer to Exhibit 3.3 in Chapter 3 for a summary of limits of liability for all types of loss.

[49] Such an analysis typically examines the company's internal strengths and weaknesses, and its external opportunities and threats concurrently with an investigation of the situation facing its customers and competitors. The purpose of a situation analysis is to identify the critical factors for a company faced with a strategic decision. Those critical factor(s) should then drive the decision-making process.

(2) Is the firm competing in an industry where opportunism is the mode of operation for most businesses? I.e., will delays mean missed opportunities and lost profits? Or is the nature of the business sufficiently stable that strategic planning allows profitable opportunities to be carefully developed?

(3) Is the firm operating in an industry where competition is global, safety stock levels are minimized, and just-in-time production raises the potential for severe consequential losses from delay in arrival of cargo or from non-delivery of a single shipment?

The purpose of these sets of questions is to identify the firm's priorities in risk assessment in multimodal transport. The answers to them will help the company to identify, in the context of its claims history and business operations, its priorities in making the choice of Multimodal Rules.

For example, if, in answering these questions, the examination of the firm's business practices reveals that physical loss and damage to its shipments are its primary concern, and that neither delay nor a JIT schedule are critical factors, the firm will be most interested in which set of Multimodal Rules provides the best terms with respect to simple cargo injuries.

The Multimodal Rules approach attributed and unattributed injuries differently, but in cases of localized cargo loss or damage, the difference in impact between the Rules is hardly significant. Indeed, in the absence of a sea leg in the movement, there is none at all.[50] Hence the cargo owner that is primarily concerned with cargo injury in selecting the preferable set of Multimodal Rules will be most concerned about their differences, in particular their limits of liability, with regard to unattributable loss and damage.

When unattributed loss or damage is incurred, Chapter 4 demonstrates that the UNCTAD/ICC Rules 1992 would grant no more and may, in fact, provide lower compensation to the cargo owner than is possible under the ICC Rules 1975.[51] In this sense, the adoption of the UNCTAD/ICC Rules 1992 must be viewed as a step backward. If loss cannot be attributed to a particular leg of the journey, the cargo owner is penalized the measure of liability being set by comparison with the low limits established for sea carriage. It is unreasonable to expect that the cargo owner will be able to prove the circumstances of the incident and it would appear that some operators gain little benefit from such localization. Although the ICC Rules 1975 have been withdrawn in favour of the UNCTAD/ICC Rules 1992, their continued use is possible by operators not updating their documentation.

---

[50] As explained supra after note 45.
[51] Consider the limits of liability tabulated in Exhibit 4.1 in Chapter 4.

If the situation analysis of the firm indicates that it is opportunistic in its approach to business, then the liability for delay under each set of Multimodal Rules will have greater priority than will their regulation of simple cargo injuries. Alternatively, if the firm has the luxury of a stable, non-opportunistic business climate, it is likely that the relative treatment of delay by each set of Multimodal Rules is of less consequence than other factors identified in the situation analysis.

The provisions of the ICC Rules 1975 are not at all acceptable to the cargo owner for whom delay is a significant economic consideration in the choice of carrier or operator, and hence the choice of a particular set of Multimodal Rules. As became obvious in the analysis of Case 3 in Chapter 6, the ICC Rules 1975 are so complex that they are almost unworkable. Also the additional delay involved in trying to resolve the claim by such a complex system also works against the interests of the cargo owner.

Particularly galling to the cargo owner must be the provision in Rule 11 of the ICC Rules 1975 that provides for compensation for delay only in instances when the delay can be attributed to a particular stage and carrier. This provision is clearly out of touch with the seamless nature of multimodal transport. A delay on one leg may be accommodated in the next and the carrier will fortuitously escape a potential claim. Alternatively, delay may be incremental, a veritable chain reaction, attributed in the final analysis to a series of events and thus to more than one stage of the journey. Delay is only incurred over the movement as a whole yet the ICC Rules 1975 fail to take account of this reality. For the consignee operating in an opportunistic business environment, such as high fashion retail, the ICC Rules 1975 are the worst possible choice on these grounds.

Furthermore, the ICC Rules 1975 are likely unacceptable to a broad range of businesses—wholesalers and retailers in industries such a packaged goods distribution, automotive sectors, high technology, computer manufacturing and assembly, and high fashion retail to name but a few. For these businesses, delay may result in significant consequential losses as well as any economic loss attributed solely to delay. For this group, however, the avoidance of the ICC Rules 1975 is not an obvious conclusion, as will be seen shortly in the discussion about consequential loss.

The MTC 1980 provides little more comfort to those cargo owners concerned about delay. Under these Multimodal Rules, the limits of liability for delay are capped at 2.5 times the amount of the freight paid. In a sector of the transport market where the value of the goods transported often far exceeds the amount of the freight paid, this ceiling on compensation is unacceptably low and usually bears little relationship to the loss actually incurred by cargo owners. It must be remembered, however, that this ceiling is higher than the one under the UNCTAD/ICC Rules 1992, which is set at the value of the freight only. None of the sets of Multimodal Rules provides adequate compensation for delay as currently structured.

Finally if, in conducting its situation analysis, the business concludes that it participates in a globally competitive industry employing minimum inventory levels within a finely tuned logistics system, in all likelihood the firm will place its highest priorities on the treatment of consequential loss and aggregate loss by each set of Multimodal Rules. What the firm may regard as a business consequence, however, may not be the kind of loss that is legally recognized. Not every loss causally consequent upon a transport casualty is compensable. Legal policy dictates that some consequential losses will be regarded as too remote to visit upon the operator. Even when compensation is payable for consequential loss, there are likely to be limits on its extent.

The inclusion of consequential loss in the UNCTAD/ICC Rules 1992 acknowledges for the first time that this form of loss is of very real concern to the cargo-owning community. Although this highlights a deficiency of the earlier sets of Multimodal Rules in meeting the needs of trade interests, the limits of liability applicable to consequential loss under the UNCTAD/ICC Rules 1992 make a mockery of its inclusion. Under these Rules, such claims are limited to the total cost of transport—clearly an insulting amount of money to most cargo owners, particularly in cases where consequential losses arise from the just-in-time inventory and delivery systems so common in high value finished goods and components parts. However, the MTC 1980 and ICC Rules 1975 do not contemplate potential claims for consequential loss.[52] Such an omission opens the way for the cargo owner to attempt to claim for such losses.

The dilemma facing cargo owners concerned about delay and other consequential loss is now clear. In a supply chain management relationship, the operator is usually kept fully informed as to the anticipated business of the cargo owner and is likely to understand the full consequences of a service failure. Some manufacturers go to extreme lengths to be sure that the carrier or third party logistical service firm is fully cognizant of the business risks faced by the firm with respect to its transport needs. In these circumstances, the cargo owner will likely find the terms and conditions applicable under the ICC Rules 1975 most unsatisfactory, especially with respect to delay. Yet it is these very same Multimodal Rules which do not appear to limit actions for consequential losses and hence the absence of such provisions may prove to be a boon.[53] As a result, the Multimodal Rules which might best benefit the cargo owner in cases of delay alone are not those serving its best interests in cases of delay causing further consequential losses!

---

[52] See Chapter 7 after note 27.

[53] Unless the operator has the power to impose a term that disclaims liability for such losses.

Unresolved Issues

There are a number of concerns which have been inadequately addressed in all three sets of Multimodal Rules. The first of these is the potential for conflict of interest. In the attribution of loss or damage to a particular stage of transport, the operator may hold the evidence to identify the mode responsible for the loss but, in providing that evidence to the shipper, it would become liable to pay a higher sum of compensation than for unattributed loss.

The second issue is the basis for calculating consequential loss. Operators would like to limit their liability under all circumstances to no more than the value of the contract to them (i.e. the freight). For cargo owners, the sum at stake may be much greater than this amount, as Case 4 illustrated. In that Case, the damage to the components in one container was responsible, in the mind of the cargo owner, for a loss of production as well as for the loss of a very large sales contract and the implied monetary contribution it would make to the profitability of the firm as a whole. Shippers have been known to argue that compensation for consequential loss, if it is to be limited, should be based at least on the value of the goods and not on the value of the freight.

The third unresolved issue concerns the application of the Multimodal Rules to consolidated cargo. The situation in Case 3 was complicated by the risk being borne by the owner of only part of the container's contents; it was a LCL shipment which arrived late. Assuming that no claim for delay is forthcoming from the balance of the shipment, does this then reduce the liability faced by the operator? How are risks to be apportioned within a consolidated shipment? Although it is true that the operator is required to exercise care while in charge of the cargo, none of the sets of Multimodal Rules addresses allocation of liability for consolidated shipments, a concern which is growing with globalization of manufacturing and fragmentation of component supply in high technology and automotive sectors of industry.

Fourth is a problem in the treatment of aggregate liability. Under the UNCTAD/ICC Rules 1992, the limit of aggregate liability is a moving target. Such uncertainty is not desirable because it leaves the cargo owner, and its insurer, uncertain as to the extent of financial risk to which they are exposed.

Finally, but not least, is a concern about the fixed nature of the limits of liability imposed. It is quite disappointing, no matter what the particular point of view of the individual cargo owner, that the authors of the UNCTAD/ICC Rules 1992 failed to recognize that inflation has ravaged the values contained in earlier sets of Multimodal Rules. Deflation in future is regarded by most economists as unlikely. Indexed limits of liability would be viewed as more appropriate by the cargo-owning community.

Final Comments

Although the principles of insurance and their application to simple cases of loss or damage have been well established for more than a century, the advent of containerization sparked concern about multimodal transport and its potential for concealed damage. In the past decade, cargo owners have increasingly followed the principles of supply chain management and adopted a wide range of negotiated relationships with their transport suppliers. It is apparent that the future area of concern to a growing number of cargo owners will be the treatment of consequential loss. More than any other type of loss, how delay and consequential loss are managed by the Multimodal Rules will be the grounds for acceptance of a particular set of Rules by business interests within globally competitive manufacturing and distributing concerns. By extension, this view will be adopted by the third-party suppliers which work on behalf of these companies.

Although the UNCTAD/ICC Rules 1992 do simplify the basis of liability for loss from the cargo owner's point of view, they still remain complex. In a step back from the MTC 1980, the UNCTAD/ICC Rules 1992 will continue to grant the operator the exception to escape liability for loss on the sea leg through fire or negligent conduct in the management of the carrying ship. Also, as a result of the continued reference to unimodal rules, shippers will still feel the need to seek advice from external parties for every cargo track (origin-destination-route combination) used, although not necessarily for every shipment on a particular track. Moreover, these simplifications in the basis of liability adopted from the MTC 1980 have been gained at the expense of its more advantageous limits of liability.

From the case studies provided in this book, cargo owners would be better off, in most situations, if the MTC 1980 had received broader acceptance. In fact, in an era of just-in-time delivery requirements and supply chain management, broader adoption would probably have resulted in reduced marine insurance premiums as the insurer is the one who pays for the spread between the limit of liability applicable to the operator and the insured value of the cargo specified in the insurance contract.

The UNCTAD/ICC Rules 1992 present a compromise that appears to offer little incentive for adoption by cargo owners. The only benefit for the cargo owner under the UNCTAD/ICC Rules 1992 initially seems to be the improved limits of liability in cases where there is no sea leg over what would be payable under the ICC Rules 1975. It appears, at first glance, that the recognition of the existence of consequential loss is an improvement. This is belittled by the limits of liability for this kind of loss being tied to the value of the freight and curtailed by the strictures on the aggregate limit of compensation. There is little gain for cargo owners to applaud and, in fact, they are better off under the MTC 1980 than under the UNCTAD/ICC Rules 1992.

Certain cargo owners may even be better off under the ICC Rules 1975 than under the UNCTAD/ICC Rules 1992 since no provision in the former expressly prevents their recovery of substantial consequential losses. However, this situation is deceptive since the absence of stated limits from both the MTC 1980 and the ICC Rules 1975 allows the operator to demand, if not to impose, its own, perhaps harsher, restrictions on compensation for such losses.

As a result, it is likely that the UNCTAD/ICC Rules 1992 will suffer a fate similar to that experienced by the MTC 1980: they will fail to acquire widespread support. From the operator's view, the ICC Rules 1975 are preferable to the UNCTAD/ICC Rules 1992. However, since the UNCTAD/ICC Rules 1992 have replaced the ICC Rules 1975 from the beginning of 1992, operators which are inclined to incorporate any of the Multimodal Rules will probably adopt the most recent set. The application of the UNCTAD/ICC Rules 1992 by trade associations in their standard model transport documents, such as the FIATA FBL, will encourage this development. Given that cargo owners tend to defer to the rules imprinted by the operator on the back of its contractual documents, the cargo owner may not have much choice about their use.

In these circumstances, the task for the cargo owner is to explore the choice of Multimodal Rules already used by its third party service providers and carriers and to work towards a choice in its own best interests. The Cases presented in this book illustrate the need for shippers also to keep the operator fully informed of their planned activities against the requirement to substantiate subsequent claims for extensive compensation. This will become even more important given that shipper-carrier partnerships and other strategic alliances will grow in number and the increasing use of JIT scheduling will require more and more operators to meet performance standards set by their customers. Cargo owners can also avail themselves of the risk reduction strategies noted previously in this chapter to assist them in the face of Multimodal Rules that fail to recognize the requirements of modern commerce.

When all is said and done, the impact of the choice of Multimodal Rules will fall on the cargo owner even in situations where a third-party service firm has undertaken responsibility to manage the logistics of the movement. All three sets of Multimodal Rules are voluntary and therefore will only favour those parties making a concerted choice to use them as the standard terms and conditions governing the contractual relationship. For the inattentive cargo owner, the rules embodied in its transport documents will be the ones chosen by the operator.

The purpose of this book was to review the international rules on multimodal transport in order to explore the differences between the alternative standards of conduct and to draw some conclusions about the significant influences affecting the choice between them. This book has served to clarify the circumstances all parties face in the course of conducting and facilitating international trade and to explain what role the perspective of the individual firm involved in multimodal transport will play.

While the book has accomplished its purpose, a general conclusion about each of the sets of Multimodal Rules becomes obvious. They are all far too complex for operational efficiency. If transport business had to be conducted this way, it would grind to a halt. Current regimes can be tolerated to regulate multimodal transport only because claims are resolved by the patchwork legal standards after the event and not during the course of day-to-day commerce. A suitable and supportive legal regime must move beyond the segmented perspective of modal regulation. What is needed is an internationally agreed regime that regards transportation services holistically. This goal has not yet been achieved. None of the available sets of Multimodal Rules, including the latest UNCTAD/ICC Rules 1992, provides those managing, using or operating the supply chain with a truly multimodal solution.

APPENDIX 1

Table of International
Unimodal Transportation Conventions

Air Carriage

Convention for the Unification of Certain Rules Relating to International
Carriage by Air, 12 October 1929, 137 L.N.T.S. 11, as amended by the Hague
Protocol, 28 September 1955, 478 U.N.T.S. 371, the Guadalajara Convention,
18 September 1961, 500 U.N.T.S. 30, the Guatemala Protocol, 8 March 1971,
65 A.J.I.L. 670, U.K. Cmnd. 4691 (1971), not in force, and the Montreal
Additional Protocols 1-4, 25 September 1975, U.K. Cmnd. 6483 (1976), not in
force.

Rail Carriage

Convention concerning International Carriage by Rail (COTIF), Appendix B:
Uniform Rules concerning the Contract for International Carriage of Goods
by Rail (CIM Uniform Rules), 9 May 1980, U.K.T.S. 1987 No. 1.

Road Carriage

Convention on the Contract for the International Carriage of Goods by Road,
19 May 1956, 399 U.N.T.S. 189, as amended by the SDR Protocol, 5 July 1978,
1208 U.N.T.S. 427.

Inter-American Convention on Contracts for the International Carriage of
Goods by Road, 15 July 1989, O.A.S.T.S. 1989 No. 72.

Sea Carriage

International Convention for the Unification of Certain Rules of Law
Relating to Bills of Lading (Hague Rules), 25 August 1924, 120 L.N.T.S. 155,
as amended by the Protocol to Amend the International Convention (Visby

Rules), 23 February 1968, U.K.T.S. 1977 No. 83, and the SDR Protocol, 21 December 1979, U.K.T.S. 1984 No. 28.

United Nations Convention on the Carriage of Goods by Sea, 1978 (Hamburg Rules), 31 March 1978, 17 I.L.M. 608.

Terminal Operations

United Nations Convention on the Liability of Operators of Transport Terminals in International Trade, 19 April 1991, 30 I.L.M. 1503, not in force.

APPENDIX 2

UNCTAD/ICC Rules For Multimodal Transport Documents

ICC Publication No. 481. Reprinted with permission.

1. APPLICABILITY

1.1 These Rules apply when they are incorporated, however this is made, in writing, orally or otherwise, into a contract of carriage by reference to the "UNCTAD/ICC Rules for multimodal transport documents," irrespective of whether there is a unimodal or a multimodal transport contract involving one or several modes of transport or whether a document has been issued or not.

1.2 Whenever such a reference is made, the parties agree that these Rules shall supersede any additional terms of the multimodal transport contract which are in conflict with these Rules, except insofar as they increase the responsibility or obligations of the multimodal transport operator.

2. DEFINITIONS

2.1 **Multimodal transport contract** means a single contract for the carriage of goods by at least two different modes of transport.

2.2 **Multimodal transport operator** (MTO) means any person who concludes a multimodal transport contract and assumes responsibility for the performance thereof as a carrier.

2.3 **Carrier** means the person who actually performs or undertakes to perform the carriage, or part thereof, whether he is identical with the multimodal transport operator or not.

2.4 **Consignor** means the person who concludes the multimodal transport contract with the multimodal transport operator.

2.5 **Consignee** means the person entitled to receive the goods from the multimodal transport operator.

2.6 **Multimodal transport document** (MT document) means a document evidencing a multimodal transport contract and which can be replaced by electronic data interchange messages insofar as permitted by applicable law and be:

(a) issued in a negotiable form; or

(b) issued in a non-negotiable form indicating a named consignee.

2.7 Taken in charge means that the goods have been handed over to and accepted for carriage by the MTO.

2.8 Delivery means:

(a) the handing over of the goods to the consignee; or

(b) the placing of the goods at the disposal of the consignee in accordance with the multimodal transport contract or with the law or usage of the particular trade applicable at the place of delivery; or

(c) the handing over of the goods to an authority or other third party to whom, pursuant to the law or regulations applicable at the place of delivery, the goods must be handed over.

2.9 Special Drawing Right (SDR) means the unit of account as defined by the International Monetary Fund.

2.10 Goods means any property including live animals as well as containers, pallets or similar articles of transport or packaging not supplied by the MTO, irrespective of whether such property is to be or is carried on or under deck.

3. EVIDENTIARY EFFECT OF THE INFORMATION CONTAINED IN THE MULTIMODAL TRANSPORT DOCUMENT

The information in the *MT document* shall be *prima facie* evidence of the taking in charge by the MTO of the goods as described by such information unless a contrary indication, such as "shipper's weight, load and count," "shipper-packed container" or similar expressions, has been made in the printed text or superimposed on the document.

Proof to the contrary shall not be admissible when the MT document has been transferred, or the equivalent electronic data interchange message has been transmitted to and acknowledged by the consignee who in good faith has relied and acted thereon.

4. RESPONSIBILITIES OF THE MULTIMODAL TRANSPORT OPERATOR

4.1   Period of responsibility. The responsibility of the MTO for the goods under these Rules covers the period from the time the MTO has taken the goods in his charge to the time of their delivery.

4.2   The liability of the MTO for his servants, agents and other persons. The multimodal transport operator shall be responsible for the acts and omissions of his servants or agents, when any such servant or agent is acting within the scope of his employment, or of any other person of whose services he makes use for the performance of the contract, as if such acts and omissions were his own.

4.3.   Delivery of the goods to the consignee. The MTO undertakes to perform or to procure the performance of all acts necessary to ensure delivery of the goods:

(a)   when the *MT document* has been issued in a negotiable form "to bearer," to the person surrendering one original of the document; or

(b)   when the *MT document* has been issued in a negotiable form "to order," to the person surrendering one original of the document duly endorsed; or

(c)   when the *MT document* has been issued in a negotiable form to a named person, to that person upon proof of his identity and surrender of one original document; if such document has been transferred "to order" or in blank the provisions of (b) above apply; or

(d)   when the *MT document* has been issued in a non-negotiable form, to the person named as consignee in the document upon proof of his identity; or

(e)   when no document has been issued, to a person as instructed by the consignor or by a person who has acquired the consignor's or the consignee's rights under the multimodal transport contract to give such instructions.

5. LIABILITY OF THE MULTIMODAL TRANSPORT OPERATOR

5.1   Basis of Liability. Subject to the defences set forth in Rule 5.4 and Rule 6, the MTO shall be liable for loss of or damage to the goods, as well as for delay in delivery, if the occurrence which caused the loss, damage or delay in delivery took place while the goods were in his charge as defined in Rule 4.1, unless the MTO proves that no fault or neglect of his own, his servants or agents or any other person referred to in Rule 4 has caused or contributed to the loss, damage or delay in delivery. However, the MTO shall not be liable for loss following from delay in delivery unless the consignor has made a declaration of interest in timely delivery which has been accepted by the MTO.

5.2   Delay in delivery. Delay in delivery occurs when the goods have not been delivered within the time expressly agreed upon or, in the absence of such agreement, within the time which it would be reasonable to require of a diligent MTO, having regard to the circumstances of the case.

5.3   Conversion of delay into final loss. If the goods have not been delivered within ninety consecutive days following the date of delivery determined according to Rule 5.2, the claimant may, in the absence of evidence to the contrary, treat the goods as lost.

5.4   Defences for carriage by sea or inland waterways. Notwithstanding the provisions of Rule 5.1, the MTO shall not be responsible for loss, damage or delay in delivery with respect to goods carried by sea or inland waterways when such loss, damage or delay during such carriage has been caused by:

- act, neglect, or default of the master, mariner, pilot or the servants of the carrier in the navigation or in the management of the ship;
- fire, unless caused by the actual fault or privity of the carrier;

however, always provided that whenever loss or damage has resulted from unseaworthiness of the ship, the MTO can prove that due diligence has been exercised to make the ship seaworthy at the commencement of the voyage.

5.5   Assessment of compensation

5.5.1 Assessment of compensation for loss of or damage to the goods shall be made by reference to the value of such goods at the place and time they are delivered to the consignee or at the place and time when, in accordance with the multimodal transport contract, they should have been so delivered.

5.5.2 The value of the goods shall be determined according to the current commodity exchange price or, if there is no such price, according to the current market price or, if there is no commodity exchange price or current market price, by reference to the normal value of goods of the same kind and quality.

6.   LIMITATION OF LIABILITY OF THE MULTIMODAL TRANS-PORT OPERATOR

6.1   Unless the nature and value of the goods have been declared by the consignor before the goods have been taken in charge by the MTO and inserted in the *MT document*, the MTO shall in no event be or become liable for any loss of or damage to the goods in an amount exceeding the equivalent of 666.67 SDR per package or unit or 2 SDR per kilogramme of gross weight of the goods lost or damaged, whichever is the higher.

6.2   Where a container, pallet or similar article of transport is loaded with more than one package or unit, the packages or other shipping units enumerated in the *MT document* as packed in such article of transport are deemed packages or shipping units. Except as aforesaid, such article of transport shall be considered the package or unit.

6.3   Notwithstanding the above-mentioned provisions, if the multimodal transport does not, according to the contract, include carriage of goods by sea or by inland waterways, the liability of the MTO shall be limited to an amount not exceeding 8.33 SDR per kilogramme of gross weight of the goods lost or damaged.

6.4   When the loss of or damage to the goods occurred during one particular stage of the multimodal transport, in respect of which an applicable international convention or mandatory national law would have provided another limit of liability if a separate contract of carriage had been made for that particular stage of transport, then the limit of the MTO's liability for such loss or damage shall be determined by reference to the provisions of such convention or mandatory national law.

6.5   If the MTO is liable in respect of loss following from delay in delivery, or consequential loss or damage other than loss of or damage to the goods, the liability of the MTO shall be limited to an amount not exceeding the equivalent of the freight under the multimodal transport contract for the multimodal transport.

6.6   The aggregate liability of the MTO shall not exceed the limits of liability for total loss of the goods.

7.   LOSS OF THE RIGHT OF THE MULTIMODAL TRANSPORT OPERATOR TO LIMIT LIABILITY

The MTO is not entitled to the benefit of the limitation of liability if it is proved that the loss, damage or delay in delivery resulted from a personal act or omission of the MTO done with the intent to cause such loss, damage or delay, or recklessly and with knowledge that such loss, damage or delay would probably result.

8. LIABILITY OF THE CONSIGNOR

8.1 The consignor shall be deemed to have guaranteed to the MTO the accuracy, at the time the goods were taken in charge by the MTO, of all particulars relating to the general nature of the goods, their marks, number, weight, volume and quantity and, if applicable, to the dangerous character of the goods, as furnished by him or on his behalf for insertion in the *MT document*.

8.2 The consignor shall indemnify the MTO against any loss resulting from inaccuracies in or inadequacies of the particulars referred to above.

8.3 The consignor shall remain liable even if the *MT document* has been transferred by him.

8.4 The right of the MTO to such indemnity shall in no way limit his liability under the multimodal transport contract to any person other than the consigner.

9. NOTICE OF LOSS OF OR DAMAGE TO THE GOODS

9.1 Unless notice of loss of or damage to the goods, specifying the general nature of such loss or damage, is given in writing by the consignee to the MTO when the goods are handed over to the consignee, such handing over is *prima facie* evidence of the delivery by the MTO of the goods as described in the *MT document*.

9.2 Where the loss or damage is not apparent, the same *prima facie* effect shall apply if notice in writing is not given within 6 consecutive days after the day when the goods were handed over to the consignee.

10. TIME-BAR

The MTO shall, unless otherwise expressly agreed, be discharged of all liability under these Rules unless suit is brought within nine months after the delivery of the goods, or the date when the goods should have been delivered, or the date when, in accordance with Rule 5.3, failure to deliver the goods would give the consignee the right to treat the goods as lost.

11. APPLICABILITY OF THE RULES TO ACTIONS IN TORT

These Rules apply to all claims against the MTO relating to the performance of the multimodal transport contract, whether the claim be founded in contract or in tort.

12. APPLICABILITY OF THE RULES TO THE MULTIMODAL TRANSPORT OPERATOR'S SERVANTS, AGENTS AND OTHER PERSONS EMPLOYED BY HIM

These Rules apply whenever claims relating to the performance of the multimodal transport contract are made against any servant, agent or other person whose services the MTO has used in order to perform the multimodal transport contract, whether such claims are founded in contract or in tort, and the aggregate liability of the MTO and such servants, agents or other persons shall not exceed the limits in Rule 6.

13. MANDATORY LAW

These Rules shall only take effect to the extent that they are not contrary to the mandatory provisions of international conventions or national law applicable to the multimodal transport contract.

APPENDIX 3

United Nations Convention On International Multimodal Transport Of Goods

UN Doc. TD/MT/CONF/17 (1980)

The States parties to this Convention,

Recognizing:

(*a*) That international multimodal transport is one means of facilitating the orderly expansion of world trade;

(*b*) The need to stimulate the development of smooth, economic and efficient multimodal transport services adequate to the requirements of the trade concerned;

(*c*) The desirability of ensuring the orderly development of international multimodal transport in the interest of all countries and the need to consider the special problems of transit countries;

(*d*) The desirability of determining certain rules relating to the carriage of goods by international multimodal transport contracts, including equitable provisions concerning the liability of multimodal transport operators;

(*e*) The need that this Convention should not affect the application of any international convention or national law relating to the regulation and control of transport operations;

(*f*) The right of each State to regulate and control at the national level multimodal transport operators and operations;

(*g*) The need to have regard to the special interest and problems of developing countries, for example, as regards introduction of new technologies, participation in multimodal services of their national carriers and operators, cost efficiency thereof and maximum use of local labour and insurance;

(*h*) The need to ensure a balance of interests between suppliers and users of multimodal transport services;

(*i*) The need to facilitate customs procedures with due consideration to the problems of transit countries;

Agreeing to the following basic principles:

(a) That a fair balance of interests between developed and developing countries should be established and an equitable distribution of activities between these groups of countries should be attained in international multimodal transport;

(b) That consultation should take place on terms and conditions of service, both before and after the introduction of any new technology in the multimodal transport of goods, between the multimodal transport operator, shippers, shippers' organizations and appropriate national authorities;

(c) The freedom for shippers to choose between multimodal and segmented transport services;

(d) That the liability of the multimodal transport operator under this Convention should be based on the principle of presumed fault or neglect;

Have decided to conclude a Convention for this purpose and have thereto agreed as follows:

PART I

General provisions

Article I

DEFINITIONS

For the purposes of this Convention:

1. "International multimodal transport" means the carriage of goods by at least two different modes of transport on the basis of a multimodal transport contract from a place in one country at which the goods are taken in charge by the multimodal transport operator to a place designated for delivery situated in a different country. The operations of pick-up and delivery of goods carried out in the performance of a unimodal transport contract, as defined in such contract, shall not be considered as international multimodal transport.

2. "Multimodal transport operator" means any person who on his own behalf or through another person acting on his behalf concludes a multimodal transport contract and who acts as a principal, not as an agent or on behalf of the consignor or of the carriers participating in the multimodal

transport operations, and who assumes responsibility for the performance of the contract.

3. "Multimodal transport contract" means a contract whereby a multimodal transport operator undertakes, against payment of freight, to perform or to procure the performance of international multimodal transport.

4. "Multimodal transport document" means a document which evidences a multimodal transport contract, the taking in charge of the goods by the multimodal transport operator, and an undertaking by him to deliver the goods in accordance with the terms of that contract.

5. "Consignor" means any person by whom or in whose name or on whose behalf a multimodal transport contract has been concluded with the multimodal transport operator, or any person by whom or in whose name or on whose behalf the goods are actually delivered to the multimodal transport operator in relation to the multimodal transport contract

6. "Consignee" means the person entitled to take delivery of the goods.

7. "Goods" includes any container, pallet or similar article of transport or packaging, if supplied by the consignor.

8. "International convention" means an international agreement concluded among States in written form and governed by international law.

9. "Mandatory national law" means any statutory law concerning carriage of goods the provisions of which cannot be departed from by contractual stipulation to the detriment of the consignor.

10. "Writing" means, *inter alia*, telegram or telex.

Article 2

SCOPE OF APPLICATION

The provisions of this Convention shall apply to all contracts of multimodal transport between places in two States, if:

(a) The place for the taking in charge of the goods by the multimodal transport operator as provided for in the multimodal transport contract is located in a Contracting State, or

(b) The place for delivery of the goods by the multimodal transport operator as provided for in the multimodal transport contract is located in a Contracting State.

Article 3

MANDATORY APPLICATION

1.   When a multimodal transport contract has been concluded which according to article 2 shall be governed by this Convention, the provisions of this Convention shall be mandatorily applicable to such contract.

2.   Nothing in this Convention shall affect the right of the consignor to choose between multimodal transport and segmented transport.

Article 4

REGULATION AND CONTROL OF MULTIMODAL TRANSPORT

1.   This Convention shall not affect, or be incompatible with, the application of any international convention or national law relating to the regulation and control of transport operations.

2.   This Convention shall not affect the right of each State to regulate and control at the national level multimodal transport operations and multimodal transport operators, including the right to take measures relating to consultations, especially before the introduction of new technologies and services, between multimodal transport operators, shippers, shippers' organizations and appropriate national authorities on terms and conditions of service; licensing of multimodal transport operators; participation in transport; and all other steps in the national economic and commercial interest.

3.   The multimodal transport operator shall comply with the applicable law of the country in which he operates and with the provisions of this Convention.

PART II

Documentation

Article 5

ISSUE OF MULTIMODAL TRANSPORT DOCUMENT

1. When the goods are taken in charge by the multimodal transport operator, he shall issue a multimodal transport document which, at the option of the consignor, shall be in either negotiable or non-negotiable form.

2. The multimodal transport document shall be signed by the multimodal transport operator or by a person having authority from him.

3. The signature on the multimodal transport document may be in handwriting, printed in facsimile, perforated, stamped, in symbols, or made by any other mechanical or electronic means, if not inconsistent with the law of the country where the multimodal transport document is issued.

4. If the consignor so agrees, a non-negotiable multimodal transport document may be issued by making use of any mechanical or other means preserving a record of the particulars stated in article 8 to be contained in the multimodal transport document. In such a case the multimodal transport operator, after having taken the goods in charge, shall deliver to the consignor a readable document containing all the particulars so recorded, and such document shall for the purposes of the provisions of this Convention be deemed to be a multimodal transport document.

Article 6

NEGOTIABLE MULTIMODAL TRANSPORT DOCUMENT

1. Where a multimodal transport document is issued in negotiable form:

(a) It shall be made out to order or to bearer;

(b) If made out to order it shall be transferable by endorsement;

(c) If made out to bearer it shall be transferable without endorsement;

(d) If issued in a set of more than one original it shall indicate the number of originals in the set;

(e) If any copies are issued each copy shall be marked "non-negotiable copy."

2.   Delivery of the goods may be demanded from the multimodal transport operator or a person acting on his behalf only against surrender of the negotiable multimodal transport document duly endorsed where necessary.

3.   The multimodal transport operator shall be discharged from his obligation to deliver the goods if, where a negotiable multimodal transport document has been issued in a set of more than one original, he or a person acting on his behalf has in good faith delivered the goods against surrender of one of such originals.

Article 7

NON-NEGOTIABLE MULTIMODAL TRANSPORT

1.   Where a multimodal transport document is issued in non-negotiable form it shall indicate a named consignee.

2.   The multimodal transport operator shall be discharged from his obligation to deliver the goods if he makes delivery thereof to the consignee named in such non-negotiable multimodal transport document or to such other person as he may be duly instructed, as a rule, in writing.

Article 8

CONTENTS OF THE MULTIMODAL TRANSPORT DOCUMENT

1.   The multimodal transport document shall contain the following particulars:

(a) The general nature of the goods, the leading marks necessary for identification of the goods, an express statement, if applicable, as to the dangerous character of the goods, the number of packages or pieces, and the gross weight of the goods or their quantity otherwise expressed, all such particulars as furnished by the consignor;

(b) The apparent condition of the goods;

(c) The name and principal place of business of the multimodal transport operator,

(d) The name of the consignor;

(e) The consignee, if named by the consignor,

(f) The place and date of taking in charge of the goods by the multimodal transport operator;

(g) The place of delivery of the goods;

(h) The date or the period of delivery of the goods at the place of delivery, if expressly agreed upon between the parties;

(i) A statement indicating whether the multimodal transport document is negotiable or non-negotiable;

(j) The place and date of issue of the multimodal transport document;

(k) The signature of the multimodal transport operator or of a person having authority from him;

(l) The freight for each mode of transport, if expressly agreed between the parties, or the freight, including its currency, to the extent payable by the consignee or other indication that freight is payable by him.

(m) The intended journey route, modes of transport and places of transhipment, if known at the time of issuance of the multimodal transport document;

(n) The statement referred to in paragraph 3 of article 28;

(o) Any other particulars which the parties may agree to insert in the multimodal transport document, if not inconsistent with the law of the country where the multimodal transport document is issued.

2.   The absence from the multimodal document of one or more of the particulars referred to in paragraph 1 of this article shall not affect the legal character of the document as a multimodal transport document provided that it nevertheless meets the requirements set out in paragraph 4 of article 1.

Article 9

RESERVATIONS IN THE MULTIMODAL TRANSPORT DOCUMENT

1.   If the multimodal transport document contains particulars concerning the general nature, leading marks, number of packages or pieces, weight or quantity of the goods which the multimodal transport operator or a person acting on his behalf knows, or has reasonable grounds to suspect, do not accurately represent the goods actually taken in charge, or if he has no reasonable means of checking such particulars, the multimodal transport operator or a person acting on his behalf shall insert in the multimodal transport document a reservation specifying these inaccuracies, grounds of suspicion or the absence of reasonable means of checking.

2. If the multimodal transport operator or a person acting on his behalf fails to note on the multimodal transport document the apparent condition of the goods he is deemed to have noted on the multimodal transport document that the goods were in apparent good condition.

Article 10

EVIDENTIARY EFFECT OF THE MULTIMODAL TRANSPORT DOCUMENT

Except for particulars in respect of which and to the extent to which a reservation permitted under article 9 has been entered:

(a) The multimodal transport document shall be *prima facie* evidence of the taking in charge by the multimodal transport operator of the goods as described therein; and

(b) Proof to the contrary by the multimodal transport operator shall not be admissible if the multimodal transport document is issued in negotiable form and has been transferred to a third party, including a consignee, who has acted in good faith in reliance on the description of the goods therein.

Article 11

LIABILITY FOR INTENTIONAL MISSTATEMENTS OR OMISSIONS

When the multimodal transport operator, with intent to defraud, gives in the multimodal transport document false information concerning the goods or omits any information required to be included under paragraph 1 *(a)* or *(b)* of article 8 or under article 9, he shall be liable, without the benefit of the limitation of liability provided for in this Convention, for any loss, damage or expenses incurred by a third party, including a consignee, who acted in reliance on the description of the goods in the multimodal transport document issued.

Article 12

GUARANTEE BY THE CONSIGNOR

1. The consignor shall be deemed to have guaranteed to the multimodal transport operator the accuracy, at the time the goods were taken in charge by the multimodal transport operator, of particulars relating to the general nature of the goods, their marks, number, weight and quantity

and, if applicable, to the dangerous character of the goods, as furnished by him for insertion in the multimodal transport document.

2.   The consignor shall indemnify the multimodal transport operator against loss resulting from inaccuracies in or inadequacies of the particulars referred to in paragraph 1 of this article. The consignor shall remain liable even if the multimodal transport document has been transferred by him. The right of the multimodal transport operator to such indemnity shall in no way limit his liability under the multimodal transport contract to any person other than the consignor.

Article 13

OTHER DOCUMENTS

The issue of the multimodal transport document does not preclude the issue, if necessary, of other documents relating to transport or other services involved in international multimodal transport, in accordance with applicable international conventions or national law. However, the issue of such other documents shall not affect the legal character of the multimodal transport document.

PART III

Liability of the multimodal transport operator

Article 14

PERIOD OF RESPONSIBILITY

1.   The responsibility of the multimodal transport operator for the goods under this Convention covers the period from the time he takes the goods in his charge to the time of their delivery.

2.   For the purpose of this article, the multimodal transport operator is deemed to be in charge of the goods:

(*a*) From the time he has taken over the goods from:
  (i)   The consignor or a person acting on his behalf; or
  (ii)   An authority or other third party to whom, pursuant to law or regulations applicable at the place of taking in charge, the goods must be handed over for transport;

(*b*) Until the time he has delivered the goods:

(i)   By handing over the goods to the consignee; or

(ii)   In cases where the consignee does not receive the goods from the multimodal transport operator, by placing them at the disposal of the consignee in accordance with the multimodal transport contract or with the law or with the usage of the particular trade applicable at the place of delivery; or

(iii) By handing over the goods to an authority or other third party to whom, pursuant to law or regulations applicable at the place of delivery, the goods must be handed over.

3. In paragraph 2 of this article, reference to the multimodal transport operator shall include his servants or agents or any other person of whose services he makes use for the performance of the multimodal transport contract, and reference to the consignor or consignee shall include their servants or agents.

Article 15

THE LIABILITY OF THE MULTIMODAL TRANSPORT OPERATOR FOR HIS SERVANTS, AGENTS AND OTHER PERSONS

Subject to article 21, the multimodal transport operator shall be liable for the acts and omissions of his servants or agents, when any such servant or agent is acting within the scope of his employment, or of any other person of whose services he makes use for the performance of the multimodal transport contract, when such person is acting in the performance of the contract, as if such acts and omissions were his own.

Article 16

BASIS OF LIABILITY

1.   The multimodal transport operator shall be liable for loss resulting from loss of or damage to the goods, as well as from delay in delivery, if the occurrence which caused the loss, damage or delay in delivery took place while the goods were in his charge as defined in article 14, unless the multimodal transport operator proves that he, his servants or agents or any other person referred to in article 15 took all measures that could reasonably be required to avoid the occurrence and its consequences.

2.   Delay in delivery occurs when the goods have not been delivered within the time expressly agreed upon or, in the absence of such agreement, within the time which it would be reasonable to require of a diligent

multimodal transport operator, having regard to the circumstances of the case.

3. If the goods have not been delivered within 90 consecutive days following the date of delivery determined according to paragraph 2 of this article, the claimant may treat the goods as lost.

Article 17

CONCURRENT CAUSES

Where fault or neglect on the part of the multimodal transport operator, his servants or agents or any other person referred to in article 15 combines with another cause to produce loss, damage or delay in delivery, the multimodal transport operator shall be liable only to the extent that the loss, damage or delay in delivery is attributable to such fault or neglect, provided that the multimodal transport operator proves the part of the loss, damage or delay in delivery not attributable thereto.

Article 18

LIMITATION OF LIABILITY

1. When the multimodal transport operator is liable for loss resulting from loss of or damage to the goods according to article 16, his liability shall be limited to an amount not exceeding 920 units of account per package or other shipping unit or 2.75 units of account per kilogram of gross weight of the goods lost or damaged, whichever is the higher.

2. For the purpose of calculating which amount is the higher in accordance with paragraph 1 of this article, the following rules apply:

(a) Where a container, pallet or similar article of transport is used to consolidate goods, the packages or other shipping units enumerated in the multimodal transport document as packed in such article of transport are deemed packages or shipping units. Except as aforesaid, the goods in such article of transport are deemed one shipping unit.

(b) In cases where the article of transport itself has been lost or damaged, that article of transport, if not owned or otherwise supplied by the multimodal transport operator, is considered one separate shipping unit.

3. Notwithstanding the provisions of paragraphs 1 and 2 of this article, if the international multimodal transport does not, according to the contract, include carriage of goods by sea or by inland waterways, the

liability of the multimodal transport operator shall be limited to an amount not exceeding 8.33 units of account per kilogram of gross weight of the goods lost or damaged.

4. The liability of the multimodal transport operator for loss resulting from delay in delivery according to the provisions of article 16 shall be limited to an amount equivalent to two and a half times the freight payable for the goods delayed, but not exceeding the total freight payable under the multimodal transport contract.

5. The aggregate liability of the multimodal transport operator, under paragraphs 1 and 4 or paragraphs 3 and 4 of this article, shall not exceed the limit of liability for total loss of the goods as determined by paragraph 1 or 3 of this article.

6. By agreement between the multimodal transport operator and the consignor, limits of liability exceeding those provided for in paragraphs 1, 3 and 4 of this article may be fixed in the multimodal transport document.

7. "Unit of account" means the unit of account mentioned in article 31.

Article 19

LOCALIZED DAMAGE

When the loss of or damage to the goods occurred during one particular stage of the multimodal transport, in respect of which an applicable international convention or mandatory national law provides a higher limit of liability than the limit that would follow from application of paragraphs 1 to 3 of article 18, then the limit of the multimodal transport operator's liability for such loss or damage shall be determined by reference to the provisions of such convention or mandatory national law.

Article 20

NON-CONTRACTUAL LIABILITY

1. The defences and limits of liability provided for in this Convention shall apply in any action against the multimodal transport operator in respect of loss resulting from loss of or damage to the goods, as well as from delay in delivery, whether the action be founded in contract, in tort or otherwise.

2. If an action in respect of loss resulting from loss of or damage to the goods or from delay in delivery is brought against the servant or agent of the multimodal transport operator, if such servant or agent proves that he acted within the scope of his employment, or against any other person of whose services he makes use for the performance of the multimodal transport contract, if such other person proves that he acted within the performance of the contract, the servant or agent or such other person shall be entitled to avail himself of the defences and limits of liability which the multimodal transport operator is entitled to invoke under this Convention.

3. Except as provided in article 21, the aggregate of the amounts recoverable from the multimodal transport operator and from a servant or agent or any other person of whose services he makes use for the performance of the multimodal transport contract shall not exceed the limits of liability provided for in this Convention.

Article 21

LOSS OF THE RIGHT TO LIMIT LIABILITY

1. The multimodal transport operator is not entitled to the benefit of the limitation of liability provided for in this Convention if it is proved that the loss, damage or delay in delivery resulted from an act or omission of the multimodal transport operator done with the intent to cause such loss, damage or delay or recklessly and with knowledge that such loss, damage or delay would probably result.

2. Notwithstanding paragraph 2 of article 20, a servant or agent of the multimodal transport operator or other person of whose services he makes use for the performance of the multimodal transport contract is not entitled to the benefit of the limitation of liability provided for in this Convention if it is proved that the loss, damage or delay in delivery resulted from an act or omission of such servant, agent or other person, done with the intent to cause such loss, damage or delay or recklessly and with knowledge that such loss, damage or delay would probably result.

PART IV

Liability of the consignor

Article 22

GENERAL RULE

The consignor shall be liable for loss sustained by the multimodal transport operator if such loss is caused by the fault or neglect of the consignor, or his servants or agents when such servants or agents are acting within the scope of their employment. Any servant or agent of the consignor shall be liable for such loss if the loss is caused by fault or neglect on his part.

Article 23

SPECIAL RULES ON DANGEROUS GOODS

1. The consignor shall mark or label in a suitable manner dangerous goods as dangerous.

2. Where the consignor hands over dangerous goods to the multimodal transport operator or any person acting on his behalf, the consignor shall inform him of the dangerous character of the goods and, if necessary, the precautions to be taken. If the consignor fails to do so and the multimodal transport operator does not otherwise have knowledge of their dangerous character:

(a) The consignor shall be liable to the multimodal transport operator for all loss resulting from the shipment of such goods; and

(b) The goods may at any time be unloaded, destroyed or rendered innocuous, as the circumstances may require, without payment of compensation.

3. The provisions of paragraph 2 of this article may not be invoked by any person if during the multimodal transport he has taken the goods in his charge with knowledge of their dangerous character.

4. If, in cases where the provisions of paragraph 2 (b) of this article do not apply or may not be invoked, dangerous goods become an actual danger to life or property, they may be unloaded, destroyed or rendered innocuous, as the circumstances may require, without payment of compensation except where there is an obligation to contribute in general average or where the multimodal transport operator is liable in accordance with the provisions of article 16.

APPENDIX 3

PART V

Claims and actions

Article 24

NOTICE OF LOSS, DAMAGE OR DELAY

1.   Unless notice of loss or damage, specifying the general nature of such loss or damage, is given in writing by the consignee to the multimodal transport operator not later than the working day after the day when the goods were handed over to the consignee, such handing over is *prima facie* evidence of the delivery by the multimodal transport operator of the goods as described in the multimodal transport document.

2.   Where the loss or damage is not apparent, the provisions of paragraph 1 of this article apply correspondingly if notice in writing is not given within six consecutive days after the day when the goods were handed over to the consignee.

3.   If the state of the goods at the time they were handed over to the consignee has been the subject of a joint survey or inspection by the parties or their authorized representatives at the place of delivery, notice in writing need not be given of loss or damage ascertained during such survey or inspection.

4.   In the case of any actual or apprehended loss or damage the multimodal transport operator and the consignee shall give all reasonable facilities to each other for inspecting and tallying the goods.

5.   No compensation shall be payable for loss resulting from delay in delivery unless notice has been given in writing to the multimodal transport operator within 60 consecutive days after the day when the goods were delivered by handing over to the consignee or when the consignee has been notified that the goods have been delivered in accordance with paragraph 2 (b) (ii) or (iii) of article 14.

6.   Unless notice of loss or damage, specifying the general nature of the loss or damage, is given in writing by the multimodal transport operator to the consignor not later than 90 consecutive days after the occurrence of such loss or damage or after the delivery of the goods in accordance with paragraph 2 (b) of article 14, whichever is later, the failure to give such notice is *prima facie* evidence that the multimodal transport operator has sustained no loss or damage due to the fault or neglect of the consignor, his servants or agents.

187

7. If any of the notice periods provided for in paragraphs 2, 5 and 6 of this article terminates on a day which is not a working day at the place of delivery, such period shall be extended until the next working day.

8. For the purpose of this article, notice given to a person acting on the multimodal transport operator's behalf, including any person of whose services he makes use at the place of delivery, or to a person acting on the consignor's behalf, shall be deemed to have been given to the multimodal transport operator, or to the consignor, respectively.

Article 25

LIMITATION OF ACTIONS

1. Any action relating to international multimodal transport under this Convention shall be time-barred if judicial or arbitral proceedings have not been instituted within a period of two years. However, if notification in writing, stating the nature and main particulars of the claim, has not been given within six months after the day when the goods were delivered or, where the goods have not been delivered, after the day on which they should have been delivered, the action shall be time-barred at the expiry of this period.

2. The limitation period commences on the day after the day on which the multimodal transport operator has delivered the goods or part thereof or, where the goods have not been delivered, on the day after the last day on which the goods should have been delivered.

3. The person against whom a claim is made may at any time during the running of the limitation period extend that period by a declaration in writing to the claimant. This period may be further extended by another declaration or declarations.

4. Provided that the provisions of another applicable international convention are not to the contrary, a recourse action for indemnity by a person held liable under this Convention may be instituted even after the expiration of the limitation period provided for in the preceding paragraphs if instituted within the time allowed by the law of the State where proceedings are instituted; however, the time allowed shall not be less than 90 days commencing from the day when the person instituting such action for indemnity has settled the claim or has been served with process in the action against himself.

Article 26

JURISDICTION

1. In judicial proceedings relating to international multimodal transport under this Convention, the plaintiff, at his option, may institute an action in a court which, according to the law of the State where the court is situated, is competent and within the jurisdiction of which is situated one of the following places:

(*a*) The principal place of business or, in the absence thereof, the habitual residence of the defendant; or

(*b*) The place where the multimodal transport contract was made, provided that the defendant has there a place of business, branch or agency through which the contract was made; or

(*c*) The place of taking the goods in charge for international multimodal transport or the place of delivery; or

(*d*) Any other place designated for that purpose in the multimodal transport contract and evidenced in the multimodal transport document.

2. No judicial proceedings relating to international multimodal transport under this Convention may be instituted in a place not specified in paragraph 1 of this article. The provisions of this article do not constitute an obstacle to the jurisdiction of the Contracting States for provisional or protective measures.

3. Notwithstanding the preceding provisions of this article, an agreement made by the parties after a claim has arisen, which designates the place where the plaintiff may institute an action, shall be effective.

4. (*a*) Where an action has been instituted in accordance with the provisions of this article or where judgement in such an action has been delivered, no new action shall be instituted between the same parties on the same grounds unless the judgement in the first action is not enforceable in the country in which the new proceedings are instituted;

(*b*) For the purposes of this article neither the institution of measures to obtain enforcement of a judgement nor the removal of an action to a different court within the same country shall be considered as the starting of a new action.

Article 27

ARBITRATION

1.   Subject to the provisions of this article, parties may provide by agreement evidenced in writing that any dispute that may arise relating to international multimodal transport under this Convention shall be referred to arbitration.

2.   The arbitration proceedings shall, at the option of the claimant, be instituted at one of the following places:

(*a*) A place in a State within whose territory is situated:
- (i)   The principal place of business of the defendant or, in the absence thereof, the habitual residence of the defendant; or
- (ii)   The place where the multimodal transport contract was made, provided that the defendant has there a place of business, branch or agency through which the contract was made; or
- (iii)   The place of taking the goods in charge for international multimodal transport or the place of delivery; or

(*b*) Any other place designated for that purpose in the arbitration clause or agreement.

3.   The arbitrator or arbitration tribunal shall apply the provisions of this Convention.

4.   The provisions of paragraphs 2 and 3 of this article shall be deemed to be part of every arbitration clause or agreement and any term of such clause or agreement which is inconsistent therewith shall be null and void.

5.   Nothing in this article shall affect the validity of an agreement on arbitration made by the parties after the claim relating to the international multimodal transport has arisen.

PART VI

Supplementary provisions

Article 28

CONTRACTUAL STIPULATIONS

1.   Any stipulation in a multimodal transport contract or multimodal transport document shall be null and void to the extent that it derogates, directly or indirectly, from the provisions of this Convention. The nullity of such a stipulation shall not affect the validity of other provisions of the contract or document of which it forms a part. A clause assigning benefit of insurance of the goods in favour of the multimodal transport operator or any similar clause shall be null and void.

2.   Notwithstanding the provisions of paragraph 1 of this article, the multimodal transport operator may, with the agreement of the consignor, increase his responsibilities and obligations under this Convention.

3.   The multimodal transport document shall contain a statement that the international multimodal transport is subject to the provisions of this Convention which nullify any stipulation derogating therefrom to the detriment of the consignor or the consignee.

4.   Where the claimant in respect of the goods has incurred loss as a result of a stipulation which is null and void by virtue of the present article, or as a result of the omission of the statement referred to in paragraph 3 of this article, the multimodal transport operator must pay compensation to the extent required in order to give the claimant compensation in accordance with the provisions of this Convention for any loss of or damage to the goods as well as for delay in delivery. The multimodal transport operator must, in addition, pay compensation for costs incurred by the claimant for the purpose of exercising his right, provided that costs incurred in the action where the foregoing provision is invoked are to be determined in accordance with the law of the State where proceedings are instituted.

Article 29

GENERAL AVERAGE

1.   Nothing in this Convention shall prevent the application of provisions in the multimodal transport contract or national law regarding the adjustment of general average, if and to the extent applicable.

2.   With the exception of article 25, the provisions of this Convention relating to the liability of the multimodal transport operator for loss of or damage to the goods shall also determine whether the consignee may refuse contribution in general average and the liability of the multimodal transport operator to indemnify the consignee in respect of any such contribution made or any salvage paid.

Article 30

OTHER CONVENTIONS

1.   This Convention does not modify the rights or duties provided for in the Brussels International Convention for the unification of certain rules relating to the limitation of the liability of owners of sea-going vessels of 25 August 1924; in the Brussels International Convention relating to the limitation of the liability of owners of sea-going ships of 10 October 1957; in the London Convention on limitation of liability for maritime claims of 19 November 1976; and in the Geneva Convention relating to the limitation of the liability of owners of inland navigation vessels (CLN) of 1 March 1973, including amendments to these Conventions, or national law relating to the limitation of liability of owners of sea-going ships and inland navigation vessels.

2.   The provisions of articles 26 and 27 of this Convention do not prevent the application of the mandatory provisions of any other international convention relating to matters dealt with in the said articles, provided that the dispute arises exclusively between parties having their principal place of business in States parties to such other convention. However, this paragraph does not affect the application of paragraph 3 of article 27 of this Convention.

3.   No liability shall arise under the provisions of this Convention for damage caused by a nuclear incident if the operator of a nuclear installation is liable for such damage:

(*a*) Under either the Paris Convention of 29 July 1960 on Third Party Liability in the Field of Nuclear Energy as amended by the Additional Protocol of 28 January 1964 or the Vienna Convention of 21 May 1963 on Civil Liability for Nuclear Damage, or amendments thereto; or

(*b*) By virtue of national law governing the liability for such damage, provided that such law is in all respects as favourable to persons who may suffer damage as either the Paris or Vienna Conventions.

4.   Carriage of goods such as carriage of goods in accordance with the Geneva Convention of 19 May 1956 on the Contract for the International

Carriage of Goods by Road in article 2, or the Berne Convention of 7 February 1970 concerning the Carriage of Goods by Rail, article 2, shall not for States Parties to Conventions governing such carriage be considered as international multimodal transport within the meaning of article 1, paragraph 1, of this Convention, in so far as such States are bound to apply the provisions of such Conventions to such carriage of goods.

Article 31

UNIT OF ACCOUNT OR MONETARY UNIT AND CONVERSION

1.   The unit of account referred to in article 18 of this Convention is the Special Drawing Right as defined by the International Monetary Fund. The amounts referred to in article 18 shall be converted into the national currency of a State according to the value of such currency on the date of the judgement or award or the date agreed upon by the parties. The value of a national currency, in terms of the Special Drawing Right, of a Contracting State which is a member of the International Monetary Fund, shall be calculated in accordance with the method of valuation applied by the International Monetary Fund, in effect on the date in question, for its operations and transactions. The value of a national currency in terms of the Special Drawing Right of a Contracting State which is not a member of the International Monetary Fund shall be calculated in a manner determined by that State.

2.   Nevertheless, a State which is not a member of the International Monetary Fund and whose law does not permit the application of the provisions of paragraph 1 of this article may, at the time of signature, ratification, acceptance, approval or accession, or at any time thereafter, declare that the limits of liability provided for in this Convention to be applied in its territory shall be fixed as follows: with regard to the limits provided for in paragraph 1 of article 18, to 13,750 monetary units per package or other shipping unit or 41.25 monetary units per kilogram of gross weight of the goods, and with regard to the limit provided for in paragraph 3 of article 18, to 124 monetary units.

3.   The monetary unit referred to in paragraph 2 of this article corresponds to 65.5 milligrams of gold of millesimal fineness nine hundred. The conversion of the amount referred to in paragraph 2 of this article into national currency shall be made according to the law of the State concerned.

4.   The calculation mentioned in the last sentence of paragraph 1 of this article and the conversion referred to in paragraph 3 of this article shall be made in such a manner as to express in the national currency of the

Contracting State as far as possible the same real value for the amounts in article 18 as is expressed there in units of account.

5. Contracting States shall communicate to the depositary the manner of calculation pursuant to the last sentence of paragraph 1 of this article, or the result of the conversion pursuant to paragraph 3 of this article, as the case may be, at the time of signature or when depositing their instruments of ratification, acceptance, approval or accession, or when availing themselves of the option provided for in paragraph 2 of this article and whenever there is a change in the manner of such calculation or in the result of such conversion.

PART VII

Customs matters

Article 32

CUSTOMS TRANSIT

1. Contracting States shall authorize the use of the procedure of customs transit for international multimodal transport.

2. Subject to provisions of national law or regulations and intergovernmental agreements, the customs transit of goods in international multimodal transport shall be in accordance with the rules and principles contained in articles I to VI of the annex to this Convention.

3. When introducing laws or regulations in respect of customs transit procedures relating to multimodal transport of goods, Contracting States should take into consideration articles I to VI of the annex to this Convention.

PART VIII

Final clauses

Article 33

DEPOSITARY

The Secretary-General of the United Nations is hereby designated as the depositary of this Convention.

Article 34

SIGNATURE, RATIFICATION, ACCEPTANCE, APPROVAL AND ACCESSION

1.   All States are entitled to become Parties to this Convention by:

(a) Signature not subject to ratification, acceptance or approval; or

(b) Signature subject to and followed by ratification, acceptance or approval; or

(c) Accession.

2.   This Convention shall be open for signature as from 1 September 1980 until and including 31 August 1981 at the Headquarters of the United Nations in New York.

3.   After 31 August 1981, this Convention shall be open for accession by all States which are not signatory States.

4.   Instruments of ratification, acceptance, approval and accession are to be deposited with the depositary.

5.   Organizations for regional economic integration, constituted by sovereign States members of UNCTAD, and which have competence to negotiate, conclude and apply international agreements in specific fields covered by this Convention, shall be similarly entitled to become Parties to this Convention in accordance with the provisions of paragraphs 1 to 4 of this article, thereby assuming in relation to other Parties to this Convention the rights and duties under this Convention in the specific fields referred to above.

Article 35

RESERVATIONS

No reservation may be made to this Convention.

Article 36

ENTRY INTO FORCE

1.   This Convention shall enter into force 12 months after the Governments of 30 States have either signed it not subject to ratification,

acceptance or approval or have deposited instruments of ratification, acceptance, approval or accession with the depositary.

2.   For each State which ratifies, accepts, approves or accedes to this Convention after the requirements for entry into force given in paragraph 1 of this article have been met, the Convention shall enter into force 12 months after the deposit by such State of the appropriate instrument.

Article 37

DATE OF APPLICATION

Each Contracting State shall apply the provisions of this Convention to multimodal transport contracts concluded on or after the date of entry into force of this Convention in respect of that State.

Article 38

RIGHTS AND OBLIGATIONS UNDER EXISTING CONVENTIONS

If, according to articles 26 or 27, judicial or arbitral proceedings are brought in a Contracting State in a case relating to international multimodal transport subject to this Convention which takes place between two States of which only one is a Contracting State, and if both these States are at the time of entry into force of this Convention equally bound by another international convention, the court or arbitral tribunal may, in accordance with the obligations under such convention, give effect to the provisions thereof.

Article 39

REVISION AND AMENDMENTS

1.   At the request of not less than one third of the Contracting States, the Secretary-General of the United Nations shall, after the entry into force of this Convention, convene a conference of the Contracting States for revising or amending it. The Secretary-General of the United Nations shall circulate to all Contracting States the texts of any proposals for amendments at least three months before the opening date of the conference.

2.   Any decision by the revision conference, including amendments, shall be taken by a two thirds majority of the States present and voting. Amendments adopted by the conference shall be communicated by the depositary to all the contracting States for acceptance and to all the States signatories of the Convention for information.

3. Subject to paragraph 4 below, any amendment adopted by the conference shall enter into force only for those Contracting States which have accepted it, on the first day of the month following one year after its acceptance by two thirds of the Contracting States. For any State accepting an amendment after it has been accepted by two thirds of the Contracting States, the amendment shall enter into force on the first day of the month following one year after its acceptance by that State.

4. Any amendment adopted by the conference altering the amounts specified in article 18 and paragraph 2 of article 31 or substituting either or both the units defined in paragraphs 1 and 3 of article 31 by other units shall enter into force on the first day of the month following one year after its acceptance by two thirds of the Contracting States. Contracting States which have accepted the altered amounts or the substituted units shall apply them in their relationship with all Contracting States.

5. Acceptance of amendments shall be effected by the deposit of a formal instrument to that effect with the depositary.

6. Any instrument of ratification, acceptance, approval or accession deposited after the entry into force of any amendment adopted by the conference shall be deemed to apply to the Convention as amended.

Article 40

DENUNCIATION

1. Each Contracting State may denounce this Convention at any time after the expiration of a period of two years from the date on which this Convention has entered into force by means of a notification in writing addressed to the depositary.

2. Such denunciation shall take effect on the first day of the month following the expiration of one year after the notification is received by the depositary. Where a longer period is specified in the notification, the denunciation shall take effect upon the expiration of such longer period after the notification is received by the depositary.

IN WITNESS WHEREOF the undersigned, being duly authorized thereto, have affixed their signatures hereunder on the dates indicated.

DONE AT Geneva, this twenty-fourth day of May, one thousand nine hundred and eighty, in one original in the Arabic, Chinese, English, French, Russian and Spanish languages, all texts being equally authentic.

ANNEX

Provisions on customs matters relating to international multimodal transport of goods

Article I

For the purposes of this Convention:

"Customs transit procedure" means the customs procedure under which goods are transported under customs control from one customs office to another.

"Customs office of destination" means any customs office at which a customs transit operation is terminated.

"Import/export duties and taxes" means customs duties and all other duties, taxes, fees or other charges which are collected on or in connection with the import/export of goods, but not including fees and charges which are limited in amount to the approximate cost of services rendered.

"Customs transit document" means a form containing the record of data entries and information required for the customs transit operation.

Article II

1.   Subject to the provisions of the law, regulations and international conventions in force in their territories, Contracting States shall grant freedom of transit to goods in international multimodal transport.

2.   Provided that the conditions laid down in the customs transit procedure used for the transit operation are fulfilled to the satisfaction of the customs authorities, goods in international multimodal transport:

(*a*) Shall not, as a general rule, be subject to customs examination during the journey except to the extent deemed necessary to ensure compliance with rules and regulations which the customs are responsible for enforcing. Flowing from this, the customs authorities shall normally restrict themselves to the control of customs seals and other security measures at points of entry and exit;

(*b*) Without prejudice to the application of law and regulations concerning public or national security, public morality or public health, shall not be subject to any customs formalities or requirements additional to those of the customs transit regime used for the transit operation.

Article III

In order to facilitate the transit of the goods, each Contracting State shall:

(a) If it is the country of shipment, as far as practicable, take all measures to ensure the completeness and accuracy of the information required for the subsequent transit operations;

(b) If it is the country of destination;

    (i)   Take all necessary measures to ensure that goods in customs transit shall be cleared, as a rule, at the customs office of destination of the goods;

    (ii)   Endeavour to carry out the clearance of goods at a place as near as is possible to the place of final destination of the goods, provided that national law and regulations do not require otherwise.

Article IV

1.   Provided that the conditions laid down in the customs transit procedure are fulfilled to the satisfaction of the customs authorities, the goods in international multimodal transport shall not be subject to the payment of import/export duties and taxes or deposit in lieu thereof in transit countries.

2. The provisions of the preceding paragraph shall not preclude:

(a) The levy of fees and charges by virtue of national regulations on grounds of public security or public health;

(b) The levy of fees and charges, which are limited in amount to the approximate cost of services rendered, provided they are imposed under conditions of equality.

Article V

1.   Where a financial guarantee for the customs transit operation is required, it shall be furnished to the satisfaction of the customs authorities of the transit country concerned in conformity with its national law and regulations and in international conventions.

2.   With a view to facilitating customs transit, the system of customs guarantee shall be simple, efficient, moderately priced and shall cover

import/export duties and taxes chargeable and, in countries where they are covered by guarantees, any penalties due.

Article VI

1.   Without prejudice to any other documents which may be required by virtue of an international convention or national law and regulations, customs authorities of transit countries shall accept the multimodal transport document as a descriptive part of the customs transit document.

2.   With a view to facilitating customs transit, customs transit documents shall be aligned, as far as possible, with the layout reproduced below. [Omitted.]

APPENDIX 4

ICC Uniform Rules For A Combined Transport Document (1975 Revision)

ICC Publication No. 298. Reprinted with permission.

GENERAL PROVISIONS

Rule 1

a) These Rules apply to every contract concluded for the performance and/or procurement of performance of combined transport of goods which is evidenced by a combined transport document as defined herein.

These Rules shall nevertheless apply even if the goods are carried by a single mode of transport contrary to the original intentions of the contracting parties that there should be a combined transport of the goods as defined hereafter.

b) The issuance of such combined transport document confers and imposes on all parties having or thereafter acquiring an interest in it the rights, obligations and defences set out in these Rules.

c) Except to the extent that it increases the responsibility or obligation of the combined transport operator, any stipulation or any part of any stipulation contained in a contract of combined transport or in a combined transport document evidencing such contract, which would directly or indirectly derogate from these Rules shall be null and void to the extent of the conflict between such stipulation, or part thereof, and these Rules. The nullity of such stipulation or part thereof shall not affect the validity of the other provisions of the contract of combined transport or combined transport document of which it forms a part.

DEFINITIONS

Rule 2

For the purpose of these Rules:

a) Combined transport means the carriage of goods by at least two different modes of transport, from a place at which the goods are taken in charge situated in one country to a place designated for delivery situated in a different country.

b) Combined transport operator (CTO) means a person (including any corporation, company or legal entity) issuing a combined transport document.

Where a national law requires a person to be authorized or licensed before being entitled to issue a combined transport document, then combined transport operator can only refer to a person so authorized or licensed.

c) Combined transport document (CT Document) means a document evidencing a contract for the performance and/or procurement of performance of combined transport of goods and bearing on its face either the heading "Negotiable combined transport document issued subject to Uniform Rules for a Combined Transport Document (ICC Brochure No. 298)" or the heading "Non-negotiable combined transport document issued subject to Uniform Rules for a Combined Transport Document (ICC Brochure No. 298)."

d) Different modes of transport means the transport of goods by two or more modes of transport, such as transport by sea, inland waterway, air, rail or road.

e) Delivery means delivering the goods to or placing the goods at the disposal of the party entitled to receive them.

f) Franc means a unit consisting of 65.5 milligrams of gold of millesimal fineness 900.

NEGOTIABLE DOCUMENT

Rule 3

Where a CT document is issued in negotiable form:

a) it shall be made out to order or to bearer;

b) if made out to order, it shall be transferable by endorsement;

c) if made out to bearer, it shall be transferable without endorsement;

d) if issued in a set of more than one original it shall indicate the number of originals in the set;

e) if any copies are issued each copy shall be marked "non negotiable copy;"

f) delivery of the goods may be demanded only from the CTO or his representative, and against surrender of the CT document duly endorsed where necessary;

g) the CTO shall be discharged of his obligation to deliver the goods if, where a CT document has been issued in a set of more than one original, he, or his representative, has in good faith delivered the goods against surrender of one of such originals.

NON-NEGOTIABLE DOCUMENT

Rule 4

Where a CT document is issued in non-negotiable form:

a) it shall indicate a named consignee;

b) the CTO shall be discharged of his obligation to deliver the goods if he makes delivery thereof to the consignee named in such non-negotiable document.

RESPONSIBILITIES AND LIABILITIES OF THE CTO

Rule 5

By the issuance of a CT document the CTO:

a) undertakes to perform and/or in his own name to procure performance of the combined transport, including all services which are necessary to such transport from the time of taking the goods in charge to the time of delivery and accepts responsibility for such transport and such services to the extent set out in these Rules;

b) accepts responsibility for the acts and omissions of his agents or servants, when such agents or servants are acting within the scope of their employment, as if such acts and omissions were his own;

c) accepts responsibility for the acts and omissions of any other person whose services he uses for the performance of the contract evidenced by the CT document;

d) undertakes to perform or to procure performance of all acts necessary to ensure delivery;

e)   assumes liability to the extent set out in these Rules for loss of or damage to the goods occurring between the time of taking them into his charge and the time of delivery, and undertakes to pay compensation as set out in these Rules in respect of such loss or damage;

f)   assumes liability to the extent set out in Rule 14 for delay in delivery of the goods and undertakes to pay compensation as set out in that Rule.

RIGHTS AND DUTIES OF THE PARTIES

Rule 6

In addition to the information specifically required by these Rules, the parties shall insert in a CT document such particulars as they may agree to be commercially desirable.

Rule 7

The Consignor shall be deemed to have guaranteed to the CTO the accuracy, at the time the goods were taken in charge by the CTO, of the description, marks, number, quantity, weight and/or volume of the goods as furnished him, and the consignor shall indemnify the CTO against all loss, damage and expense arising or resulting from inaccuracies in or inadequacy of such particulars.

The right of the CTO to such indemnity shall in no way limit his responsibility under the CT Document to any person other than the consignor.

Rule 8

The consignor shall comply with rules which are mandatory according to the national law or by reason of international Convention relating to the carriage of goods of a dangerous nature and shall in any case inform the CTO in writing of the exact nature of the danger before goods of a dangerous nature are taken in charge by the CTO and indicate to him, if need be, the precautions to be taken.

If the consignor fails to provide such information and the CTO is unaware of the dangerous nature of the goods and the necessary precautions to be taken and if, at any time, they are deemed to be a hazard to life or property, they may at any place be unloaded, destroyed or rendered harmless, as circumstances may require, without compensation, and the consignor shall be liable for all loss, damage, delay or expenses arising out of their being taken in charge, or their carriage, or of any service incidental thereto.

The burden of proving the CTO knew the exact nature of the danger constituted by the carriage of the said goods shall rest upon the person entitled to the goods.

Rule 9

The CTO shall clearly indicate in the CT document, at least by quantity and/or weight and/or volume and/or marks, the goods he has taken in charge and for which he accepts responsibility.

Subject to paragraph 1 of this Rule, if the CTO has reasonable grounds for suspecting that the CT document contains particulars concerning the description, marks, number, quantity, weight and/or volume of the goods which do not represent accurately the goods actually taken in charge, or if he has no reasonable means of checking such particulars, the CTO shall be entitled to enter his reservations in the CT document, provided he indicates the particular information to which such reservations apply

The CT document shall be *prima facie* evidence of the taking in charge by the CTO of the goods as therein described. Proof to the contrary shall not be admissible when the CT document is issued in negotiable form and has been transferred to a third party acting in good faith.

Rule 10

Except in respect of goods treated as lost in accordance with Rule 15 hereof the CTO shall be deemed *prima facie* to have delivered the goods described in the CT document unless notice of loss of, or damage to, the goods, indicating the general nature of such loss or damage, shall have been given in writing to the CTO or to his representative at the place of delivery before or at the time of removal of the goods into the custody of the person entitled to delivery thereof under the CT document, or, if the loss or damage is not apparent, within seven consecutive days thereafter.

LIABILITY FOR LOSS OR DAMAGE

A.   Rules applicable when the stage of transport where the loss or damage occurred is not known.

Rule 11

When in accordance with Rule 5 (e) hereof the CTO is liable to pay compensation in respect of loss of, or damage to the goods and the stage of transport where the loss or damage occurred is not known:

a)   such compensation shall be calculated by reference to the value of such goods at the place and time they are delivered to the consignee or at the place and time when, in accordance with the contract of combined transport, they should have been so delivered;

b)   the value of the goods shall be determined according to the current commodity exchange price or, if there is no such price, according the current market price, or, if there is no commodity exchange price or current market price, by reference to the normal value of goods of the same kind and quality;

c)   compensation shall not exceed 30 francs per kilo of gross weight of the goods lost or damaged, unless, with the consent of the CTO, the consignor has declared a higher value for the goods and such higher value has been stated in the CT document, in which case such higher value shall be the limit.

However, the CTO shall not, in any case, be liable for an amount greater than the actual loss to the person entitled to make the claim.

Rule 12

When the stage of transport where the loss or damage occurred is not known, the CTO shall not be liable to pay compensation in accordance with Rule 5 (e) hereof if the loss or damage was caused by:

a)   an act or omission of the consignor or consignee, or person other than the CTO acting on behalf of the consignor or consignee, or from whom the CTO took the goods in charge;

b)   insufficiency or defective condition of the packing or marks;

c)   handling, loading, stowage or unloading of the goods by the consignor or the consignee or any person acting on behalf of the consignor or the consignee;

d)   inherent vice of the goods;

e)   strike, lockout, stoppage or restraint of labour, the consequences of which the CTO could not avoid by the exercise of reasonable diligence;

f)   any cause or event which the CTO could not avoid and the consequences of which he could not prevent by the exercise of responsible diligence;

g)   a nuclear incident if the operator of a nuclear installation or a person acting for him is liable for this damage under an applicable international Convention or national law governing liability in respect of nuclear energy.

The burden of proving that the loss or damage was due to one or more of the above causes or events shall rest upon the CTO.

When the CTO establishes that, in the circumstances of the case, the loss or damage could be attributed to one or more of the causes or events specified in (b) to (d) above, it shall be presumed that it was so caused. The claimant shall, however, be entitled to prove that the loss or damage was not, in fact, caused wholly or partly by one or more of these causes or events.

B.   Rules applicable when the stage of transport where the loss or damage occurred is known.

Rule 13

When in accordance with Rule 5 (e) hereof the CTO is liable to pay compensation in respect of loss or damage to the goods and the stage of transport where the loss or damage occurred is known, the liability of the CTO in respect of such loss or damage shall be determined:

a)   by the provisions contained in any international Convention or national law, which provisions:
   i)   cannot be departed from by private contract, to the detriment of the claimant, and
   ii)   would have applied if the claimant had made a separate and direct contract with the CTO in respect of the particular stage of transport where the loss or damage occurred and received as evidence thereof any particular document which must be issued in order to make such international Convention or national law applicable; or

b)   by the provisions contained in any international Convention relating to the carriage of goods by the mode of transport used to carry the goods at the time when the loss or damage occurred, provided that:

> i) no other international Convention or national law would apply by virtue of the provisions contained in sub-paragraph (a) of this Rule, and that
>
> ii) it is expressly stated in the CT Document that all the provisions contained in such Convention shall govern the carriage of goods by such mode of transport; where such mode of transport is by sea, such provisions shall apply to all goods whether carried on deck or under deck; or

c) by the provisions contained in any contract of carriage by inland waterways entered into between the CTO and any sub-contractor, provided that:

> i) no international Convention or national law is applicable under sub-paragraph (a) of this Rule, or is applicable, or could have been made
>
> ii) it is expressly stated in the CT Document that such contract provisions shall apply; or

d) by the provisions of Rules 11 and 12 in cases where the provisions of sub-paragraphs (a), (b) and (c) above do not apply.

Without prejudice to the provisions of Rule 5 (b) and (c), when, under the provisions of the preceding paragraph, the liability of the CTO shall be determined by the provisions of any international Convention or national law, this liability shall be determined as though the CTO were the carrier referred to in any such Convention or national law. However, the CTO shall not be exonerated from liability where the loss or damage is caused or contributed to by the acts or omissions of the CTO in his capacity as such, or his servants or agents when acting in such capacity and not in the performance of the carriage.

LIABILITY FOR DELAY

Rule 14

The CTO is liable to pay compensation for delay only when the stage of transport where a delay occurred is known, and to the extent that there is liability under any international Convention or national law, the provisions of which:

> i) cannot be departed from by private contract to the detriment of the claimant;
>
> ii) would have applied if the claimant had made a separate and direct contract with the CTO as operator of that stage of transport and received as evidence thereof any particular document which

must be issued in order to make such international Convention or national law applicable.

However, the amount of such compensation shall not exceed the amount of the freight for that stage, provided that this limitation is not contrary to any applicable international Convention or national law.

MISCELLANEOUS PROVISIONS

Rule 15

Failure to effect delivery within 90 days after the expiry of a time limit agreed and expressed in a CT Document or, where no time limit is agreed and so expressed, failure to effect delivery within 90 days after the time it would be reasonable to allow for diligent completion of the combined transport operation shall, in the absence of proof to the contrary, give to the party entitled to receive delivery the right to treat the goods as lost.

Rule 16

The defences and limits of liability provided for in these Rules shall apply in any action against the CTO for loss of, damage, or delay to the goods whether the action be founded in contract or in tort.

Rule 17

The CTO shall not be entitled to the benefit of the limitation of liability provided for in Rule 11 hereof if it is proved that the loss or damage resulted from an act or omission of the CTO done with intent to cause damage or recklessly and with knowledge that damage would probably result.

Rule 18

Nothing in these Rules shall prevent the CTO from including in the CT document provisions for protection of his agents or servants or any other person whose services he uses for the performance of the contract evidenced by the CT document, provided such protection does not extend beyond that granted to the CTO himself.

TIME-BAR

Rule 19

The CTO shall be discharged of all liability under these Rules unless suit is brought within nine months after,

    i)   the delivery of the goods, or,

    ii) the date when the goods should have been delivered, or

    iii) the date, when in accordance with Rule 15, failure to deliver the goods would, in the absence of evidence to the contrary, give to the party entitled to receive delivery the right to treat the goods as lost.